The Learning Works

I LOVE LISTS!

Grades 1–6

Updated & Expanded Second Edition

More than 200 fun-filled lists for reading, science, math, geography, history, music, art, sports, and lots more!

Written by
Linda Schwartz

Illustrated by
Beverly Armstrong

LIBRARY OF AGS
ANNE C. SUDOR

The Learning Works

Cover Design:

Andy Blinn

Dedicated with love
to
Stan, Stephen, Michael,
and
Mom and Dad—
special people at the top
of my list.

The purchase of this book entitles the individual teacher to reproduce copies for use in the classroom. The reproduction of any part for an entire school or school system or for commercial use is strictly prohibited. No form of this work may be reproduced or transmitted or recorded without written permission from the publisher. Inquiries should be addressed to the Permissions Department.

Copyright © 1996
The Learning Works, Inc.
P.O. Box 6187
Santa Barbara, California 93160

ISBN: 0-88160-285-X

Introduction

I Love Lists! is a remarkable collection of more than two hundred separate lists drawn from all major subject areas. This book includes lists related to art, astronomy, careers, chemistry, computers, dance, geography, geology, health, history, hobbies, law, literature, measurement, medicine, metrics, music, numerals, nutrition, phonics, politics, space, sports, theater, and more. There are lists of architects, artists, and authors; lists of careers, codes, and comets; lists of flowers, Internet words, phobias, and firsts; lists of people, places, and palindromes; lists of similes, suffixes, and synonyms. And there are lists of things—things to celebrate, things to collect, things to celebrate, things to collect, things to eat, things to wear, and things to write about. At the end of many lists are instructions for follow-up activities tailored to the actual list content.

Within this book, the lists are arranged in six major sections entitled **Language Arts**, **Social Studies**, **Science**, **Math**, **The Arts and Sports**, and **Just for Fun**. In each section, closely related lists are grouped in subsections and alphabetized by title or topic. For example, a two-page list of Animals appears near the end of the Animals subsection within the Science section. And a three-page list of Astronauts opens the Space subsection of the Science section. In addition to an amazing array of lists, many of the six sections contain a page of Bonus Ideas for using the lists within that section in interesting and creative ways and a page that offers readers an opportunity to add to the section by creating their own special lists.

The lists in this book can be used in a variety of ways. Not only do they make ideal resources for reference, but they can also serve as the bases for quiz and game questions and as topics for research. They may be used to develop skill in alphabetizing, chronologizing, classifying, and comparing. And they are guaranteed to inspire creative expression in the form of centers, charts, displays, graphs, illustrations, paintings, plays, poems, posters, stories, and time lines. They will help students explore word origins and meanings, increase their vocabularies, and expand their knowledge of the world around them. In short, *I Love Lists!* gives readers of all ages more than two hundred reasons to do exactly that—love lists!

Protoceratops · yoga · jack-in-the-box
kunzite · prestidigitation · frogmouth · all
pewter · chorizo · duodecillion · Zambezi
nerd · Kenya · eucalyptus · dancer · Vizsla

Contents

Contents
(continued)

Contents
(continued)

Language Arts

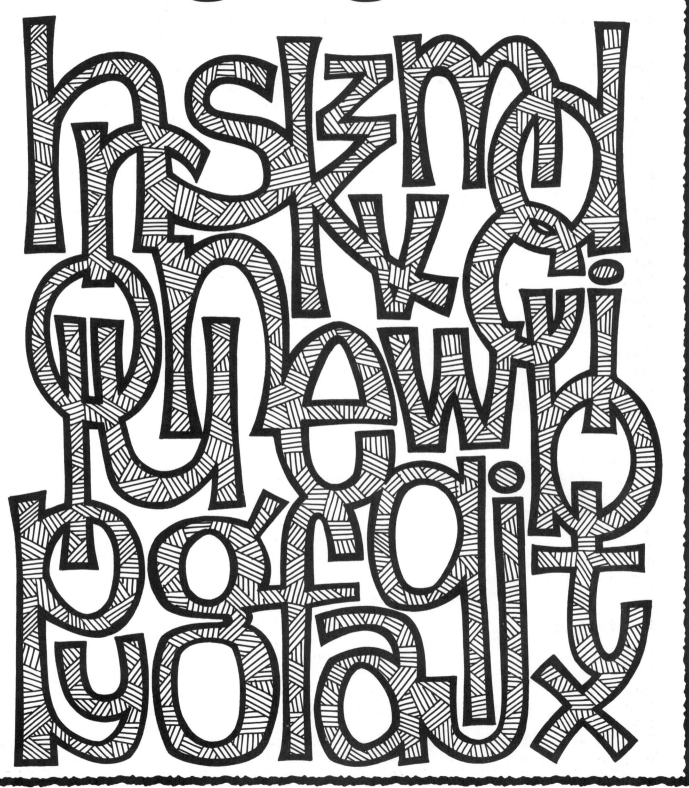

I Love Lists!
© The Learning Works, Inc.

Abbreviations

An **abbreviation** is a shortened or contracted form of a word or phrase.

abbr.	abbreviated, abbreviation	ibid.	Latin *ibidem*, in the same place
acct.	account, accountant	i.e.	Latin *id est*, that is
adj.	adjective	illust.	illustrated, illustration
adv.	adverb	inc.	incomplete, incorporated
A.M.	Latin *ante meridiem*, before noon	interj.	interjection
amt.	amount	I.O.U.	I owe you
anon.	anonymous, anonymously	I.Q.	intelligence quotient
approx.	approximate, approximately	lat.	latitude
appt.	appoint, appointed, appointment	mfg.	manufacturing
apt.	apartment, aptitude	misc.	miscellaneous
assn.	association	mo.	month
assoc.	associate	M.P.G.	miles per gallon
asst.	assistant	M.P.H.	miles per hour
avdp.	avoirdupois	mt.	mount, mountain
avg.	average	n.	noun
bldg.	building	no.	north, number
chap.	chapter	nos.	numbers
co.	company	p.	page
C.O.D.	cash on delivery, collect on delivery	pd.	paid
conj.	conjunction	pkg.	package
contd.	continued	pl.	plural
corp.	corporation	P.M.	Latin *post meridiem*, after noon
dept.	department	P.O.	post office, purchase order
dist.	distance, district	pp.	pages
ea.	each	ppd.	postpaid, prepaid
e.g.	Latin *exempli gratia*, for example	pr.	pair, price, printed
elem.	elementary	pron.	pronoun
encyc.	encyclopedia	P.S.	Latin *postscriptum*, postscript
esp.	especially	univ.	universal, university
est.	established, estimate, estimated	v.	verb
etc.	Latin *et cetera*, and others (of the same kind), and so forth	v., vs.	versus
		vss.	verses, versions
fig.	figure, meaning picture or illustration	wk.	week
		yr.	year
govt.	government		

bldg.conj.encyc.fig.ibid.n.wk.

Abbreviations
(continued)

Addresses and Directions

Ave.	Avenue
Blvd.	Boulevard
E.	East
Frwy.	Freeway
Hwy.	Highway
Ln.	Lane
N., No.	North
Pkwy.	Parkway
Pl.	Place
Rd.	Road
Rte.	Route
S., So.	South
Sq.	Square
St.	Street
Terr.	Terrace

Days of the Week

Sun.	Sunday
Mon.	Monday
Tues.	Tuesday
Wed.	Wednesday
Thurs.	Thursday
Fri.	Friday
Sat.	Saturday

Months of the Year

Jan.	January
Feb.	February
Mar.	March
Apr.	April
May	May
June	June
July	July
Aug.	August
Sept.	September
Oct.	October
Nov.	November
Dec.	December

Titles

Adm.	Admiral
atty.	attorney
dent.	dentist
Capt.	Captain
Col.	Colonel
Dr.	Doctor
Gen.	General
Gov.	Governor
Hon.	Honorable
Jr.	Junior
Lt.	Lieutenant
Maj.	Major
mgr.	manager
Miss	(unmarried woman)
Mr.	Mister
Mrs.	Mistress (married woman)
Pres.	President
Rep.	Representative
Rev.	Reverend
Secy.	Secretary
Sr.	Senior
Supt.	Superintendent

Units of Measure

a.	acre	m	meter
bbl.	barrel	mg	milligram
bu.	bushel	mi.	mile
C.	Celsius, Centigrade	min.	minute
c.	cup	ml	milliliter
cm	centimeter	mm	millimeter
d.	day	mo.	month
deg.	degree	oz.	ounce
doz.	dozen	pk.	peck
F	Fahrenheit	pt.	pint
ft.	foot	qt.	quart
gal.	gallon	rd.	rod
gm	gram	sec.	second
hr.	hour	T.	tablespoon
ht.	height	t.	teaspoon
in.	inch	tbsp.	tablespoon
kg	kilogram	tsp.	teaspoon
kl	kiloliter	vol.	volume
l	liter	wt.	weight
lb.	pound	yd.	yard
		yr.	year

Acronyms

An **acronym** is a word formed from the initial letter or letters of words in a phrase. It is often written entirely in capital letters and is usually pronounced as a word.

AIDS	acquired immune deficiency syndrome
ASAP	as soon as possible
AWOL	absent without leave
CAT	computerized axial tomography
CORE	Congress of Racial Equality
loran	long-range navigation
MADD	Mothers Against Drunk Driving
maser	microwave amplification by stimulated emission of radiation
NASA	National Aeronautics and Space Administration
NASCAR	National Association of Stock Car Auto Racing
NATO	North Atlantic Treaty Organization
NOW	National Organization for Women
OPEC	Organization of Petroleum Exporting Countries
OSHA	Occupational Safety and Health Administration
radar	radio detecting and ranging
RAM	random access memory
ROM	read only memory
SADD	Students Against Drunk Driving
SALT	Strategic Arms Limitation Talks
SAT	Scholastic Aptitude Test
scuba	self-contained underwater breathing apparatus
SEATO	Southeast Asia Treaty Organization
sonar	sound navigation ranging
STOL	short takeoff and landing
SWAT	special weapons and tactics
UNESCO	United Nations Educational, Scientific, and Cultural Organization
UNICEF	United Nations International Children's Emergency Fund
VISTA	Volunteers in Service to America
Wac	Women's Army Corps; a member of the Women's Army Corps
Waf	Women in the Air Force; a member of the women's component of the Air Force formed after World War II
WHO	World Health Organization
zip	zone improvement plan

Adjectives

An **adjective** is a word that describes a noun or a pronoun. An adjective tells which one, what kind, or how many.

absent	jubilant	regal
absurd	juicy	resourceful
basic	keen	silky
belligerent	kindly	slender
casual	lazy	thick
crooked	lovely	tireless
damp	massive	unhappy
delightful	mellow	usual
eligible	nervous	versatile
enormous	nice	vivid
faithful	obscure	windy
fleshy	obvious	wiry
gaunt	poignant	xenolithic
gloomy	previous	xeric
healthy	quaint	young
helpful	queasy	youthful
icy		zany
idle		zestful

lazy lovely lizard

Adverbs

An **adverb** is a word that describes a verb, an adjective, or another adverb. An adverb tells how, when, where, or to what degree.

angrily	jointly	rather
away	justly	regularly
barely	keenly	sharply
boastfully	knowingly	slyly
casually	legally	thoughtfully
cheerfully	lustily	truthfully
daintily	merely	upstairs
deceptively	moderately	uselessly
excitedly	neglectfully	violently
expectantly	nowhere	visibly
falsely	obviously	weakly
fearfully	orderly	wishfully
gloomily	passively	xenially
guiltily	possibly	xenocentrically
hastily	quickly	yearly
humbly	quietly	yes
immediately		zealously
inwardly		zestfully

The vulture vaulted violently.

Antonyms

Antonyms are words that are opposite in meaning.

abate-increase	comply-resist	inferior-superior
above-below	crooked-straight	join-separate
absent-present	dark-light	joy-grief
accept-refuse	day-night	kind-cruel
achieve-fail	decrease-increase	large-small
active-passive	deep-shallow	leave-stay
advance-retreat	defeat-victory	long-short
alike-different	difficult-easy	loose-tight
allow-forbid	down-up	lose-win
always-never	dry-wet	many-few
ambitious-lazy	early-late	maximum-minimum
appear-vanish	easy-hard	noisy-quiet
arrival-departure	empty-full	offense-defense
ascent-descent	evil-good	often-seldom
asleep-awake	exact-vague	on-off
attack-defend	exterior-interior	part-whole
back-front	fancy-plain	permanent-temporary
beautiful-ugly	far-near	plentiful-scarce
before-after	fast-slow	polite-rude
begin-end	first-last	pull-push
believe-doubt	flimsy-solid	regular-irregular
beneficial-harmful	foe-friend	rich-poor
best-worst	foolish-wise	rough-smooth
bold-timid	forget-remember	save-spend
bottom-top	fragile-sturdy	short-tall
bright-dull	fresh-stale	shrink-swell
busy-idle	give-take	start-stop
calm-excited	guilty-innocent	strong-weak
cheerful-somber	happy-sad	tame-wild
clean-dirty	hard-soft	thick-thin
close-open	healthy-sick	true-false
cold-hot	heavy-light	usual-unusual
common-rare	high-low	wide-narrow
complex-simple	include-omit	zenith-nadir

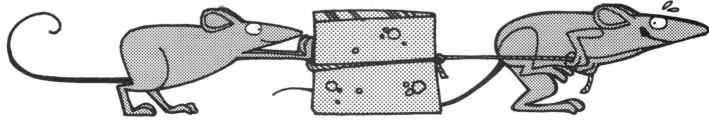

Bi- Words

The prefix **bi-** means "two, twice, coming or occurring every two, or coming or occurring twice." Below is a list of words that start with this prefix. How many words can you add to the list?

biangular	biennial	binomial
biannual	bifacial	binuclear
biarticulate	bifanged	bipartisan
biaxial	bifilar	bipartite
bicentennial	biflagellate	biped
bicephalous	bifocal	biplane
bicolor	bifoliate	bipolar
bicorn	bilabial	bipropellant
bicorporal	bilateral	biradiate
bicultural	bimolecular	bireme
bicuspid	binary	bisect
bicycle		biweekly

Here are some other prefixes that indicate numbers. Select one of these prefixes and list ten or more words in which it is used.

tri-	three	*sept-, septi-*	seven
quad-	four	*octa-, octo-*	eight
penta-, quint-	five	*novem-*	nine
hexa-, hex-, sext-	six	*deca-, dec-, deka-*	ten

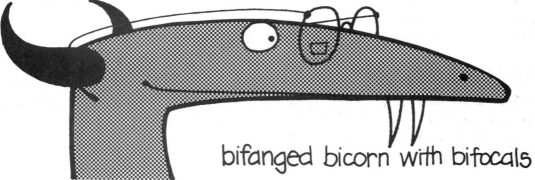

bifanged bicorn with bifocals

Compound Words

absentminded	battleship	checkerboard	driftwood	football
aftermath	bedroom	cheeseburger	driveway	footnote
afternoon	bedspread	chessboard	drugstore	footprint
aircraft	bedtime	classroom	drumstick	forever
airfield	beehive	coastline	dugout	framework
airline	beside	coffeepot	earache	freshman
airmail	birthday	copyright	eardrum	frostbite
airplane	birthmark	countdown	earmark	fullback
airport	birthplace	courthouse	earthbound	gaslight
airstrip	blackberry	courtyard	earthquake	gatehouse
airtight	blackbird	cowboy	eggnog	gatekeeper
alongside	blackboard	crowbar	eggplant	getaway
angelfish	blackmail	cupcake	eggshell	gingerbread
another	blackout	daybreak	elsewhere	glassware
anybody	blindfold	daytime	evergreen	goldfish
anyone	bluebell	deckhand	everybody	grapefruit
anything	bluebird	deerskin	everyone	grapevine
applesauce	bluegrass	dewdrop	everything	hairbrush
armband	boathouse	dishpan	eyebrow	halfway
armchair	boldface	dodgeball	eyelash	handbook
armhole	brainstorm	dogcart	eyelid	handcuff
backbone	brakeman	doorbell	fairground	handshake
backfire	breakfast	doormat	fairway	hangnail
background	briefcase	doorway	farewell	headline
backhand	broomstick	doubleheader	farmhand	highway
bagpipe	buckskin	downhill	farmhouse	hilltop
bareback	bulldog	downpour	farmland	homework
barefoot	bullfight	downstairs	farmyard	horseback
barnyard	butterfly	downstream	fingernail	houseboat
baseball	buttermilk	downtown	fingerprint	housefly
baseman	campfire	dragonfly	fireplace	household
basketball	campground	drainpipe	fireworks	however
bathrobe	candlestick	drawback	flagpole	icebox
bathroom	catfish	drawbridge	flashlight	icecap
bathtub	cattleman	drawstring	flowerpot	inchworm
battlefield	chalkboard	dressmaker	foolproof	innkeeper

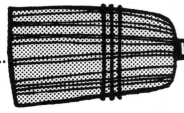

Compound Words
(continued)

inside	mouthpiece	peanut	scarecrow	toothpick
into	necktie	peppercorn	scoutmaster	trademark
jackpot	newspaper	peppermint	seafood	tugboat
jaywalk	nightfall	pickpocket	seaport	turnpike
jellyfish	nightgown	pigtail	seashore	typewriter
junkyard	nobody	pillowcase	seesaw	undergo
kettledrum	notebook	pineapple	shipmate	underground
keyboard	oatmeal	pipeline	shipwreck	underline
keyhole	offshore	pitchfork	shortstop	underwater
kickoff	outboard	playground	skyline	upright
laborsaving	outdoors	popcorn	slipknot	vineyard
ladybug	outfit	postmark	smallpox	wallpaper
landmark	outguess	quicksand	snowball	wastebasket
landslide	outlaw	railroad	starboard	watermelon
lifeboat	outline	railway	steamboat	waterway
lifeline	outrage	rainbow	sunburn	weekend
lifetime	outside	raincoat	sunshine	whatever
liftoff	overdose	raindrop	supermarket	widespread
lighthouse	overdue	rainfall	surfboard	wildfire
limestone	overgrowth	rattlesnake	tablespoon	windmill
locksmith	overtime	roadblock	tadpole	within
lookout	overweight	roadside	tailbone	without
mailbox	paintbrush	roommate	takeoff	wolfhound
mainstream	pancake	rosebud	teaspoon	woodshed
masterpiece	paperback	rowboat	textbook	woodwork
moonlight	paperweight	runway	themselves	worldwide
motorboat	parkway	sailboat	tightrope	yardstick
motorcycle	password	sandbox	toenail	

Select ten compound words from the list on pages 15 and 16. Illustrate each word on a separate page of a booklet. Do *not* write the word. Give your booklet to a friend to see if he or she can use the pictures you drew to identify the compound words you selected.

Conjunctions

A **conjunction** is a word that joins together individual words or groups of words in a sentence.

Coordinating	Correlative	Subordinating
and	either . . . or	after
but	neither . . . nor	as
for	not only . . . but also	because
nor		if
or		when

Interjections

An **interjection** is a word that expresses emotion and has no grammatical relation to other words in a sentence.

Ah!	Ouch!
Alas!	Phooey!
Bah!	Pooh!
Dear me!	Pshaw!
Farewell!	Shoo!
Good-bye!	Shame!
Heavens!	Tut!
Help!	Ugh!
My goodness!	Well!
Oh!	Whew!

Contractions

A **contraction** is a shortened form of a single word or of a word pair. An apostrophe is used to show where a letter or letters have been omitted to create the shortened form.

Be

I'm	I am
you're	you are
he's	he is
she's	she is
it's	it is
we're	we are
they're	they are

Have

I've	I have
you've	you have
we've	we have
they've	they have

Not

isn't	is not
aren't	are not
won't	will not
can't	cannot
wouldn't	would not
don't	do not
doesn't	does not
haven't	have not
hasn't	has not
hadn't	had not
shouldn't	should not
mightn't	might not
mustn't	must not
oughtn't	ought not
wasn't	was not
weren't	were not

Will

I'll	I will
you'll	you will
he'll	he will
she'll	she will
it'll	it will
we'll	we will
they'll	they will
who'll	who will

Would

I'd	I would
you'd	you would
he'd	he would
she'd	she would
we'd	we would
they'd	they would

And More

I'd	I had
he'd	he had
let's	let us
that's	that is
	that has
what's	what is
	what has
where's	where is
	where has
who's	who is
	who has

Ex- Words

exacerbate	exhort	expound
exact	exhumation	express
exaggerate	exigency	expropriation
exalt	exiguity	expulsion
examination	exile	expunge
example	exist	exquisite
exasperate	exit	extant
excavate	exonerate	extemporaneous
exceed	exorbitant	extend
excellence	exorcism	extensive
except	exotic	extent
excess	expand	extenuating
exchange	expatiate	exterior
exchequer	expect	exterminate
excise	expedient	external
excite	expel	extinct
exclaim	expenditure	extinguish
exclude	expensive	extirpate
excrete	experience	extol
exculpate	experiment	extortion
excursion	expert	extra
excuse	expiate	extract
execrate	expire	extradite
execute	explain	extraneous
exegesis	explicable	extraordinary
exegetical	explicit	extravagance
exemplary	explode	extreme
exempt	exploit	extremity
exercise	explore	extricate
exert	explosion	extrinsic
exhale	expose	exuberance
exhaustion	expostulate	exude
exhibit	exposure	exultant
exhilarate		

Expressions

all gussied up
backseat driver
baker's dozen
bated breath
bed of roses
behind the eight ball
big cheese
bite the dust
bone to pick
bring down the house
castles in Spain
charley horse
cut the mustard
Davy Jones's locker
dead as a doornail
dead duck
the deep six
devil's advocate
diamond in the rough
dog days
duck soup
egg money
elbow grease
eleventh hour
face the music
fall in love
fast and loose

a feather in one's cap
feel one's oats
a fly in the ointment
fly off the handle
forty acres and a mule
four corners of the earth
full of beans
get one's fingers burned
get one's goat
handwriting on the wall
hit the road
humble pie
in a pickle
it's Greek to me
Johnny-come-lately
kit and caboodle
lame duck
let George do it
mad as a hatter
make hay while the sun shines
Monday-morning quarterback
month of Sundays
out of kilter
over the hill
play second fiddle
pretty kettle of fish
pull the wool over one's eyes

rain cats and dogs

Choose five of these expressions. For each one you choose, draw two pictures. In one picture, show what the expression makes you think of. In the other picture, illustrate what the expression really means.

Homophones

Homophones are words that sound alike but have different spellings and meanings.

acts, ax	capital, capitol	flea, flee
ad, add	carat (karat), carrot	flew, flu, flue
aerie, airy	cell, sell	floe, flow
aid, aide	cellar, seller	flour, flower
ail, ale	cent, scent, sent	for, fore, four
air, err, heir	cereal, serial	foreword, forward
aisle, isle	cheap, cheep	forth, fourth
all, awl	chews, choose	foul, fowl
allowed, aloud	chili, chilly	franc, frank
altar, alter	chord, cord	frays, phrase
ant, aunt	chute, shoot	friar, fryer
arc, ark	cite, sight, site	gait, gate
ate, eight	clause, claws	genes, jeans
auricle, oracle	close, clothes	gild, guild
aye, eye, I	coarse, course	gilt, guilt
bail, bale	colonel, kernel	gored, gourd
bald, balled, bawled	core, corps	gorilla, guerrilla
band, banned	counsel, council	grate, great
bare, bear	creak, creek	groan, grown
barren, baron	currant, current	guessed, guest
base, bass	cymbal, symbol	guise, guys
be, bee	dear, deer	hail, hale
beach, beech	descent, dissent	hair, hare
beat, beet	desert, dessert	hall, haul
been, bin	dew, do, due	halve, have
bell, belle	die, dye	hangar, hanger
berry, bury	doe, dough	hay, hey
berth, birth	dual, duel	heal, heel, he'll
better, bettor	ducked, duct	hear, here
billed, build	earn, urn	heard, herd
blew, blue	ewe, yew, you	he'd, heed
bloc, block	eyelet, islet	hew, hue
boar, bore	faint, feint	hi, high
board, bored	fair, fare	higher, hire
bold, bowled	faun, fawn	him, hymn
boll, bowl	faze, phase	hoard, horde
bough, bow	feat, feet	hoarse, horse
bread, bred	find, fined	hole, whole
bridal, bridle	fir, fur	hostel, hostile
buy, by	flair, flare	hour, our

Homophones
(continued)

idle, idol	pail, pale	serf, surf
in, inn	pain, pane	sew, so, sow
jam, jamb	pair, pare, pear	shear, sheer
jinks, jinx	palate, palette, pallet	shone, shown
key, quay	pause, paws	sighs, size
knead, need	peace, piece	slay, sleigh
knew, new	peak, peek	soar, sore
knight, night	peal, peel	sole, soul
knot, not	pedal, peddle	some, sum
know, no	peer, pier	son, sun
knows, nose	pi, pie	staid, stayed
lain, lane	plain, plane	stair, stare
laps, lapse	plum, plumb	stake, steak
lead, led	pole, poll	stationary, stationery
leak, leek	pore, pour	steal, steel
lessen, lesson	pray, prey	step, steppe
lie, lye	pride, pried	straight, strait
links, lynx	prince, prints	suite, sweet
lo, low	principal, principle	tail, tale
load, lode	profit, prophet	taper, tapir
loan, lone	quarts, quartz	taught, taut
made, maid	rain, reign, rein	tea, tee
mail, male	raise, rays	team, teem
main, mane	rap, wrap	tear, tier
maize, maze	read, reed	their, there, they're
mall, maul	read, red	threw, through
manner, manor	real, reel	throne, thrown
marshal, martial	right, write	thyme, time
meat, meet, mete	ring, wring	to, too, two
medal, meddle, metal	road, rode	toe, tow
might, mite	roe, row	vail, vale, veil
moan, mown	root, route	vain, vane, vein
moose, mousse	rose, rows	wade, weighed
muscle, mussel	rote, wrote	waist, waste
naval, navel	rough, ruff	wait, weight
nay, neigh	rung, wrung	walk, wok
none, nun	rye, wry	war, wore
oh, owe	sac, sack	ware, wear
one, won	sail, sale	we, wee
or, ore	scene, seen	weak, week
overdo, overdue	sea, see	who's, whose
paced, paste	seam, seem	wood, would
packed, pact		yoke, yolk

Hyphenated Words

A **hyphen** is a punctuation mark that is used to divide words into syllables or to connect them to make compound words. When compound words are first formed, they are written with hyphens. Eventually, however, their spelling changes so that they are written as single words, closed up, without hyphens. See, for example, the list of compound words on pages 15 and 16. Hyphens are still used in writing the compound words listed below.

all-out	half-mast	push-up
baby-sit	hide-and-seek	quick-tempered
brand-new	jack-in-the-box	quick-witted
brother-in-law	jack-o'-lantern	right-handed
by-product	king-size	run-in
cold-blooded	know-it-all	second-guess
cross-eyed	life-size	self-conscious
custom-built	light-footed	self-made
deep-sea	made-to-order	self-service
double-cross	made-up	small-time
double-decker	middle-aged	thin-skinned
drive-in	old-fashioned	third-rate
dry-clean	one-half	walkie-talkie
father-in-law	one-sided	walk-up
go-between	on-line	well-fixed
go-getter	out-of-date	well-groomed
grown-up	pinch-hit	worn-out
half-baked	ping-pong	would-be

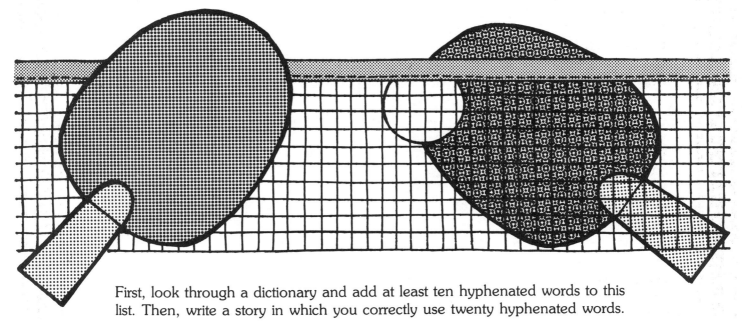

First, look through a dictionary and add at least ten hyphenated words to this list. Then, write a story in which you correctly use twenty hyphenated words.

Nouns

A **noun** is the name of a person, place, thing, quality, or idea.

appetite	igloo	river
audience	jacket	signature
bachelor	journalism	sociology
bobcat	kangaroo	territory
committee	knowledge	trestle
Congress	Linda	unicycle
deputy	literature	Utah
disease	macaroni	Venus
errand	misery	virus
example	nostalgia	weevil
fender	nucleus	wrath
florist	ocean	xylem
gasoline	organization	xylophone
ghost	photography	yam
hat	pleasure	yogurt
heart	quadrangle	zephyr
idea	quota	zest
	reconstruction	

Plurals

A **noun** is the name of a person, place, thing, quality, or idea. A noun that is **singular** names only one person, place, thing, quality, or idea. A noun that is **plural** names more than one.

The plurals of many singular nouns are formed simply by adding the letter *s* to the end of the noun.

ant	ants	monster	monsters
book	books	pencil	pencils
card	cards	pool	pools
girl	girls	ring	rings
hat	hats	school	schools

The plurals of most nouns ending in the letters *ch*, *s*, *sh*, *x*, and *z* are formed by adding the letters *es* to the end of the noun.

ax	axes	guess	guesses
box	boxes	match	matches
branch	branches	sandwich	sandwiches
bush	bushes	speech	speeches
church	churches	tax	taxes
fox	foxes	watch	watches
gas	gases	wish	wishes

To form the plural of a noun ending in *y* preceded by a vowel, add the letter *s* to the end of the noun.

boy	boys	monkey	monkeys
chimney	chimneys	tray	trays
donkey	donkeys	trolley	trolleys
journey	journeys	turkey	turkeys
key	keys	volley	volleys

To form the plural of a noun ending in *y* preceded by a consonant, change the *y* to *i* and add the letters *es*.

berry	berries	lily	lilies
body	bodies	penny	pennies
bunny	bunnies	sky	skies
city	cities	story	stories
daisy	daisies	tragedy	tragedies

To form the plural of a noun ending in *f* preceded by a vowel, simply add the letter *s* to the end of the noun.

belief	beliefs	reef	reefs
chef	chefs	roof	roofs

Plurals
(continued)

To form the plural of a noun ending in *f* preceded by a consonant, change the *f* to *v* and add the letters *es*.

calf	calves	self	selves
elf	elves	shelf	shelves
half	halves	wharf	wharves
	wolf	wolves	

To form the plural of a noun ending in *o* preceded by a vowel, simply add the letter *s* to the end of the noun.

bamboo	bamboos	radio	radios
cameo	cameos	ratio	ratios
folio	folios	rodeo	rodeos
portfolio	portfolios	studio	studios

To form the plural of a noun ending in *o* preceded by a consonant, add the letters *es* to the end of the noun.

cargo	cargoes	mosquito	mosquitoes
echo	echoes	potato	potatoes
embargo	embargoes	tomato	tomatoes
hero	heroes	veto	vetoes

Some nouns ending in *o* preceded by a consonant are an exception to this rule. The plurals of these nouns are formed simply by adding the letter *s*.

alto	altos	piano	pianos
Eskimo	Eskimos	soprano	sopranos

For some nouns, the singular and plural forms are exactly the same.

corps
deer
fowl
moose
salmon
sheep

For some nouns, the plurals cannot be formed by following the rules. These nouns are irregular, and their plurals must be memorized.

child	children	man	men
foot	feet	mouse	mice
goose	geese	ox	oxen
	woman	women	

Plurals of English Words Derived From Latin

In Latin, nouns have gender. They can be masculine, feminine, or neuter. In general, singular masculine nouns end in the letters *us*. The plural form of these nouns is made by changing this word ending from *us* to *i*. Singular feminine nouns end in the letter *a*. The plural form of these nouns is made by changing this ending from *a* to *ae*. Singular neuter nouns end in the letters *um*. The plural form of these nouns is made by changing the ending from *um* to either *a* or *i*.

In some instances, words that have come into English from Latin have retained their Latin plural form exclusively. In other instances, an English plural has been added to the Latin one so that the word actually has two acceptable plural forms.

Singular Form	Plural Forms	
	Latin	**English**
alga	algae	algas
alumna	alumnae	
alumnus	alumni	
aquarium	aquaria	aquariums
bacterium	bacteria	
cactus	cacti	cactuses
candelabrum	candelabra	candelabrums
curriculum	curricula	curriculums
datum	data	
gladiolus	gladioli	gladioluses
hiatus	hiati	hiatuses
hippopotamus	hippopotami	hippopotamuses
larva	larvae	
nebula	nebulae	nebulas
octopus	octopi	octopuses
paramecium	paramecia	parameciums
radius	radii	radiuses
stratum	strata	
syllabus	syllabi	syllabuses
vertebra	vertebrae	vertebras

Prefixes

A **prefix** is a letter or sequence of letters attached to the beginning of a word, base, or phrase.

Prefixes	Definitions	Examples
a-	in, on	abed, ashore
ab-, abs-	from, away, off	absent, absolve
alti-	high, height	altimeter, altitude
ambi-	both	ambidextrous, ambiguous
ante-	before	antebellum, antecedent
anti-	against, opposite of	antifreeze, antislavery, antiwar
aut-, auto-	self, same one	autograph, automobile
ben-, bene-	good, well	benediction, benefactor, benefit
bi-	two, occurring every two, twice	bicycle, biweekly
biblio-	book	bibliography, bibliophile
bio-	life, living matter	biography, biology
circum-	around	circumnavigate, circumscribe
co-	with, together, joint, jointly	coauthor, coexist
contra-, contro-	against, contrary, contrasting	contradict, controversy
demi-	half	demigod, demitasse
dis-	do the opposite of, exclude from, opposite or absence of, not	disable, disappear, disbelief
dys-	abnormal, difficult, bad	dyslexia, dystrophy
equi-	equal, equally	equidistant, equivalent
ex-	from, out of, not, former	export, ex-president, extend
extra-	outside, beyond	extracurricular, extraneous, extraordinary
fore-	in front of, previous	forecast, forehead
geo-	earth	geography, geology
hemi-	half	hemisphere, hemistich
hydro-	water	hydrofoil, hydroplane
hyper-	too much, over	hyperactive, hypersensitive
il-, im-, in-	not, without	illegal, impossible
inter-	between, among, jointly, together	interlock, international, interstate
intra-	within, inside	intramural, intrastate
mal-	bad, badly, abnormal, inadequate	maladjusted, malevolent

Prefixes
(continued)

Prefixes	Definitions	Examples
micr-, micro-	small, minute, minutely	microcosm, microphone
mis-	bad, badly, wrong, wrongly	misbehave, misdeed, misprint
mono-	single, one	monologue, monosail
multi-	many, multiple, more than two	multicolored, multiplex
non-	not	nonsense, nonstop
oct-, octa-, octo-	eight	octagon, octave, octet
orth-, ortho-	straight, upright, vertical, correct, corrective	orthodontics, orthodox
over-	above, more than is necessary, excessive, excessively	overact, overcoat
pan-	all	panacea, panorama
ped-, pedi-	foot, feet	pedal, pedicure, pedigree
per-	throughout, thoroughly	perfection, perform
poly-	many, several, much	polygon, polyhedral
post-	after, subsequent, later	posthumous, postpone
pre-	prior to, before, in front of	prefix, preschool
pro-	earlier than, forward, in front of, taking the place of, favoring	pro-American, proceed, proclaim, profess, pronate
pseud-, pseudo-	false, spurious	pseudonym, pseudopodium
re-	again, anew, back, backward	rebound, recall
retro-	backward, back, situated behind	retroactive, retrospect
sub-	under, beneath, below, subordinate, secondary, next lower than or inferior to	submarine, subtract
super-	over and above; higher in quality, quantity, or degree; more than	superbowl, superior
tele-	far	telescope, television
trans-	across, beyond, through	transfer, transport
tri-	three, once in every three	triangle, triplets
ultra-	beyond, extreme, extremely	ultramodern, ultraviolet
un-	not, do the opposite of, deprive of	unfinished, unlucky
uni-	one, single	unicycle, unilateral
vice-	acting for, next in rank to	vice-president, viceroy

Prepositions

A **preposition** is a word that can be combined with a noun or pronoun to form a phrase that tells something about some other word in a sentence.

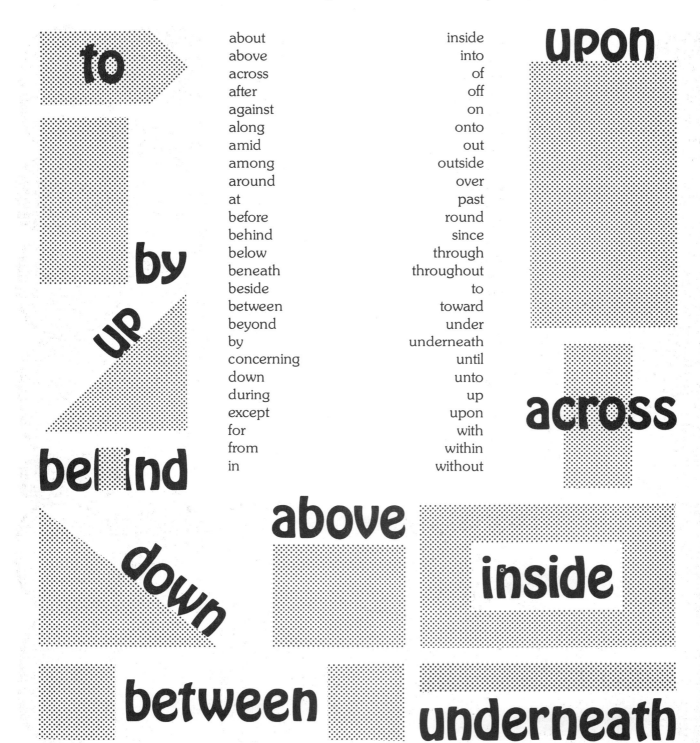

about	inside
above	into
across	of
after	off
against	on
along	onto
amid	out
among	outside
around	over
at	past
before	round
behind	since
below	through
beneath	throughout
beside	to
between	toward
beyond	under
by	underneath
concerning	until
down	unto
during	up
except	upon
for	with
from	within
in	without

to
by
up
behind
down
between
upon
across
above
inside
underneath

Pronouns

A **pronoun** is a word used in place of a noun. A pronoun may stand for the name of a person, place, thing, quality, or idea.

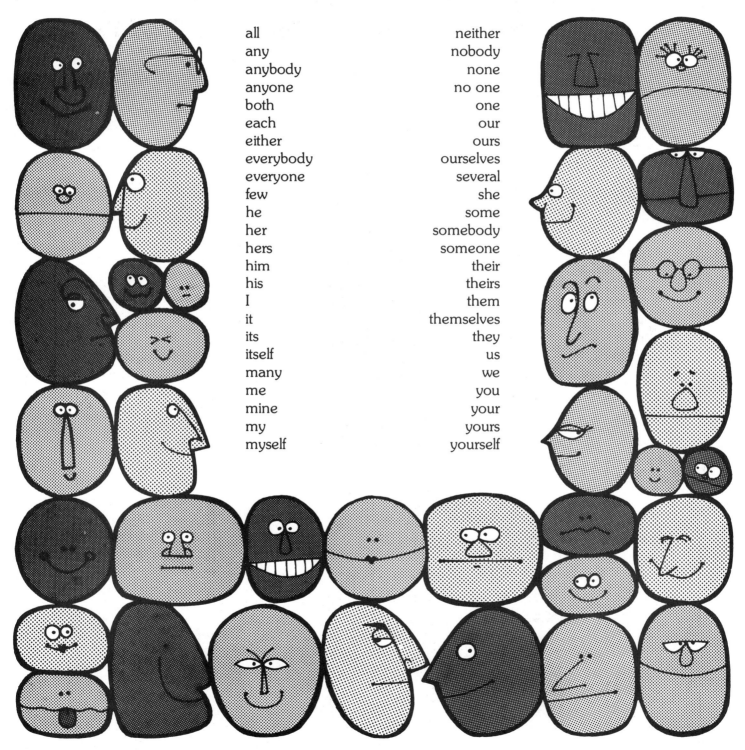

all	neither
any	nobody
anybody	none
anyone	no one
both	one
each	our
either	ours
everybody	ourselves
everyone	several
few	she
he	some
her	somebody
hers	someone
him	their
his	theirs
I	them
it	themselves
its	they
itself	us
many	we
me	you
mine	your
my	yours
myself	yourself

Punctuation Rules

Use a *period* •

- after a sentence that is a statement or command.
- after an abbreviation.
- after an initial.

Use a *comma* ,

- in a date to separate the day from the year and the year from the rest of the sentence.
- between words or phrases in a series.
- to set off *yes* and *no* at the beginning of a sentence.
- when giving a location or an address to separate the name of a city from the name of a state, the name of a state from the name of a country, and the name of a state or country from the rest of the sentence.
- before a conjunction when it joins two independent clauses.
- after the words *however* and *therefore* when they are used to join clauses in a compound sentence.
- in direct address to separate the name of the person being spoken to from what is being said.
- to separate a quotation from the rest of the sentence unless a question mark or exclamation point is needed.
- after the greeting in a personal letter and after the closing in all letters.

Use a *question mark* ?

- after a sentence that asks a question.
- after a question in a quotation.

Use an *exclamation point* !

- after a word, sentence, or quotation that shows strong feeling.

Punctuation Rules
(continued)

Use a *colon* :

- after the greeting in a business letter.
- at the beginning of a list of things in a sentence.
- to separate hours and minutes when writing times.

Use a *semicolon* ;

- in a compound sentence between principal clauses that are not joined by a conjunction.
- in a compound sentence before a conjunction that joins clauses in which there is internal punctuation.
- before the words *however* and *therefore* when they are used to join clauses in a compound sentence.

Use an *apostrophe* '

- to show that one or more letters have been left out of a word.
- with the letter *s* to form the possessive case of most singular nouns.

Use *quotation marks* " "

- before and after words that are being or have been spoken or written by someone.
- before and after the titles of articles, chapters, short poems, short stories, and songs.

Use *parentheses* ( )

- to enclose parts of a sentence, such as explanations or comments, that could be omitted without making the sentence incomplete or changing its meaning.

Use a *hyphen* -

- at the end of a line in a word that is broken and continued on the following line.
- when dividing words into syllables for spelling or pronunciation purposes.

Roots and Combining Forms

A **root** is the simple element from which a more complex word is derived, often by means of the addition of prefixes, suffixes, and/or other combining forms.

Roots	Definitions	Examples
act	do	action
-agogue	leader	demagogue
agr-, ager	field	agriculture
altus, alte	high	altitude
alter	other (of two)	alternate
annus, anno	year	annual
anthrop-, anthropo-, -anthrop	human being, man	misanthrop
aqui, aqua-	water	aquatic
arch-	chief, principal	anarchy
astr-, astro-	star	astronomy
aut-, auto-	self, same one	autobiography
brevi-	short	abbreviation
cand	white, bright, shining	incandescent
captus	take, seize, hold	capture
caput, capitis	head	cap, capital
cent	hundred	century, percent
chron-, chrono-	time	chronological
citare	put in motion, summon	citation
clarus	clear	clarity
cogito	turn over in the mind, think	cogitate
cogna-, cogni-	know	recognize
cosm-, cosmo-, -cosm	order, world	cosmopolitan
cred-	believe	incredible
culpa	blame, guilt, sin	culprit
cycle	circle, ring, wheel	bicycle
dem-, demo-	people, populace, population	democracy
derm-, derma, -derm	skin	epidermis
dict-	say, speak	diction, edict
doc-, doct-	instruct, teach	docent, doctor
dominus	master of the house, lord, ruler	dominate

Roots and Combining Forms
(continued)

Roots	Definitions	Examples
flex	bend	flexible
flor, flora	flower	floral, florist
flux	flow	influx
fort	strong	fortify
fragilis	frail; easily broken	fragile
fus-	pour, melt	fusion
-gon	angle	polygon
-gram	drawing, writing	telegram
gratus	pleasing, thankful	gratitude, gratuitous
gregarius	of or relating to a crowd, flock, or herd	gregarious
hem-, hema-, hemo-	blood	hemorrhage
hydr-, hydro-	water	hydrofoil
iacto	to throw, cast, or fling away	eject, interject
is-, iso-	equal, homogeneous, uniform	isometric
liber	to free	liberate
locus	a single place	location
logos, logi	*word, words*	*monologue*
magnus	great, large	magnify, magnitude
manus	the hand	manufacture
mare	the sea	marine, maritime
mega-	great, large	megaphone
mitto, mittere	to send or dispatch	missive, remit, transmit
mobilito	to set in motion	mobilize
navigo	to sail	navigate
ne-, neo-	new	neoclassic
nego, negare	to say no	negate, negative
-nomy	system of laws governing or sum or knowledge regarding	agronomy, autonomy
novus	fresh, new, young, inexperienced	novel, novice
ocul-, oculo-	having to do with the eye	binoculars, ocular
pan-	all	Pan-American, panorama

Roots and Combining Forms
(continued)

Roots	Definitions	Examples
paed-, ped-	child	pediatrics
phil-, philo-	loving; having an affinity for	philanthropist
phon-, phono-	sound, voice, speech	phonograph
phot-, photo-	light	photography, photon
porto, portare	to bear, bring, or carry	portable, transport
prior, primus	former, first	primacy, primary
psych-, psycho-	brain, mind, soul, spirit	psychic, psychoanalysis, psychotherapy
pyr-, pyro-	fire, heat	pyrogenic, pyromania
rogo, rogare	to ask or question	interrogate
rumpere, ruptum	to break or shatter	interrupt, rupture
scribere, scriptum	to write	prescribe, script
secare, sectum	to cut	dissect, intersection
solus, soli	alone, only	solely, solitary
somnus	sleep, slumber	insomnia, somnambulate
sono, sonare	to sound, resound, or make a noise	resonant, sonata, sonorous, unison
struo, struere, structum	to put together, to put in order, to build	construct, destructive, structure
techno-	art, craft, skill	technique, technology
tempus, temporis	a period of time	contemporary, temporal
tenuo, tenuare	to make thin, fine, slender, or slight	attenuated, tenuous
termino, terminare	to bound, limit, or make an end to	coterminous, terminate
terra	earth, land	terrain, terrarium
testor, testare	to bear witness to; to give evidence of	testify
therm-, thermo-	heat	thermos, thermometer
torquare, tortum	to twist, wind, or wrench	contort, distort, torsion
tribuere, tributum	to divide out or allot; to assign, give, or pay to	tributary, tribute
turbo, turbare	to agitate, to throw into disorder or confusion	disturb, turbulence

Similes

A **simile** is a statement in which one thing is said to be like, or the same as, another thing.

as big as all outdoors
as black as coal
as blind as a bat
as brave as a lion
as brown as a berry
as busy as a bee
as clean as a whistle
as clear as crystal
as cool as a cucumber
as easy as pie
as flat as a pancake
as fresh as a daisy
as good as gold
as happy as a lark
as hard as a rock
as high as a kite
as light as a feather
as mad as a hornet
as meek as a lamb

as neat as a pin
as old as the hills
as pale as a ghost
as pretty as a picture
as proud as a peacock
as quick as a wink
as quiet as a mouse
as red as a beet
as sharp as a tack
as slippery as an eel
as slow as molasses in January
as sly as a fox
as smooth as silk
as stiff as a board
as straight as an arrow
as strong as an ox
as stubborn as a mule
as warm as toast
as white as a sheet

as wise as an owl

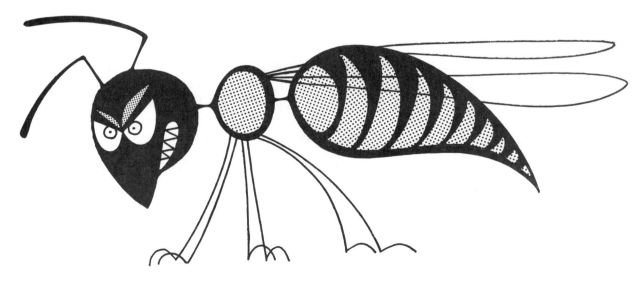

Just for fun, think of or make up some other similes and write them down. Then, select five similes from the ones listed on this page or the ones you have written and draw a picture to illustrate each one.

Slang

airhead	someone who is empty-headed; dumb
blast	a good time; a wild party
blow it	miss an opportunity; fail
boom box	large portable stereo ususally with tape/CD/radio combination
boonies	backwoods; middle of nowhere; an out-of-the-way place
bummer	a bad break; a nasty experience
burn-out	to do something so long and so intensely that you get sick and tired of doing it; also used in the phrase "burn yourself out"
cheesy	poor quality
chill out	to calm down; take it easy; relax
cool	great or fine
cop out	to give up or take the easy way out
couch potatoes	those who are content to spend large amounts of their free time at home watching television; also known as "sofa spuds"
crib	home; the place where someone lives
fresh	fine; very good
hacker	a skilled and enthusiastic user of computers; a person who illicitly uses or changes information in a computer system
psych	to intimidate or frighten psychologically, or make nervous, as in "to psych out the competition"
scarf	to consume quickly; for example, to scarf up a pizza
spin doctor	a public relations person with the proven ability to put a certain slant or a story across
spin-off	a creation which is the by-product of something else
wanna be	someone who is on the edge of something that he or she wants to be a part of
yuppies	young urban professionals with a taste for expensive cars and clothes, imported bottled water, and fashionable restaurants

Suffixes

A **suffix** is a letter or sequence of letters that has a specific definition and may be added to the end of a word, base, or phrase to change its meaning.

Suffixes	Definitions	Examples
-able, -ible	capable or worthy of	changeable, collectible
-age	action or process; rate of; fee	dosage, postage
-ance, -ancy	act, process, or state of being	brilliance, fragrance
-ant, -ent	one who performs a specified action	confidant, defendant
-dom	office; state or fact of being	dukedom, freedom
-ence	act, process, or state of being	absence
-er, -or	one who; that which	banker, editor
-ful	full of; number or quantity that fills	cupful, roomful, shameful
-fy	to make; to invest with the attributes of	simplify, citify
-hood	condition, time, or instance of	boyhood, motherhood
-ion	act, condition, state, or process of	exploration, operation
-ish	characteristic of or relating to	girlish
-ism	belief or practice of	intellectualism
-ist	one who performs a specified action; one who advocates a particular doctrine or position	communist, florist
-ity, -ty, -y	quality, state, or degree of	civility
-ive	tending to	supportive
-ize	to cause to conform to; to become like; to engage in	theorize, westernize
-logue, -log	speech or discourse; student or specialist	monologue, dialogue, ideologue
-logy	oral or written expression; doctrine, theory, or study of	biology, criminology
-ment	act, process, or state of being; concrete result of an action	entanglement, government
-ness	state, condition, quality, or degree of	happiness
-ory	having the quality of; being characterized by; a place or thing for	compulsory, laboratory
-osis	act, condition or process of	metamorphosis
-ous, -ose	full of, having, or possessing the qualities of	anxious, comatose
-ship	state of being; the art, office, or skill of	brinksmanship, friendship
-some	causing or characterized by	awesome, lonesome
-tude	state, condition, quality, or degree of	gratitude
-ward	in the direction of	upward
-y	characterized by, full of, like, or inclined to	dusty, sleepy

Syllables

Here is a list of rules for dividing words into syllables.

1. A syllable is a group of letters sounded together.

2. Each syllable must have at least one vowel sound; a word cannot have more syllables than vowel sounds.

3. Words pronounced as one syllable should not be divided.

    dive   helped   through

4. A word containing two consonants between two vowels (**vccv**) is divided between the two consonants.

    vc cv   vc cv   vc cv
    cor-rect   pret-ty   sis-ter

5. In a two-syllable word containing a single consonant between two vowels (**vcv**), the consonant usually begins the second syllable.

    v cv   v cv
    po-tion   to-day

6. In a word ending in **-le**, the consonant immediately preceding the **-le** usually begins the last syllable.

    can-<u>d</u>le   mar-<u>b</u>le   ta-<u>b</u>le

7. Compound words usually are divided between their word parts.

    down-stairs   rain-bow   sun-shine

Here is a list of rules for the way syllables are accented.

1. In a two-syllable word containing a double consonant, the first syllable is usually accented.

    hap′ py   rib′ bon

2. In a two-syllable word where the second syllable has two vowels, the second syllable is usually accented.

    con ceive′   de fraud′   pre mier′

3. In words ending in **-ion**, **-tion**, **-sion**, **-ial**, and **-ical**, the syllable preceding these endings is usually accented.

    dis cus′ sion   ex ten′ sion   of fi′ cial

4. In a word containing a prefix, the accent usually falls on or within the root word.

    com pose′   in doors′   re ply′

5. In a compound word, the accent usually falls on or within the first word.

    black′ board   court′ house   farm′ hand

but-ter-scotch ma-ple pep-per-mint

lic-o-rice lime choc-o-late tof-fee

Synonyms

abrupt-sudden	false-untrue	obvious-apparent
adjust-fix	fast-quick	odor-smell
aid-assist	fear-fright	often-frequently
alone-solitary	fierce-ferocious	opinion-view
anger-rage	forgive-excuse	oppose-resist
answer-reply	genuine-real	pain-ache
arouse-awaken	gleam-shine	peculiar-odd
beg-plead	govern-rule	petty-trivial
blank-empty	grief-sorrow	piece-part
brave-fearless	happen-occur	promise-pledge
buy-purchase	hardy-strong	quiver-shake
calm-serene	honest-sincere	reasonable-fair
caution-warn	hurry-rush	recall-remember
choice-option	identical-alike	refuse-decline
clear-plain	ill-sick	reimburse-repay
close-near	imitate-copy	sensible-wise
coarse-rough	inquire-ask	separate-disconnect
coy-shy	late-tardy	severe-harsh
danger-peril	leave-depart	shiver-shake
decline-refuse	liberty-freedom	silly-foolish
decrease-lessen	limp-slack	small-tiny
dense-thick	marvelous-wonderful	task-job
desire-want	meek-mild	teach-instruct
detach-separate	mend-repair	tease-taunt
disappear-vanish	merit-worth	tight-snug
divulge-disclose	misty-foggy	timid-shy
dubious-doubtful	mix-blend	tranquil-peaceful
easy-simple	modern-recent	useless-worthless
elect-choose	moist-damp	value-worth
empty-vacant	necessary-essential	verdict-judgment
enemy-rival	need-require	whole-entire
enormous-gigantic	nimble-spry	worthy-honorable
extraordinary-unusual	normal-ordinary	zone-area

Tricky Words

accede, *verb:* to agree
exceed, *verb:* to surpass

accept, *verb:* to receive
except, *verb:* to leave out

adapt, *verb:* to change or adjust
adept, *adv.:* expert, proficient, skillful
adopt, *verb:* to accept; to receive as one's own

affect, *verb:* to influence
effect, *verb:* to bring about
effect, *noun:* the result

aisle, *noun:* a passageway between sections of seats
isle, *noun:* a small island

all ready, *adj.:* completely prepared
already, *adv.:* before now, previously

allude, *verb:* to make brief or vague reference
elude, *verb:* to dodge or slip away from
illude, *verb:* to trick or deceive in the manner of a magician

allusion, *noun:* a reference
illusion, *noun:* something that deceives, misleads, or plays tricks upon

all ways, *adv.:* in every possible way
always, *adv.:* at all times; forever

annual, *adj.:* occurring yearly
biannual, *adj.:* occurring twice a year
biennial, *adj.:* occurring once every two years

ascent, *noun:* the act of climbing or going up
assent, *noun:* agreement or approval

assay, *verb:* to analyze or test
essay, *verb:* to attempt

avenge, *verb:* to punish in just payment for wrong done
revenge, *noun:* a personal attempt to get even

berth, *noun:* a resting place
birth, *noun:* the beginning of life

beside, *prep.:* at the side of; next to
besides, *prep.:* in addition to; moreover

capital, *noun:* a city that is the seat of government
capitol, *noun:* the building in which a legislative body deliberates

complement, *noun:* a completing part
compliment, *noun:* an expression of admiration

confidant, *noun:* a person in whom one confides
confident, *adj.:* certain

conscience, *noun:* sense of right
conscientious, *adj.:* governed by conscience; meticulous, careful
conscious, *adj.:* aware of an inward state and/or an outward fact

consul, *noun:* a government representative
council, *noun:* an assembly of persons convened for deliberation
counsel, *noun:* advice

Tricky Words
(continued)

continual, *adj.:* recurring in steady and rapid succession
continuous, *adj.:* uninterrupted

decent, *adj.:* conforming to standards of propriety, good taste, or morality
descent, *noun:* the act of going from a higher to a lower level
dissent, *noun:* difference of opinion; disagreement

deduct, *verb:* to take away an amount or quantity from a total
subtract, *verb:* to take one number from another

deprecate, *verb:* to express disapproval or regret
depreciate, *verb:* to lessen in value

directions, *noun:* guidance or step-by-step instructions for reaching a goal, place, or destination
instructions, *noun:* an outline of procedures for the accomplishment of a task

discreet, *adj.:* wise, prudent, judicious
discrete, *adj.:* disconnected, separate

elicit, *verb:* to draw forth or bring out; to evoke
illicit, *adj.:* not permitted; unlawful

eliminate, *verb:* to get rid of
illuminate, *verb:* to supply with light

emigrate, *verb:* to leave one's own country for another
immigrate, *verb:* to come into a country of which one is not a native for permanent residence

former, *adj.:* the first of two
latter, *adj.:* the second of two; the end, last, or final

imply, *verb:* to express indirectly; to hint at or suggest
infer, *verb:* to draw a conclusion or conclusions based on facts or premises

incredible, *adj.:* unbelievable
incredulous, *adj.:* skeptical, disbelieving

ingenious, *adj.:* skillful in contriving; inventive
ingenuous, *adj.:* artless, naïve, innocent

lay, *verb:* to place
lie, *verb:* to recline

mania, *noun:* a craze
phobia, *noun:* a fear

persecute, *verb:* to oppress or harass
prosecute, *verb:* to initiate criminal action against

precede, *verb:* to be, come, or go ahead or in front of
proceed, *verb:* to continue after a pause; to go on in an orderly way

principal, *adj.:* most important
principal, *noun:* a chief or head man or woman
principle, *noun:* a rule or code of conduct

rout, *noun:* an overwhelming defeat
route, *noun:* a line or direction of travel

stationary, *adj.:* immovable
stationery, *noun:* letter paper and/or other materials for writing

turbid, *adj.:* foul, muddy
turgid, *adj.:* swollen

Verbs

A **verb** is a word that expresses an act, occurrence, or state of being.

ask	interpret	recognize
assist	invite	recommend
banish	justify	stimulate
beg	jut	think
conceal	kindle	trample
cringe	know	transgress
dandle	levitate	unclench
detain	liberate	usurp
divulge	magnetize	vandalize
enter	meddle	visualize
extinguish	navigate	wobble
feel	nestle	wrote
flew	ooze	X-ray
frighten	overcome	yank
give	participate	yawn
grow	prowl	yield
hear	quake	zap
hire	quibble	zero

Helping Verbs

An **auxiliary verb**, or **helping verb**, is a verb that accompanies another verb and typically expresses mood, number, person, or tense. See if you can memorize these helping verbs in the order in which they are listed below.

am	has	will
is	have	should
are	had	would
was	do	may
were	does	might
be	did	must
being	shall	can
been		could

Verb Tenses

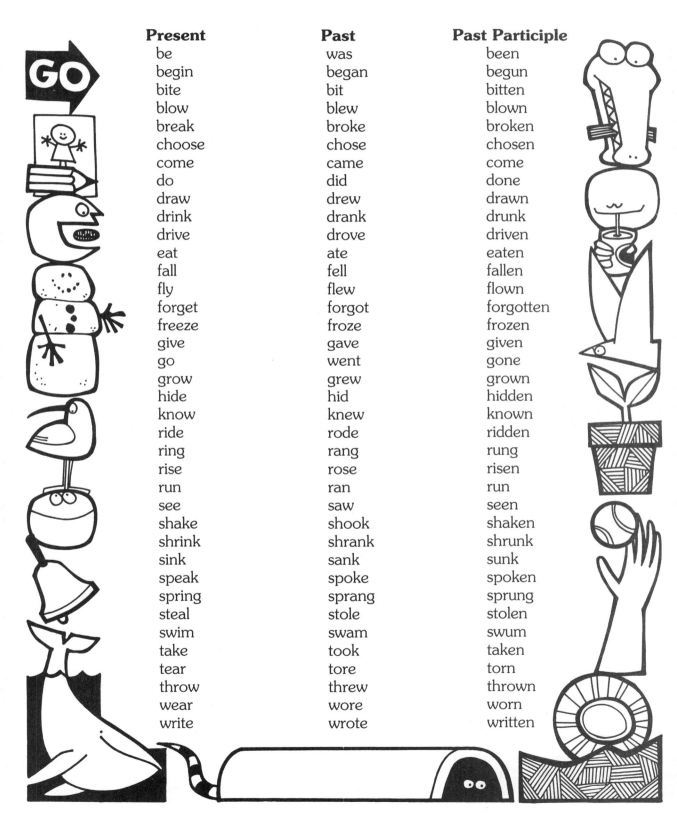

Present	Past	Past Participle
be	was	been
begin	began	begun
bite	bit	bitten
blow	blew	blown
break	broke	broken
choose	chose	chosen
come	came	come
do	did	done
draw	drew	drawn
drink	drank	drunk
drive	drove	driven
eat	ate	eaten
fall	fell	fallen
fly	flew	flown
forget	forgot	forgotten
freeze	froze	frozen
give	gave	given
go	went	gone
grow	grew	grown
hide	hid	hidden
know	knew	known
ride	rode	ridden
ring	rang	rung
rise	rose	risen
run	ran	run
see	saw	seen
shake	shook	shaken
shrink	shrank	shrunk
sink	sank	sunk
speak	spoke	spoken
spring	sprang	sprung
steal	stole	stolen
swim	swam	swum
take	took	taken
tear	tore	torn
throw	threw	thrown
wear	wore	worn
write	wrote	written

Words for Sensations

Sound

bang	growl	shriek
boom	gurgle	sizzle
brouhaha	hiss	slam
bubble	howl	smack
buzz	hum	snap
cackle	jingle	sniff
chatter	moan	splash
chime	murmur	sputter
clang	mutter	squeak
clatter	plink	squeal
click	plop	swish
clop	pop	thud
crackle	purr	thump
crash	rattle	tick
croak	ring	tinkle
crunch	roar	twang
din	rumble	wail
drone	rustle	wheeze
fizz	scream	whimper
flap	screech	whine
flutter	shout	whisper
grind		yell

Touch

brittle	oily
bumpy	prickly
coarse	ribbed
cold	rough
cool	rubbery
crumbly	sandy
damp	satiny
dirty	scaly
fluffy	scratchy
furry	sharp
fuzzy	silky
greasy	slippery
gritty	smooth
gummy	soft
hairy	spiny
hard	squishy
heavy	sticky
hot	stringy
knobbed	velvety
light	warm
lumpy	woolly
moist	wrinkled

Sight

bright	gloomy
clear	glow
cloudy	muddy
dark	murky
dim	opaque
dull	pale
dusk	radiant
faded	scintillate
gleam	shimmer
glimmer	shine
glint	shiny
glisten	sparkle
glitter	twinkle

Smell

acrid	pungent
aroma	rancid
bouquet	rank
foul	reek
fragrance	scent
fragrant	smoky
moldy	stench
musty	stink
odor	stuffy
odoriferous	sulfurous
perfume	

Taste

acid
ambrosial
bitter
delicious
peppery
piquant
salty
savory
sour
spicy
sweet
tangy
tart
vinegary
zesty

Word of the Week

Here is a list of new words to add to your vocabulary. If you learn one word each week, you'll have the entire list mastered in a year!

adorn (ə - dôrn´) *verb*—to add beauty to; decorate: *I will* **adorn** *my hat with ribbons.*

apathy (ap´ - ə - thē) *noun*—lack of feeling or interest; indifference: *He was filled with* **apathy** *after losing his job.*

bawl (bôl) *verb*—to shout or cry loudly: *I heard her* **bawl** *when she cut her finger.*

bountiful (boun´ - tə - fəl) *adj.*—more than enough; plentiful; abundant: *The farmer was proud of his* **bountiful** *crop.*

chasm (kaz´ - əm) *noun*—deep opening or crack in the earth; gap; gorge: *We could not cross the wide* **chasm**.

condone (kən - dōn´) *verb*—to forgive or overlook: *I cannot* **condone** *your bad manners.*

diligent (dil´ - ə - jənt) *adj.*—steady and careful; hardworking and industrious: *She is a* **diligent** *student.*

dwindle (dwin´ - dəl) *verb*—to become smaller or less; to shrink: *Lack of rain caused the water supply to* **dwindle**.

eccentric (ek - sen´ - trik) *adj.*—different; odd; peculiar: *Everyone laughed at the* **eccentric** *woman who dyed her hair green.*

explicit (ek - splis´ - ət) *adj.*—clearly expressed; distinctly stated; definite: *We found the house easily because of his* **explicit** *directions.*

flit (flit) *verb*—to move lightly and quickly from one place to another; dart: *We saw the hummingbird* **flit** *among the flowers.*

frivolous (friv´ - ə - ləs) *adj.*—not serious; silly: **Frivolous** *behavior is out of place in a church or courtroom.*

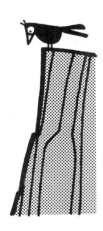

Word of the Week
(continued)

girder (gur′ - dər) *noun*—a large, horizontal beam of concrete, steel, or wood used as a main support: *The construction worker lowered the **girder** in place to support the floor.*

gnarled (närld) *adj.*—having a rough, twisted or knotted look: *There is a **gnarled** oak tree in the park. His leathery hands had been **gnarled** by time and hard work.*

heifer (hef′ - ər) *noun*—a young cow that has not had a calf: *The **heifer** was grazing in the pasture.*

humiliate (hyo͞o - mil′ - ē - āt) *verb*—make feel ashamed: *I will not **humiliate** you in front of your friends.*

impudent (im′ - pyə - dənt) *adj.*—not well mannered; shamelessly bold; very rude: *The **impudent** student argued with the professor.*

isolate (ī′ - sə - lāt) *verb*—separate from others; place or set apart: *It is wise to **isolate** patients with contagious diseases.*

jovial (jō′ - vē - əl) *adj.*—full of fun; jolly: *The child was in a **jovial** mood on her birthday.*

jubilant (jo͞o′ - bə - lənt) *adj.*—expressing or showing joy: *The team members were **jubilant**.*

katydid (kā′ - tē - did) *noun*—a large, green grasshopper: *The **katydid** hopped on our grass.*

knoll (nōl) *noun*—a small, rounded hill; mound: *We had a picnic on the grassy **knoll**.*

loiter (loi′ - tər) *verb*—stand around; linger idly: *Do not **loiter** in the halls.*

luminous (lo͞o′ - mə - nəs) *adj.*—shining by its own light; full of light; bright: *The sun and stars are **luminous**.*

melancholy (mel′ - ən - kol - ē) *adj.*—sad or gloomy; low in spirits: *She was in a **melancholy** mood.*

Word of the Week
(continued)

mumble (mum′ - bəl) *verb*—speak softly and unclearly: *If you **mumble**, I cannot understand you.*

nimble (nim′ - bəl) *adj.*—light and quick in movement; active and surefooted; agile: *The ballerina was graceful and **nimble**.*

noble (nō′ - bəl) *adj.*—being of high birth, rank, or title; showing greatness of mind or character; possessing superior qualities, magnificent: *Although his beginning was humble, his actions were **noble**.*

ominous (om′ - ə - nəs) *adj.*—unfavorable; threatening; telling of bad luck or trouble to come: *The **ominous** clouds warned us that a storm was approaching.*

optional (op′ - shə - nəl) *adj.*—not required; left to one's choice: *The chemistry class was **optional** for juniors.*

pulsate (pul′ - sāt) *verb*—beat; throb; move rhythmically: *The doctor could see the artery **pulsate** with each beat of his patient's weakened heart.*

punctual (pungk′ - chōō - əl) *adj.*—on time; prompt: *He makes a habit of being **punctual** no matter where he goes.*

quench (kwench) *verb*—put an end to by satisfying: *On a hot, dry day, you can **quench** your thirst by drinking lemonade.*

querulous (kwer′ - əl - əs) *adj.*—complaining; fretful: *The sick boy was very **querulous**.*

relic (rel′ - ik) *noun*—a thing left from the past: *The vase was a **relic** from grandmother's day.*

rustic (rus′ - tik) *adj.*—belonging to the country rather than the city; rural; simple, plain, unsophisticated: *They live in a **rustic** farmhouse.*

scant (skant) *adj.*—inadequate in size or amount; barely enough: *It was hard for us to give our patients adequate treatment because we had a **scant** supply of medicine.*

stifle (stī′ - fəl) *verb*—to hold back; suppress; stop: *Vainly I tried to **stifle** my yawn.*

Word of the Week
(continued)

tapir (tā′ - pər) *noun*—a large piglike mammal with a long nose: *The **tapir** lives in tropical America and southern Asia.*

tedious (tē′ - dē - əs) *adj.*—long and tiring: *Her job on the assembly line was very **tedious**.*

uncanny (un - kan′ - ē) *adj.*—strange and mysterious: *He had an **uncanny** ability to predict the future.*

urban (ər′ - bən) *adj.*—having to do with cities or city life: *They missed their **urban** life-style when they moved to the farm.*

valiant (val′ - yənt) *adj.*—brave; courageous: *The fire fighter put up a **valiant** battle against the flames.*

verge (vərj) *noun*—the point at which something begins; brink; border: *She was on the **verge** of falling asleep when the phone rang.*

wilt (wilt) *verb*—droop or fade; become limp: *The delicate flower will **wilt** in this hot sun.*

witty (wit′ - ē) *adj.*—amusing in a clever way: *The comedian told a **witty** joke.*

xylem (zī′ - ləm) *noun*—fleshy or woody part of plants: *The **xylem** carries water and minerals absorbed by the roots up through the plant.*

xylophone (zī′ - lə - fōn) *noun*—a musical instrument made of metal or wooden bars of varying lengths, which are sounded by striking: *She played the **xylophone** in the school band.*

yearn (yərn) *verb*—feel a deep desire or longing: *I **yearn** to go on a long vacation.*

yowl (youl) *noun*—long, loud wailing sound: *The **yowl** of the wolf could be heard throughout the forest.*

zeal (zēl) *noun*—eagerness; enthusiasm: *She worked with **zeal** on her science fair project.*

zephyr (zef′ - ər) *noun*—soft, gentle wind; mild breeze: *A **zephyr** blew across the plains.*

Consonant Blends—Final

-ck

back	hock
black	lack
block	lick
brick	lock
buck	luck
clack	mock
click	nick
clock	pack
crack	pick
crock	pluck
deck	quick
duck	rack
flack	sack
fleck	sock
flock	tack

-ct

abstract	elect
act	enact
affect	exact
collect	expect
conduct	fact
conflict	indict
connect	inflict
convict	inject
correct	insect
deduct	neglect
depict	object
detect	select
direct	suspect
effect	tact
eject	tract

-ft

aft
cleft
craft
draft
drift
gift
graft
left
lift
loft
raft
rift
shaft
shift
swift

-ld

bald
bold
build
child
cold
field
guild
hold
mild
mold
scald
shield
told
wild
yield

-mp

blimp	primp
bump	pump
camp	ramp
champ	romp
chimp	scamp
chomp	shrimp
cramp	skimp
damp	slump
dump	stamp
grump	stomp
jump	stump
lamp	thump
limp	tramp
lump	trump
plump	vamp

-nd

and	found
band	friend
behind	gland
bend	grind
beyond	ground
blend	hand
blond	hind
command	land
contend	mound
defend	remind
demand	round
depend	send
end	strand
expand	trend
extend	wind

Consonant Blends — Final
(continued)

-ng		**-nk**		**-nt**
bang	sang	bank	pink	agent
bring	sing	blank	plank	aunt
clang	slang	blink	prank	bent
cling	sling	brink	rank	cent
fang	slung	bunk	rink	chant
fling	spring	clink	sank	client
gang	sprung	crank	sink	count
hang	sting	drank	skunk	current
hung	string	drink	slink	decent
king	strong	flank	spank	dent
long	stung	frank	spunk	distant
lung	sung	junk	stink	event
pang	swing	link	sunk	front
rang	wing	mink	tank	glint
ring	zing	monk	think	grant
				haunt
				hint

-pt	**-sk**	**-st**		hunt
adapt	ask	adjust	honest	implant
adept	bask	artist	host	infant
adopt	brisk	best	invest	instant
attempt	cask	boast	just	joint
concept	desk	cast	last	lent
corrupt	disk	coast	least	moment
disrupt	dusk	contest	must	print
erupt	flask	crest	nest	sent
except	frisk	dentist	past	splint
interrupt	husk	dust	roast	tent
kept	mask	enlist	suggest	vacant
prompt	musk	feast	toast	went
receipt	risk	fist	vest	
slept	task	frost	yeast	
wept	tusk	gust	zest	

Consonant Blends—Initial

bl

black	blimp
blade	blind
blame	blink
blanch	bloat
blank	block
blanket	blond
blare	blood
blast	bloom
blaze	blouse
bleach	blow
bleak	blown
bleat	blue
bleed	bluff
blend	blur
bless	blush

br

brace	brick
brag	bride
braid	bright
brain	brim
brake	bring
bran	brink
branch	broad
brand	broke
brass	brook
brave	broom
bread	broth
break	brother
breed	brown
breeze	browse
bribe	brush

ch

chain	cheese
chair	chest
chalk	chew
champ	chick
chance	chief
change	chill
chant	chimp
chap	chin
charm	china
chart	chip
chase	chirp
chat	choke
cheap	choose
cheat	chop
check	chum
cheek	chunk
cheer	churn

cl

clack	clever
clad	click
claim	climb
clammy	clinch
clamp	cling
clash	cloak
clasp	clock
class	clog
claw	close
clay	clot
clean	cloth
clear	clove
cleat	clown
clench	clump
clerk	clutch

Consonant Blends—Initial
(continued)

cr		dr		fl	
crab	crept	drab	dried	flab	flex
crack	crest	draft	drift	flag	flick
craft	crew	drag	drill	flake	flier
cramp	crib	dragon	drink	flame	flinch
crane	crime	drain	drip	flank	fling
crash	crisp	drake	drive	flap	flip
crate	crook	drama	drizzle	flare	float
crater	crop	drank	drone	flash	flock
crawl	cross	drape	droop	flat	floor
craze	crow	draw	drop	flavor	flop
creak	crowd	drawer	drove	flaw	flour
cream	crown	dread	drug	flea	flow
crease	cruel	dream	drum	fleck	flower
credit	cruise	drench	drunk	fled	flown
creep	crust	dress	dry	flesh	fly

fr		gl		gr	
frail	fritter	glacier	glint	grab	greet
frame	fro	glad	glitter	grace	grid
fray	frock	glamour	gloat	grade	grief
freak	frog	glance	glob	grain	grill
freckle	frolic	gland	globe	grand	grim
free	from	glare	gloom	grant	grin
freeze	frond	glass	glory	grape	grind
fresh	front	glaze	gloss	graph	grip
fret	frontier	gleam	glossary	grass	grit
friction	frost	glean	glove	grate	groan
friend	frown	glee	glow	grave	groom
frill	froze	glib	glue	gray	ground
fringe	fruit	glide	glum	graze	group
frisk	fry	glimmer	glut	grease	grow
		glimpse		great	growl
				greed	gruff
				green	grunt

Consonant Blends — Initial
(continued)

pl

place	pleat
plague	pledge
plaid	plenty
plain	plod
plan	plot
plane	plow
planet	plug
plank	plum
plant	plumb
plaster	plump
plate	plunge
play	plural
plaza	plus
plead	ply
please	

pr

praise	prime
pram	prince
prance	print
prank	prior
preach	private
premium	prize
prep	probe
press	prod
pretend	profit
pretty	prone
pretzel	proof
prey	prop
price	prose
pride	proud
prim	pry

sh

shack	shell
shade	shift
shake	shine
shall	ship
shame	shirt
shape	shop
share	shore
shark	short
shave	shot
shawl	should
she	shout
shed	shove
sheep	show
sheet	shut
shelf	shy

sl

slab	slid
slack	slim
slam	slink
slander	slip
slang	sliver
slant	slob
slap	slosh
slash	slot
slat	slow
slate	slug
slave	slum
sled	slur
sleek	slush
sleep	sly
slick	

sm

smack	smock
small	smog
smart	smoke
smash	smolder
smear	smooch
smell	smother
smile	smudge
smirk	smuggle
smite	

th

that	thing
thaw	think
the	third
their	thirty
them	this
then	those
there	though
these	thought
they	thud
thick	thumb
thin	thump

st

stab	stitch
stack	stock
staff	stole
stair	stomp
stake	stone
stale	stop
stamp	store
stand	street
stare	stress
stash	strict
stem	struck
step	stuff
stick	stump
still	stun
sting	stunt

wh

whale	which
wharf	while
what	whine
wheat	whip
wheel	whirl
when	white
where	why

Long Words
Five Syllables

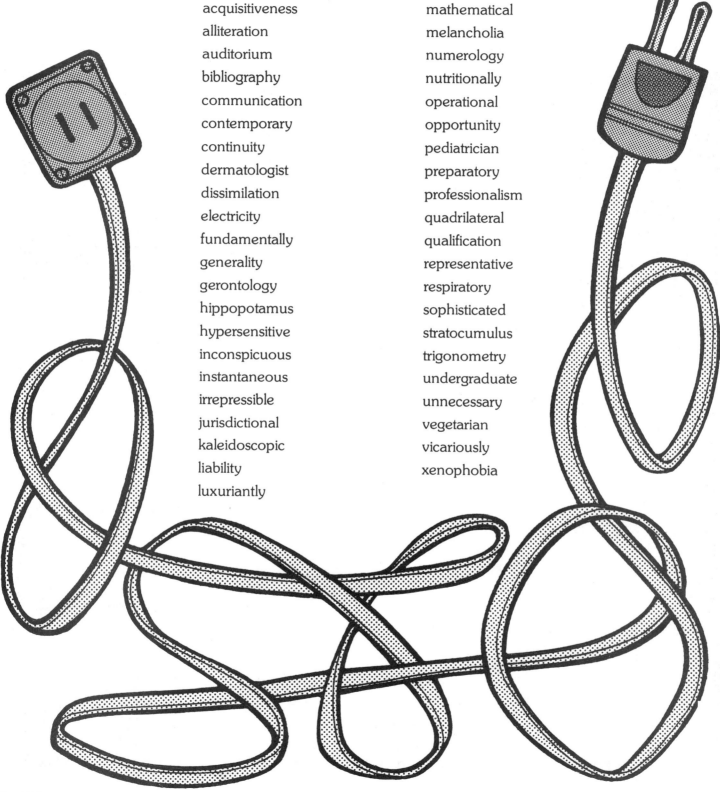

acquisitiveness
alliteration
auditorium
bibliography
communication
contemporary
continuity
dermatologist
dissimilation
electricity
fundamentally
generality
gerontology
hippopotamus
hypersensitive
inconspicuous
instantaneous
irrepressible
jurisdictional
kaleidoscopic
liability
luxuriantly

mathematical
melancholia
numerology
nutritionally
operational
opportunity
pediatrician
preparatory
professionalism
quadrilateral
qualification
representative
respiratory
sophisticated
stratocumulus
trigonometry
undergraduate
unnecessary
vegetarian
vicariously
xenophobia

Longer Words
Six Syllables

autobiography	neuropsychiatry
beneficiary	nonparticipating
bioenergetics	onomatopoeia
compartmentalizing	originality
compatibility	paleontology
congregationalism	parenthetically
conversationalist	prestidigitation
convertability	pronunciamento
disciplinarian	reorganization
disproportionally	representational
ecclesiasticism	respectability
encyclopedia	sentimentality
equivocatory	sesquicentennial
eventuality	subordinationism
exemplification	susceptibility
externalization	territorialism
extraprofessional	totalitarian
gyrostabilizer	transubstantiation
hallucinatory	ultramicroscopic
inconsequentially	unintelligible
intercommunicate	unsophisticated
jurisdictionally	unsuitability
metaphysically	vegetarianism
microscopically	vulnerability
mythologically	

Longest Words
Seven Syllables or More

axiomatically
differentiability
electrotherapeutics
hydrometeorology
incorrigibility
indefensibility
insusceptibility
micropaleontology
microphotometrically
neurophysiology
nonrepresentationalism
onomasiology
psychobiological
septuagenarian
territoriality
thermoelectromotive
unapologetically
unceremoniously
unreliability
utilitarianism

1. Use a dictionary to discover the meanings of at least five of the words on this list.

2. Use a dictionary to help you add ten words to this list.

3. Use a dictionary to find and list words with nine or ten syllables.

Rhyming Words

-ab	-ack	-ag	-ake	-all	-am
cab	back	bag	bake	all	am
fab	black	flag	brake	ball	bam
gab	crack	gag	cake	call	dam
grab	flack	hag	drake	fall	ham
jab	lack	jag	fake	gall	jam
lab	pack	lag	flake	hall	lamb
nab	quack	nag	lake	mall	Pam
slab	rack	rag	make	pall	ram
stab	sack	sag	quake	small	Sam
tab	slack	shag	rake	stall	tam
	smack	snag	sake	tall	yam
	stack	tag	shake	wall	
			snake		
			stake		
			take		
			wake		

-an	-ank	-ap	-at	-ay
an	bank	cap	at	bay
ban	blank	clap	bat	clay
bran	crank	flap	brat	day
can	drank	gap	cat	fray
clan	flank	lap	chat	gay
Dan	frank	map	fat	gray
fan	hank	nap	flat	hay
Jan	plank	rap	gnat	jay
man	rank	sap	hat	lay
Nan	sank	slap	mat	may
pan	spank	tap	Nat	pay
plan	tank	trap	pat	play
ran	thank	wrap	rat	pray
scan	yank	yap	sat	ray
tan		zap	scat	say
than			slat	stay
van			spat	sway
			that	tray
			vat	way

Rhyming Words
(continued)

-eak	-ear	-eat	-ed	-end	-et	-ick	-ig
beak	clear	beat	bed	bend	bet	brick	big
cheek	dear	cheat	bled	blend	get	chick	dig
leak	drear	cleat	bred	end	jet	flick	fig
meek	ear	eat	dead	fend	let	kick	gig
peak	fear	feat	fed	lend	met	lick	jig
peek	gear	heat	fled	mend	net	nick	pig
reek	hear	meat	led	send	pet	pick	rig
seek	leer	meet	red	spend	set	sick	twig
sleek	rear	neat	said	tend	vet	slick	wig
weak	sear	pleat	shed	trend	wet	stick	
week	shear	seat	shred	vend	yet	tick	
	sneer	sheet	sled			trick	
	spear	treat	sped			wick	
	tear	wheat	wed				
	year						

-est	-ill	-in	-ing	-ink	-ip	-it	-ob
best	bill	bin	bring	blink	dip	bit	bob
chest	chill	din	cling	clink	drip	fit	cob
jest	dill	fin	ding	drink	flip	flit	gob
nest	drill	gin	fling	link	hip	hit	job
pest	fill	kin	king	mink	lip	kit	knob
rest	gill	pin	ring	pink	nip	knit	mob
test	hill	sin	sing	rink	rip	lit	rob
vest	ill	skin	sling	sink	sip	mitt	slob
west	kill	spin	spring	stink	slip	nit	snob
wrest	mill	thin	sting	think	snip	pit	sob
zest	nil	tin	swing	wink	strip	sit	throb
	pill	win	thing		tip	slit	
	quill		wing		trip	wit	
	skill		wring		whip	writ	
	spill				zip		
	still						
	will						

Rhyming Words
(continued)

-ock	-od	-og	-oom	-op	-ot	-y
block	clod	cog	bloom	bop	cot	by
clock	cod	dog	boom	cop	dot	cry
dock	God	flog	broom	crop	got	die
flock	mod	fog	doom	drop	hot	eye
hock	nod	frog	fume	fop	jot	fly
knock	plod	hog	gloom	hop	lot	fry
lock	pod	jog	groom	lop	not	high
mock	prod	log	loom	mop	pot	I
rock	rod	smog	room	plop	rot	lie
sock	shod	tog	tomb	pop	shot	my
	sod		zoom	prop	slot	pie
	Todd			slop	sot	rye
				sop	spot	sigh
				stop	tot	sty
				top		tie
						try
						why

-ud	-ug	-un	-unk	-ut
bud	bug	bun	bunk	but
cud	dug	done	clunk	cut
dud	hug	fun	drunk	gut
flood	jug	gun	dunk	hut
Jud	lug	none	hunk	jut
mud	mug	one	junk	nut
thud	pug	pun	punk	putt
	rug	run	stunk	rut
	slug	son	sunk	shut
	tug	sun	trunk	Tut
		ton		
		won		

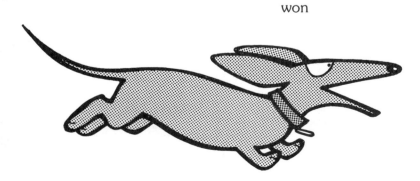

Name _____

Create a Language List

Think of a language-related topic that interests you. On the lines below, create a list that reflects this topic. Illustrate your list and give it a title.

_____

_____

_____

_____

_____

_____

_____

_____

_____

_____

_____

Social Studies

Chief Justices of the U.S. Supreme Court

Name, appointed from	Term	Years	Appointed by
John Jay (NY)	1789–1795	5	Washington
John Rutledge (SC)	1795	—	Washington
Oliver Ellsworth (CT)	1796–1800	4	Washington
John Marshall (VA)	1801–1835	34	John Adams
Roger B. Taney (MD)	1836–1864	28	Jackson
Salmon P. Chase (OH)	1864–1873	8	Lincoln
Morrison R. Waite (OH)	1874–1888	14	Grant
Melville W. Fuller (IL)	1888–1910	21	Cleveland
Edward D. White (LA)	1910–1921	10	Taft
William H. Taft (CT)	1921–1930	8	Harding
Charles E. Hughes (NY)	1930–1941	11	Hoover
Harlan F. Stone (NY)	1941–1946	5	F. D. Roosevelt
Frederick M. Vinson (KY)	1946–1953	7	Truman
Earl Warren (CA)	1953–1969	16	Eisenhower
Warren E. Burger (VA)	1969–1986	17	Nixon
William H. Rehnquist (AZ)	1986–		Reagan

Explorers

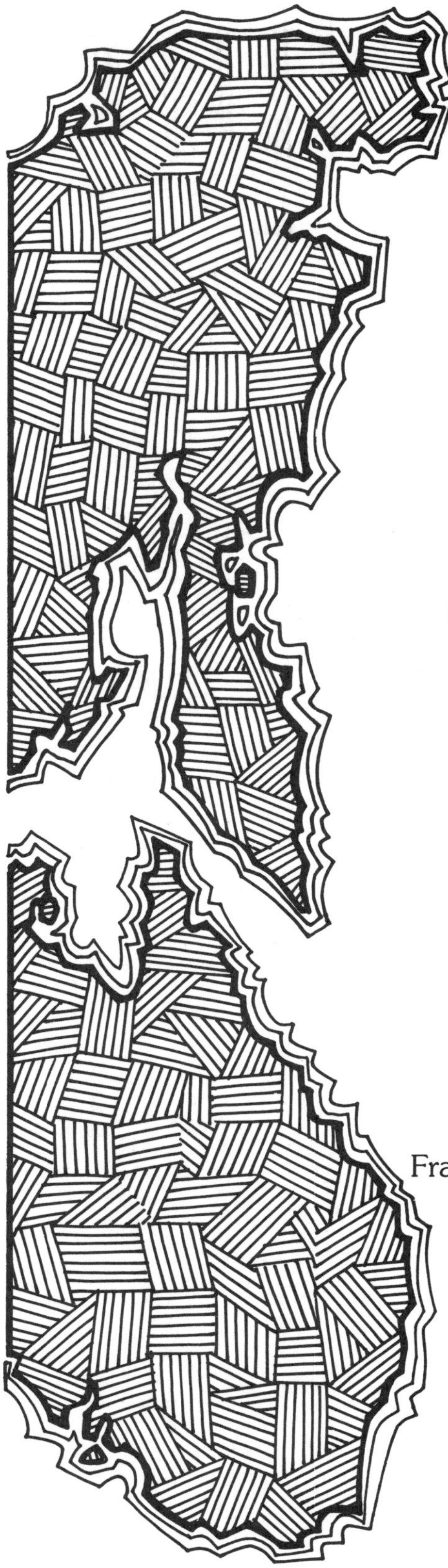

Edwin E. Aldrin, Jr.

Neil A. Armstrong

Lucas Vásquez de Ayllon

William Baffin

Vasco Núñez de Balboa

Robert A. Bartlett

Charles William Beebe

Vitus Bering

Daniel Boone

James Bowie

James Bridger

James Bruce

Robert O'Hara Burke

Sir Richard Francis Burton

Richard E. Byrd

John Cabot

Pedro Álvares Cabral

Juan Rodríquez Cabrillo

René Auguste Caillié

Kit Carson

Jacques Cartier

Samuel de Champlain

Hugh Clapperton

William Clark

Christopher Columbus

James Cook

Francisco Vásquez de Coronado

Hernando Cortes

Jacques Cousteau

William Dampier

Hernando de Soto

Bartholomeu Dias

Sir Francis Drake

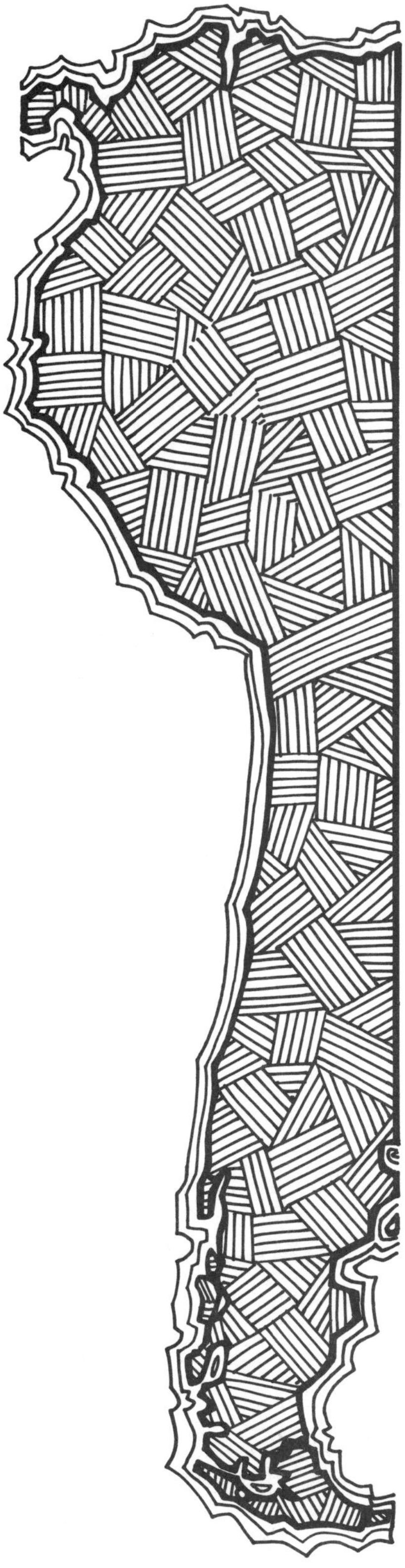

Explorers
(continued)

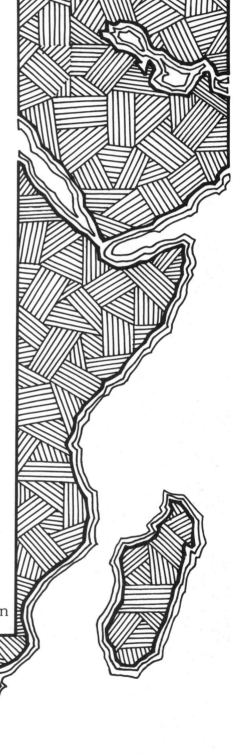

Sieur Duluth
Leif Ericson
Edward John Eyre
Sir John Franklin
John C. Frémont
Sir Martin Frobisher
Yuri A. Gagarin
Vasco da Gama
Louis Hennepin
Sir Edmund Hillary
Henry Hudson
Louis Jolliet
Sieur de La Salle
Alexei A. Leonov
Meriwether Lewis
David Livingstone
James A. Lovell, Jr.
Ferdinand Magellan
Jacques Marquette
Shirley Metz
Victoria Murden
Tenzing Norgay
Mungo Park
Robert E. Peary
Zebulon Pike
Francisco Pizarro
Sir Walter Raleigh
Robert Falcon Scott
Sir Ernest Henry Shackleton

Explorers
(continued)

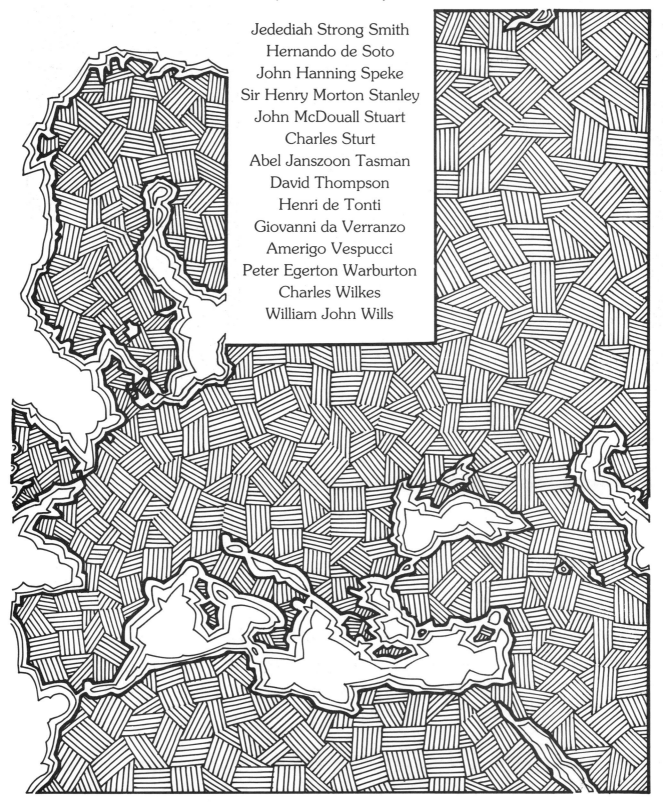

Jedediah Strong Smith
Hernando de Soto
John Hanning Speke
Sir Henry Morton Stanley
John McDouall Stuart
Charles Sturt
Abel Janszoon Tasman
David Thompson
Henri de Tonti
Giovanni da Verranzo
Amerigo Vespucci
Peter Egerton Warburton
Charles Wilkes
William John Wills

Famous African Americans

Rev. Dr. Ralph David Abernathy (1926-1990) organizer (1957) and former president of the Southern Christian Leadership Conference

Maya Angelou (1928-   ) author; recited her poem, *On the Pulse of Morning,* at President Bill Clinton's inauguration

James P. Beckwourth (1798-c.1867) western fur trader; scout, for whom Beckwourth Pass in northern California is named

Dr. Mary McCleod Bethune (1875-1955) advisor to presidents Franklin Roosevelt and Harry Truman; founder and president of Bethune-Cookman College

Guion S. Bluford, Jr. (1942-   ) astronaut; first African American in space (1983)

Thomas Bradley (1917-   ) mayor of Los Angeles, CA from 1973-1993

Dr. Ralph Bunche (1904-1971) first African American to win the Nobel Peace Prize (1950)

George Washington Carver (1861-1943) botanist and educator; his experiments in soil building and plant diseases revolutionized the economy of the South

Shirley Chisholm (1924-   ) first African-American woman elected to the House of Representatives, Brooklyn, NY (1968)

Rev. James Cleveland (1931-1991) composer and musician; first African-American gospel artist to appear at Carnegie Hall

Frederick Douglass (1817-1895) author, editor, orator, and diplomat; edited the abolitionist weekly, *The North Star*, in Rochester, NY

William Edward Burghardt (W.E.B.) Du Bois (1868-1963) historian and sociologist; a founder of the NAACP and founder of its magazine, *The Crisis*

Marian Wright Edelman (1939-   ) founder, president of Children's Defense Fund

Barbara Harris (1931-   ) first female Episcopal bishop

Benjamin L. Hooks (1925-   ) first African-American member of the Federal Communications Commission; executive director of the NAACP from 1977-1993

Langston Hughes (1902-1967) poet, writer, and lyricist; a major influence in the Harlem Renaissance of the 1920s

Rev. Jesse Jackson (1941-   ) campaigned for the Democratic presidential nomination in 1984 and 1988; president and founder of the Rainbow Coalition

Famous African Americans
(continued)

Maynard Jackson (1938-   ) mayor of Atlanta, GA, 1973-1981, 1989-1993

John H. Johnson (1918-   ) publisher and editor of *Ebony, Jet,* and *Ebony, Jr.* magazines

Barbara Jordan (1936-1996) former congresswoman from Texas; former member of the House Judiciary Committee

Rev. Dr. Martin Luther King, Jr. (1929-1968) organized a boycott of the Montgomery, AL transit system that led to the 1956 U.S. Supreme Court decision making segregation on buses unconstitutional; major organizer of massive March on Washington, where he delivered famous "I Have a Dream" speech (August, 1963); awarded Nobel Peace Prize (1964)

Malcolm X (1925-1965) Black Muslim leader and black nationalist whose ideas and oratory contributed to the black pride and black power movements in the 1960s

Thurgood Marshall (1908-1993) first African-American justice of the U.S. Supreme Court (1967-1991)

Toni Morrison (1931-   ) novelist whose books include *Song of Solomon, Sula,*and *Tar Baby*; first African-American woman to win the Nobel Prize in literature (1993)

Carol Moseley-Braun (1947-   ) first African-American woman elected to the U.S. Senate (1992)

Rosa Parks (1913-   ) Montgomery, AL resident arrested for refusing to move to the back of the bus, December 1, 1955, bringing about a boycott of the transit system

Colin Powell (1937-   ) first African-American National Security Advisor, 1987-1988; first African-American chairman of the Joint Chiefs of Staff (1989-1993)

Harriet Tubman (1823-1913) Underground Railroad conductor; served as nurse and spy for Union Army during the Civil War

Alice Walker (1944-   ) writer and essayist; awarded the Pulitzer Prize for fiction for *The Color Purple* (1983)

Booker T. Washington (1856-1915) founder (1881) and first President of Tuskegee Institute at Tuskegee, AL; author of *Up From Slavery* (1901)

Famous Americans

Maude Adams
Jane Addams
Marian Anderson
Susan B. Anthony
Virginia Apgar
John Jacob Astor
John James Audubon
Clara Barton
Alexander Graham Bell
Mary McLeod Bethune
Elizabeth Blackwell
Erma Bombeck
Daniel Boone
Ed Bradley
David Brinkley
Dr. Joyce Brothers
Margaret Wise Brown
Pearl S. Buck
Luther Burbank
Andrew Carnegie
Hattie Carnegie
Emma Perry Carr
George Washington Carver
Mary Cassatt
Willa Cather
Julia Child
Henry Clay
Katharine Cornell
Walter Cronkite
Hilda Doolittle (H. D.)
Amelia Earhart
Thomas Alva Edison
Ralph Waldo Emerson
Edna Ferber
Geraldine Ferraro

Dorothy Canfield Fisher
Henry Ford
Stephen Symonds Foster
Benjamin Franklin
Betty Friedan
Robert Fulton
William Lloyd Garrison
Theodor Geisel
Elizabeth Meriwether Gilmer
John H. Glenn, Jr.
Ulysses S. Grant
Alex Haley
Sonja Henie
Patrick Henry
Elias Howe
Lee Iacocca
Mahalia Jackson
Helen Keller
Francis Scott Key
Martin Luther King, Jr.
Ann Landers
Dorothea Lange
Emma Lazarus
Norman Lear
Robert E. Lee
Henry Wadsworth Longfellow
Amy Lowell
Clare Boothe Luce
Douglas MacArthur
Carson McCullers
Hattie McDaniel
Horace Mann
James Wilson Marshall
John Marshall
Thurgood Marshall

Famous Americans
(continued)

Margaret Mead
Samuel F. B. Morse
Anna Mary Robertson Moses
Ralph Nader
Sandra Day O'Connor
Georgia O'Keefe
Dorothy Parker
Linus Pauling
Emily Post
Joseph Pulitzer
Paul Revere
Sally Ride
John D. Rockefeller
Anna Eleanor Roosevelt
Elihu Root
Nellie Tayloe Ross
Helena Rubinstein
Jonas Edward Salk
Beverly Sills
B. F. Skinner

Cornelia Otis Skinner
Gloria Steinem
Harriet Beecher Stowe
Maria Tallchief
Henry David Thoreau
James Thurber
Ted Turner
Abigail Van Buren
Barbara Walters
Daniel Webster
Noah Webster
Dr. Ruth Westheimer
Marcus Whitman
Walt Whitman
Eli Whitney
Laura Ingalls Wilder
Thornton Niven Wilder
Roger Williams
Charles E. Yeager
Brigham Young

Famous Asian Americans

Jose Aruego (1932-   ) Filipino author and illustrator of more than sixty children's books; favorite titles are *Whose Mouse Are You?*, *Owliver*, and *Leo the Late Bloomer*

Michael Chang (1972-   ) tennis player; youngest male ever to win a Grand Slam tournament; first American to win the French Open (1989) in more than forty years

Connie Chung (1946-   ) news anchor and reporter; known for her work on *Eye to Eye with Connie Chung* and as co-anchor with Dan Rather on *CBS Evening News*

Myung-Whun Chung (1953-   ) Korean-born musician and music director; named conductor of the Opera de la Bastille, Paris (1989)

Midori Goto (1971-   ) concert violinist; popular both as a performer and a recording artist; debuted at Carnegie Hall in 1990 at the age of nineteen

Wendy Lee Gramm (1945-   ) Korean-American economist; approved for second term as Chair of the Commodity Futures Trading Commission in 1990

Sessue (Kintaro) Hayakawa (1890-1973) silent film star from the 1920s; also known for his role in *Tokyo Joe* and his Oscar-nominated performance in *Bridge on the River Kwai*

James Wong Howe (1899-1976) former boxer who became a cinematographer; best known for *The Charge of the Light Brigade*, *Yankee Doodle Dandy*, and *Casablanca*

Daniel K. Inouye (1924-   ) U.S. senator for more than thirty years; highly decorated veteran of World War II

June Kuramoto (1948-   ) talented musician, known for her work incorporating the sounds of the koto (a Japanese musical instrument) with western instruments in contemporary pop and jazz compositions

Bruce Lee (1940-1973) martial artist and actor; best known for roles in *The Green Hornet*, *Fists of Fury*, and *Enter the Dragon*

Sammy Lee (1920-   ) Korean-born doctor, Olympic diver, and coach; elected to the U.S. Olympic Hall of Fame in 1990

Andy Leonard (1968-   ) Vietnamese-born power weight lifter who holds records for the bench press, squat, and dead lift in the Special Olympics

Lydia Liliuokalani (1838-1917) Hawaii's queen from 1891-1898; talented musician who wrote *Aloha Oe* and the Hawaiian National Anthem, *He Mele Lahui Hawaii*

Famous Asian Americans
(continued)

Greg Louganis (1960-   ) Olympic-diving champion who overcame many obstacles, including learning disabilities, to win gold medals in the 1984 and 1988 Olympics

Yo-Yo Ma (1955-   ) world-reknown concert cellist who performs as a soloist and works as a recording artist

Zubin Mehta (1936-   ) musical conductor who has served as director of the Los Angeles Philharmonic, the Montreal Symphony, and the New York Philharmonic

Ellison S. Onizuka (1946-1986) astronaut and aerospace engineer; 1985, first Asian-American in space

Ieoh Ming (I.M.) Pei (1917-   ) Chinese-American architect best known for his construction work with glass designs; well-known projects include the new terminal at New York's JFK Airport, Dallas City Hall, and the extension of the Louvre Museum in Paris

Dith Pran (1942-   ) Cambodian-born journalist whose journey of survival in the 1970s in Khmer-Rouge-occupied Cambodia was depicted in the Oscar-winning film, *The Killing Fields*; currently a news photographer for the *New York Times*

Dalip Singh Saund (1899-1973) first Asian-Pacific American elected to Congress; appointed to the House Foreign Affairs Committee in 1955, where he showed concern for Asian (particularly Indian) issues

Amy Tan (1952-   ) novelist; known for *The Joy Luck Club* and *The Kitchen God's Wife*

An Wang (1920-1990) computer wizard and philanthropist; founded Wang Laboratories in 1955

Kristi Yamaguchi (1971-   ) world-champion figure skater; gold medalist at the 1992 Olympics in Albertville, France

Minoru Yamasaki (1912-1986) Japanese-American architect; his best-known designs are the Century Plaza Complex in Los Angeles, Rainier Square in Seattle, and the World Trade Center in New York

Famous Hispanic Americans

Everett Alvarez, Jr. (1937-   ) businessman and navy pilot; first American P.O.W. captured in the Vietnam War (held prisoner for eight and a half years)

Luis Alvarez (1911-1988) physicist who worked on the development of radar and the atomic bomb; won the Nobel Prize for physics, 1968

Desi Arnaz (1917-1986) Cuban bandleader; star of *I Love Lucy* with wife, Lucille Ball, from 1951-1961; co-creator of Desilu Productions

Joan Baez (1941-   ) political activist and popular singer; known as the Queen of Folk Music; well-known hits include "Blowing in the Wind" and "The Night They Drove Old Dixie Down"

Ruben Blades (1948-   ) Panamanian-born singer, composer, and actor; recorded *Buscando America* (*Searching for America*), a combination of jazz, soul, rock, and reggae (1984)

Michael Carbajal (1968-   ) international boxing star in the light flyweight division; winner of a silver medal in the 1988 Olympics; won the International Boxing Federation world title in 1990

Pablo Casals (1876-1973) cellist, composer, and conductor; known for recitals given at both the United Nations and the White House

Cesar Chavez (1927-1993) leader for Chicano migrant farm workers, particularly in the grape industry; founder of the United Farm Workers of America Union

Dennis Chavez (1888-1962) first Hispanic-American elected to the U.S. Senate (1935, New Mexico); worked to abolish racial and religious workplace discrimination

Evelyn Cisneros (1958-   ) prima ballerina with the San Francisco Ballet Company; known for her performances in *The Tempest*, *Swan Lake*, and *Sleeping Beauty*

Henry Cisneros (1947-   ) politician; elected mayor of San Antonio, TX (1981); appointed Secretary of Housing and Urban Development by President Bill Clinton

Roberto Clemente (1934-1972) baseball player; winner of four National League batting championships; elected to the Baseball Hall of Fame in 1973

David Glasgow Farragut (1801-1870) decorated American admiral and Civil War hero highly regarded for his naval heroics

Richard "Pancho" Gonzales (1928-   ) tennis player; world Professional Singles Champion from 1954 -1961

Famous Hispanic Americans
(continued)

Oscar Hijuelos (1948-   ) novelist; awarded the Pulitzer Prize in Literature (1989) for *The Mambo Kings Play Songs of Love*, the story of two Cuban musicians who want to appear on the *I Love Lucy* TV show

Manuel Lisa (1772-1820) explorer of the upper Midwest; among the first to do business with Native American tribes; later became an Indian agent for the U.S. government

Rita Moreno (1931-   ) actress, singer, and dancer; won Best Supporting Actress in 1960 for her role in *West Side Story*; has won an Oscar, an Emmy, a Tony, and a Grammy

Ellen Ochoa (1959-   ) first Hispanic-American female chosen by NASA to become an astronaut

Linda Ronstadt (1946-   ) one of the top female pop vocalists of the mid-1970s; known for her strong voice and versatile style

Ruben Salazar (1928-1970) journalist; worked to close the gap between the Mexican and Anglo committees in Los Angeles

Father Junipero Serra (1713-1784) Spanish missionary who taught Christianity to Indians in Mexico before coming to California in 1767; founded nine of California's missions

Martin Sheen (1940-   ) accomplished actor known for his work in television, the theater, and films; starred in *Catch-22*, *Apocalypse Now*, and *Wall Street*

Loreta Janeta Velázquez (aka Harry Buford) (1842-?) Confederate spy who disguised herself as a man and actively fought as a lieutenant in the Civil War; her autobiography is entitled *The Woman in Battle*

Luis Valdes (1940-   ) playwright; wrote *Zoot Suit* for the Broadway stage and the screenplay for *La Bamba*, a film about the career of Ritchie Valens

Ritchie Valens (1942-1959) singer, guitarist, and songwriter; best known for his rock version of the traditional Mexican folk song "La Bamba"

Famous Jewish Americans

Woody Allen (1935-   ) film director, screen writer, playwright, actor, and author; best known for *Sleeper*, *Annie Hall*, and *Manhattan*

Isaac Asimov (1920-   ) scientist and science-fiction writer; well-known works include *I, Robot*, *The Robots of Dawn*, and *Foundation Trilogy*

Leonard Bernstein (1918-1990) conductor, composer, pianist, lecturer, author, music educator, and spokesperson for the arts; music director for the New York Philharmonic for many years

Louis D. Brandeis (1856-1941) lawyer, teacher, advocate, and Supreme Court Justice from 1916 to 1939; Brandeis University is named for him

Eddie Cantor (1892-1964) popular comedian and dancer; performed in vaudeville and movies and on Broadway, radio, and television

Aaron Copland (1900-1990) symphony composer and music educator; best known for *Billy the Kid*, *Rodeo*, *Appalachian Spring*, and *Lincoln Portrait*; won the Kennedy Center Award in 1979

Albert Einstein (1879-1955) one of the most important physicists of modern times; formed the Special and General Theories of Relativity; won the Nobel Prize in physics in 1921

Felix Frankfurter (1882-1965) served as a Justice on the U.S. Supreme Court from 1939-1962; known for his pursuit of equal protection under the law for minorities

George Gershwin (1898-1937) one of America's favorite popular-music composers; best-known works include *Rhapsody in Blue*, *An American in Paris*, and *Porgy and Bess*

Benny Goodman (1909-1986) popular jazz clarinet player, band leader, and arranger; known as "the King of Swing;" his "big band" performed regularly from 1935 until the end of World War II

Armand Hammer (1898-1990) industrialist and entrepreneur; president and CEO of Occidental Petroleum Corporation from 1956-1973

Henry A. Kissinger (1923-   ) writer, lecturer, Harvard professor, and political strategist; served as Secretary of State from 1973-1977

Emma Lazarus (1849-1887) poet and essayist; best known for her sonnet, *The New Colossus* (1883), inscribed at the base of the Statue of Liberty

Famous Jewish Americans
(continued)

The Marx Brothers—Groucho (1890-1977), **Chico** (1887-1961), **Harpo** (1888-1964), and **Zeppo** (1901-1979) Groucho, Chico, and Harpo performed in vaudeville; Zeppo joined his brothers to form a popular comedy team famous for their performances on stage, screen, and radio; best-known films are *Monkey Business*, *Horsefeathers*, and *Duck Soup*

Arthur Miller (1915-   ) one of America's most important dramatic playwrights; two of his works are considered classics of the modern theatre, *Death of a Salesman* (1949) and *The Crucible (*1953)

Adolph S. Ochs (1858-1935) civic leader and newspaperman; long-time publisher of the *New York Times*

Billy Rose (1899-1966) impressario, theatrical producer, newspaper columnist, and nightclub owner; best remembered as a songwriter with such hits as "That Old Gang of Mine," "Without a Song," and "Me and My Shadow"

Julius Rosenwald (1862-1932) merchant and philanthropist; considered responsible for the success of Sears Roebuck; worked to encourage interracial understanding and a quality education for all people

Jonas Edward Salk (1914-1995) physician and scientist; credited with the discovery of the first vaccine for polio

Neil Simon (1927-   ) playwright; best known for his television, movie, and Broadway comedies; among his hits are *Barefoot in the Park*, *The Odd Couple*, and *Biloxi Blues*

Isaac Bashevis Singer (1904-1991) Yiddish fiction writier; won the Nobel Prize in literature in 1978

Lillian Wald (1867-1940) social worker, nurse, and sociologist; worked to provide medical care for all people, especially the poor; the creation of public health nursing is largely credited to her

Rabbi Stephen S. Wise (1874-1949) rabbi, Zionist, and social reformer; worked in support of America's labor movement; promoted equality for all those who worship in the synagogue

Famous Native Americans

Joseph Brant (c.1742-1807) Mohawk name was Thayendanegea; chief, British soldier, and Christian missionary; because of strong ties with both the Indians and the British, he often had divided loyalties between them; translated parts of the Bible into the Mohawk language

Crazy Horse (1842-1877) Lakota war chief; known for his flamboyant appearance going into battle; monument in South Dakota honors him

Charles Alexander Eastman (1858-1939) Santee Dakota physician and writer; one of the first Indians ever to receive an M.D.; instrumental in establishing more than forty Indian YMCAs; helped to found the Boy Scouts of America

Geronimo (1829-1909) Apache patriot and resistance leader; his name became a war cry because of his unyielding aggressiveness in battle; ultimately made a living through public appearances and autographed pictures; rode in Teddy Roosevelt's inaugural parade in 1905

Ira Hayes (1922-1955) Pima (O'odam) soldier and World War II hero; Marine paratrooper photographed with other men raising the U.S. flag on Iwo Jima

Iron Eyes Cody (1904-   ) of Cherokee and Cree descent; born on a reservation in Oklahoma; long associated with the "Keep America Beautiful" campaign; veteran of more than 200 western movies; sometimes called "the crying Indian"

Wilma Mankiller (1945-   ) first woman elected Principal Chief of the Cherokee nation; worked to develop educational opportunities and economic self-sufficiency for Cherokees

Maria Martinez (c. 1884-1980) San Ildefonso Pueblo potter; known particularly for producing "blackware;" provided link between the modern world and the ancestral ways

Billy Mills (1938-   ) Oglala Lakota Olympic athlete; won the 10,000 meters in Tokyo in 1964, setting a new world record, in an upset victory; only American to ever win a gold medal in this event; his life story is told in the 1983 movie *Running Brave*

Carlos Montezuma (c.1867-1823) Yavapai orphan who became a well-known physician and Indian rights leader; strong opponent of the reservation system and the Bureau of Indian Affairs

Osceola (1804-1838) Seminole patriot and resistance leader; led the Seminoles in a guerrilla campaign against the U.S. government in its attempt to move them out of Florida to Oklahoma

Ely Samuel Parker (1828-1895) Seneca chief; first American Indian to become Commissioner of Indian Affairs; educated as an attorney; served on Ulysses S. Grant's headquarters staff during the Civil War

Pocohontas (c.1595-1617) story is told that she saved the life of Captain John Smith by pleading with her father; she later married another colonist, John Rolfe; her name means "she is playful"

Famous Native Americans
(continued)

Ben Reifel (1906-1990) Brule Lakota U.S. Congressman; first Native-American member of Congress; worked with the Bureau of Indian Affairs for a number of years encouraging Native Americans to adapt cultural patterns for the present and future

Will Rogers (1879-1935) Cherokee cowboy humorist, writer, and actor; known for his rope tricks; performed on Broadway, in movies, on weekly radio broadcasts, and as part of the Ziegfeld Follies; wrote books with his commentary on life and the common man

Buffy Sainte-Marie (1942-   ) Cree musician, songwriter, and activist; 1960s folk singer known for her protest songs "Universal Soldier" and "Now That the Buffalo's Gone"and for her appearances on *Sesame Street* in the 1970s

Samoset (c.1590-c.1653) name means "he walks over much;" first man to greet Pilgrims upon their arrival in the New World; he and Unongoit signed the first treaty between the Indians and the Europeans

Will Sampson (1934-1987) Creek actor and painter; starred in *One Flew Over the Cuckoo's Nest, Orca,* and *Poltergeist II: The Other Side,* among other movies; his painted works have been exhibited in one-man shows at The Smithsonian and The Library of Congress

Sequoyah (1770-1843) used symbols to create a Cherokee writing system/alphabet; a talented silversmith; California's giant redwood tree, the sequoia, is named in his honor

Sitting Bull (1831-1890) Hunkpapa Lakota tribal and spiritual leader; during the Sun Dance, he had a vision of a battle wherein his people were victorious; this later happened in the Battle of Little Big Horn; briefly toured Europe with Buffalo Bill's Wild West Show in the 1880s

Tecumseh (1768-1813) Shawnee war chief, political leader, and orator; worked to have prisoners treated humanely; encouraged the formation of one unified Indian nation from Canada to Mexico

Jim Thorpe (1888-1953) Sac and Fox Olympic athlete; only Olympic athlete to win the pentathlon and decathlon; also participated in baseball, football, track, hockey, lacrosse, boxing, and swimming; named best American athlete for the first half of the twentieth century

Nancy Ward (c. 1738-1822) Cherokee leader and peace advocate; credited with introducing dairy farming to the Cherokees, which helped their economy

Sarah Winnemucca (c. 1844-1891) Paiute activist, scout, interpreter, teacher, and writer; traveled widely throughout the U.S. promoting Indian rights

Wovoka (c. 1858-1932) Paiute visionary responsible for the birth and expansion of the Ghost Dance religion; some called him "the Red Man's Christ;" his name means "one who makes life"

Famous Native-American Tribes

Tribe	Location	Tribe	Location
Algonquin	Far North	Menominee	Northeast
Apache	Southwest	Miami	Northeast
Arapaho	Plains	Micmac	Far North
Arikara	Plains	Miwok	California-Intermountain
Assiniboine	Plains	Modoc	California-Intermountain
Bannock	California-Intermountain	Mohave	California-Intermountain
Bella Coola	Northwest Coast	Mohegan	Northeast
Beothuk	Far North	Montagnais	Far North
Blackfeet	Plains	Munsee	Northeast
Caddo	Plains	Narragansett	Northeast
Cherokee	Southeast	Naskapi	Far North
Cheyenne	Plains	Natchez	Southeast
Chickasaw	Southeast	Navajo	Southwest
Chinook	Northwest	Nez Perce	California-Intermountain
Chippewa	Notheast/Far North	Nootka	Northwest Coast
Choctaw	Southeast	Osage	Plains
Chumash	California-Intermountain	Paiute	California-Intermountain
Comanche	Plains	Pawnee	Plains
Cree	Far North	Pima	Southwest
Creek	Southeast	Pomo	California-Intermountain
Crow	Plains	Potawatomi	Northeast
Delaware	Northeast	Powhatan	Southeast
Gros Ventre	Plains	Pueblo:	
Haida	Northwest Coast	Hopi	Southwest
Illinois	Northeast	Zuni	Southwest
Iowa	Plains	Quapaw	Plains
Iroquois:		Quechan	Southwest
Cayuga	Northeast	Salish	Northwest/California
Mohawk	Northeast	Sauk	Northeast
Seneca	Northeast	Seminole	Southeast
Kansa	Plains	Shawnee	Northeast
Kickapoo	Plains	Shoshone	California-Intermountain
Kiowa	Plains	Sioux	Plains
Klamath	California-Intermountain	Tlingit	Northwest Coast
Kutenal	California-Intermountain	Tsimshian	Northwest Coast
Kwakiutl	Northwest Coast	Ute	California-Intermountian
Lumbee	Southeast	Winnebago	Northest
Mahican	Northwest	Wintun	California-Intermountain
		Yaqui	Southwest

Firsts for American Women

Jane Addams	first American woman to win the Nobel Peace Prize
Marian Anderson	first African-American woman to sing with the Metropolitan Opera
Clara Barton	founder of the American Red Cross
Antoinette Brown Blackwell	first ordained minister in the United States (1853 in New York state)
Elizabeth Blackwell	first woman doctor of medicine in modern times
Pearl S. Buck	first American woman to win the Nobel Prize in literature
Shirley Chisholm	first African-American woman to serve in the U.S. Congress
Isadora Duncan	first American woman interpretive dancer
Amelia Earhart	American aviatrix who became the first woman to cross the Atlantic Ocean in an airplane
Rebecca Latimer Felton	became, by appointment, the first woman to serve in the U.S. Senate
Patricia Harris	first African-American woman to serve as a U.S. ambassador
Clare Boothe Luce	first woman to represent the United States in a major diplomatic post
Susanna Madora	first woman elected mayor in the United States
Maria Mitchell	first woman astronomer and discoverer of a comet
Sandra Day O'Connor	first woman justice of the U.S. Supreme Court
Frances Perkins	first woman appointed to serve in a presidential cabinet
Jeannette Rankin	first woman elected to the U.S. Congress
Janet Reno	first woman to serve as Attorney General of the United States
Sally K. Ride	first American woman to travel in space (in June of 1983 on the space shuttle *Challenger*)
Nellie Tayloe Ross	first woman governor in the United States
Elizabeth Cochrane Seaman around (pseudonym: Nellie Bly)	American journalist who set a record in 1890 by traveling around the world in 72 days, 6 hours, and 11 minutes
Mary Edwards Walker	first female to receive the Medal of Honor, the highest military award given by the U.S. government; pioneer woman physician who gave treatment to Union soldiers during the Civil War
Victoria Clafin Woodhull	first woman to run for president of the United States

Leaders of the Revolutionary War

John Adams

Samuel Adams

Ethan Allen

Benedict Arnold

John Barry

George Rogers Clark

George Clinton

Silas Deane

Henry Dearborn

Benjamin Franklin

Horatio Gates

Nathanael Greene

Nathan Hale

John Hancock

Patrick Henry

Esek Hopkins

John Jay

Thomas Jefferson

John Paul Jones

Henry Knox

Charles Lee

Henry Lee

Richard Henry Lee

Robert R. Livingston

Francis Marion

George Mason

Robert Morris

William Moultrie

James Otis

Thomas Paine

Israel Putnam

Rufus Putnam

Paul Revere

Arthur St. Clair

Haym Salomon

Philip J. Schuyler

John Stark

Artemas Ward

Seth Warner

Joseph Warren

George Washington

Anthony Wayne

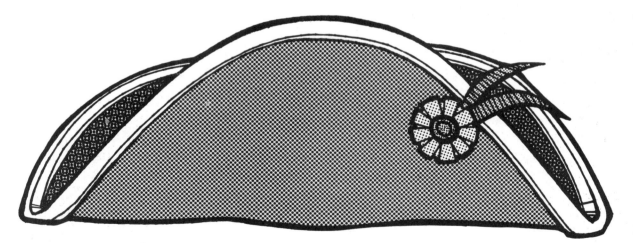

Do the research necessary to classify the people on this list as either military leaders or civilian leaders.

Presidents of the United States

Name	Term	Party
1. George Washington	1789-1797	Federalist
2. John Adams	1797-1801	Federalist
3. Thomas Jefferson	1801-1809	Democratic-Republican
4. James Madison	1809-1817	Democratic-Republican
5. James Monroe	1817-1825	Democratic-Republican
6. John Quincy Adams	1825-1829	Democratic-Republican
7. Andrew Jackson	1829-1837	Democrat
8. Martin Van Buren	1837-1841	Democrat
9. William H. Harrison	1841	Whig
10. John Tyler	1841-1845	Whig
11. James K. Polk	1845-1849	Democrat
12. Zachary Taylor	1849-1850	Whig
13. Millard Fillmore	1850-1853	Whig
14. Franklin Pierce	1853-1857	Democrat
15. James Buchanan	1857-1861	Democrat
16. Abraham Lincoln	1861-1865	Republican
17. Andrew Johnson	1865-1869	Democrat
18. Ulysses S. Grant	1869-1877	Republican
19. Rutherford B. Hayes	1877-1881	Republican
20. James A. Garfield	1881	Republican
21. Chester A. Arthur	1881-1885	Republican
22. Grover Cleveland	1885-1889	Democrat
23. Benjamin Harrison	1889-1893	Republican
24. Grover Cleveland	1893-1897	Democrat
25. William McKinley	1897-1901	Republican

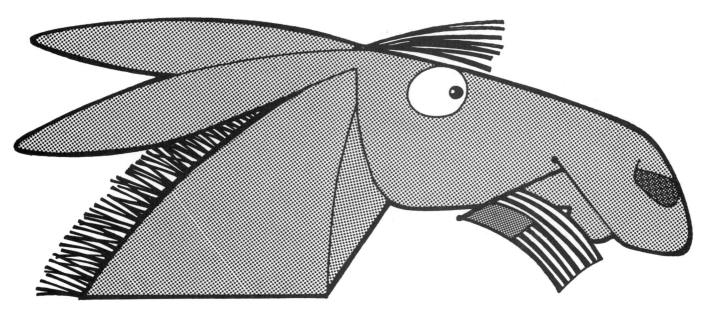

Presidents of the United States
(continued)

Name	Term	Party
26. Theodore Roosevelt	1901 - 1909	Republican
27. William Howard Taft	1909 - 1913	Republican
28. Woodrow Wilson	1913 - 1921	Democrat
29. Warren G. Harding	1921 - 1923	Republican
30. Calvin Coolidge	1923 - 1929	Republican
31. Herbert C. Hoover	1929 - 1933	Republican
32. Franklin D. Roosevelt	1933 - 1945	Democrat
33. Harry S. Truman	1945 - 1953	Democrat
34. Dwight D. Eisenhower	1953 - 1961	Republican
35. John F. Kennedy	1961 - 1963	Democrat
36. Lyndon B. Johnson	1963 - 1969	Democrat
37. Richard M. Nixon	1969 - 1974	Republican
38. Gerald R. Ford	1974 - 1977	Republican
39. James Earl ("Jimmy") Carter	1977 - 1981	Democrat
40. Ronald W. Reagan	1981 - 1989	Republican
41. George Herbert Walker Bush	1989 - 1993	Republican
42. William ("Bill") Clinton	1993 -	Democrat

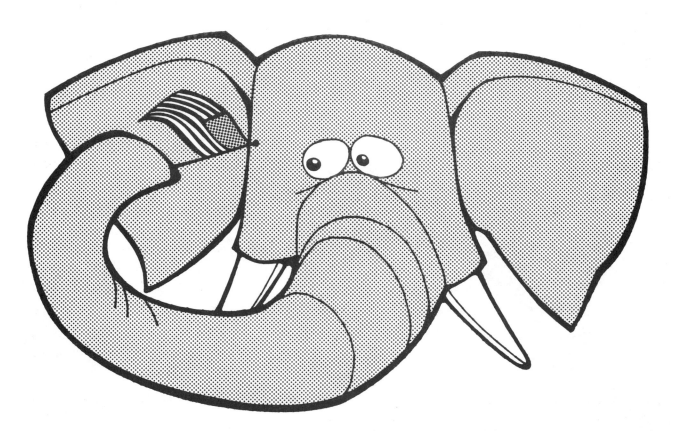

Presidents' Wives—The First Ladies

Name	Birth/Death	Name	Birth/Death
Martha Washington	1732-1802	Caroline Harrison	1832-1892
Abigail Adams	1744-1818	Ida McKinney	1847-1907
Martha Jefferson	1748-1782	Alice Roosevelt	1861-1884
"Dolly" Madison	1768-1849	Edith Roosevelt	1861-1948
Elizabeth Monroe	1768-1830	Helen Taft	1861-1943
Louisa Adams	1775-1852	Ellen Wilson	1860-1914
Rachel Jackson	1767-1828	Edith Wilson	1872-1961
Hannah Van Buren	1783-1819	Florence Harding	1860-1924
Anna Harrison	1775-1864	Grace Coolidge	1879-1957
Letitia Tyler	1790-1842	Lou Hoover	1875-1944
Julia Tyler	1820-1889	Eleanor Roosevelt	1884-1962
Sarah Polk	1803-1891	Bess Truman	1885-1982
Margaret Taylor	1788-1852	Mamie Eisenhower	1896-1979
Abigail Fillmore	1798-1853	Jacqueline Kennedy	1929-1994
Jane Pierce	1806-1863	Claudia "Lady Bird" Johnson	1912-
Mary Todd Lincoln	1818-1882	Patricia Nixon	1912-1993
Eliza Johnson	1810-1876	Elizabeth "Betty" Ford	1918-
Julia Grant	1826-1902	Rosalynn Carter	1927-
Lucy Hayes	1831-1889	Nancy Reagan	1921-
Lucretia Garfield	1832-1918	Barbara Bush	1925-
Ellen Arthur	1837-1880	Hillary Clinton	1947-
Frances Cleveland	1864-1947		

1. Prior to becoming a First Lady, Hillary Clinton was a partner in a Little Rock, Arkansas, law firm. She was voted one of the "100 Most Influential Lawyers in America" by the National Law Journal. How many other First Ladies had careers apart from the work they shared with their famous husbands? Who were they and what did they do?

2. Throughout history, many First Ladies have favored particular causes. Elizabeth Monroe worked toward improving America's diplomatic stature. Abigail Fillmore established the first White House Library. More recently, "Lady Bird" Johnson dedicated herself to a "Beautification" program for the highway system. Nancy Reagan instituted "Just Say No" for drug education. Barbara Bush became an advocate for American literacy. Hillary Clinton has worked toward health care reform for the nation.

   Investigate the lives of some of the other women listed above. Did other First Ladies support causes? What were they? How did they reflect the political climate of the country at that time?

Signers of the Declaration of Independence

Fifty-six members of the Continental Congress signed the Declaration of Independence, the historic document in which the American colonies declared their freedom from British rule.

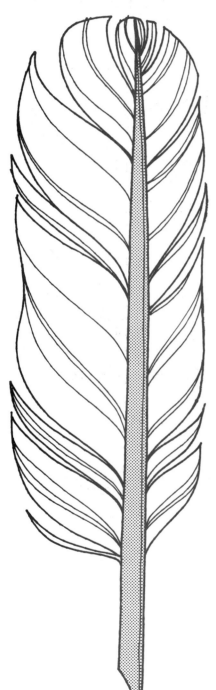

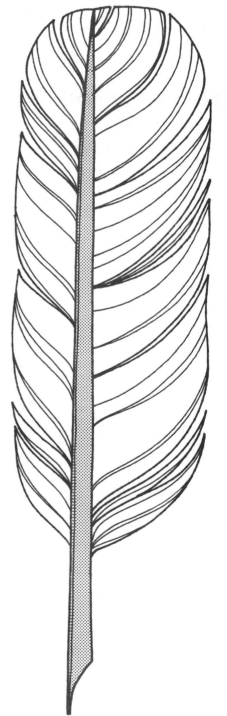

John Adams	Massachusetts
Samuel Adams	Massachusetts
Josiah Bartlett	New Hampshire
Carter Braxton	Virginia
Charles Carroll	Maryland
Samuel Chase	Maryland
Abraham Clark	New Jersey
George Clymer	Pennsylvania
William Ellery	Rhode Island
William Floyd	New York
Benjamin Franklin	Pennsylvania
Elbridge Gerry	Massachusetts
Button Gwinnett	Georgia
Lyman Hall	Georgia
John Hancock	Massachusetts
Benjamin Harrison	Virginia
John Hart	New Jersey
Joseph Hewes	North Carolina
Thomas Heyward, Jr.	South Carolina
William Hooper	North Carolina
Stephen Hopkins	Rhode Island
Francis Hopkinson	New Jersey
Samuel Huntington	Connecticut
Thomas Jefferson	Virginia
Francis Lightfoot Lee	Virginia
Richard Henry Lee	Virginia
Francis Lewis	New York
Philip Livingston	New York

Signers of the Declaration of Independence
(continued)

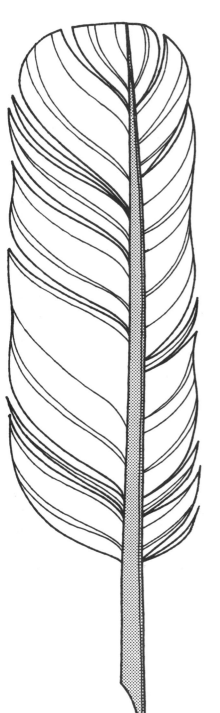
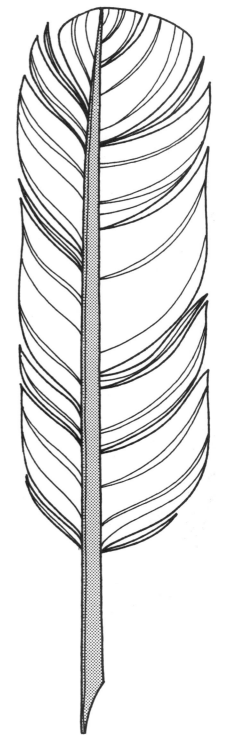

Thomas Lynch, Jr.	South Carolina
Thomas McKean	Delaware
Arthur Middleton	South Carolina
Lewis Morris	New York
Robert Morris	Pennsylvania
John Morton	Pennsylvania
Thomas Nelson, Jr.	Virginia
William Paca	Maryland
Robert T. Paine	Massachusetts
John Penn	North Carolina
George Read	Delaware
Caesar Rodney	Delaware
George Ross	Pennsylvania
Benjamin Rush	Pennsylvania
Edward Rutledge	South Carolina
Roger Sherman	Connecticut
James Smith	Pennsylvania
Richard Stockton	New Jersey
Thomas Stone	Maryland
George Taylor	Pennsylvania
Matthew Thornton	New Hampshire
George Walton	Georgia
William Whipple	New Hampshire
William Williams	Connecticut
James Wilson	Pennsylvania
John Witherspoon	New Jersey
Oliver Wolcott	Connecticut
George Wythe	Virginia

1. Pick one of the signers on this list and do research to learn more about him.

2. Make a chart or bar graph showing how many signers were from each colony.

World-Famous Leaders

Konrad Adenauer (1876-1967)
Alexander the Great (356-323 B.C.)
Yasir Arafat (1929-   )
Attila the Hun (c. 406-453)
Menahem Begin (1913-   )
David Ben-Gurion (1886-1973)
Otto von Bismarck (1815-1898)
Simón Bolívar (1783-1830)
Ralph Bunche (1904-1971)
Gaius Julius Caesar (100-44 B.C.)
Fidel Castro (1927-   )
Charlemagne (742-814)
Chiang Kai-shek (1887-1975)
Winston Churchill (1874-1965)
Cleopatra (69-30 B.C.)
Crazy Horse (1849-1877)
Oliver Cromwell (1599-1658)
Cyrus the Great (c. 600-529 B.C.)
Dalai Lama: Tenzin Gyatso (1935-   )
Moshe Dayan (1915-1981)
Charles de Gaulle (1890-1970)
F. W. de Klerk (1936-   )
Mikhail Gorbachev (1931-   )
Porfirio Díaz (1830-1915)
Dwight D. Eisenhower (1890-1969)
Elizabeth I (1523-1603)
Elizabeth II (1926-   )
Valery Giscard d'Estaing (1926-   )
Farouk I (1920-1965)
Frederick the Great (1712-1786)
Genghis Khan (1162-1227)
Indira Nehru Gandhi (1917-1984)
Mahatma Gandi (1869-1948)

Geronimo (1829-1909)
Henry VII (1491-1547)
Hirohito (1901-   )
Adolf Hitler (1889-1945)
Ho Chi Minh (1890-1969)
Chief Joseph (c. 1840-1904)
Benito Pablo Juarez (1806-1872)
Nikita Khrushchev (1894-1971)
Thomas E. Lawrence (1888-1935)
Nikolai Lenin (1870-1924)
Louis XIV (1638-1715)
Douglas MacArthur (1880-1964)
Nelson Mandela (1918-   )
Mao Tse-tung (1893-1976)
Golda Meir (1898-1978)
Mother Teresa (1910-   )
Benito Mussolini (1883-1945)
Napoleon I (1769-1821)
George S. Patton (1885-1945)
Pope John Paul II (1920-   )
Yitzak Rabin (1922-1995)
Erwin Rommel (1891-1944)
Franklin D. Roosevelt (1882-1945)
Anwar el-Sadat (1918-1981)
Santa Anna (c. 1795-1876)
Joseph Stalin (1879-1953)
Tecumseh (c. 1768-1813)
Margaret Thatcher (1925-   )
Tutankhamen (c. 1358 B.C.)
Bishop Desmond Tutu (1931-   )
Lech Walesa (1943-   )
Deng Xiaoping (1904-   )
Boris Yeltsin (1931-   )

Ancient Civilizations

Name	Approx. Dates	Location	Major Cities
Akkadian	2350-2230 B.C.	Mesopotamia, parts of Syria, Asia Minor, Iran	Akkad, Ur, Erich
Assyrian	1800-889 B.C.	Mesopotamia, Syria	Assur, Niveneh, Calah
Babylonian	1728-1686 B.C. (old) 625-539 B.C. (new)	Mesopotamia, Syria Palestine	Babylon
Cimmerian Asia Minor	750-500 B.C.	Caucasus, northern	——————
Egyptian	2850-715 B.C.	Nile Valley	Thebes, Memphis, Tanis
Etruscan	900-396 B.C.	Northern Italy	——————
Greek	900-200 B.C.	Greece	Athens, Sparta, Thebes, Mycenae, Corinth
Hittite	1640-1200 B.C.	Asia Minor, Syria	Hattusas, Nesa
Indus Valley	3000-1500 B.C.	Pakistan, North-western India	——————
Lydian	700-547 B.C.	Western Asia Minor	Sardis, Miletus
Mede	835-550 B.C.	Iran	Media
Minoan	3000-1100 B.C.	Crete	Knossos
Persian	559-330 B.C.	Iran, Asia Minor, Syria	Persepolis, Pasargadae
Phoenician	1100-332 B.C.	Palestine (colonies: Gibraltar, Carthage, Sardinia)	Tyre, Sidon, Byblos
Phrygian	1000-547 B.C.	Central Asia Minor	Gordion
Roman	500 B.C.–A.D. 300	Italy, Mediterranean region, Asia Minor, western Europe	Rome, Byzantium
Scythian	800-300 B.C.	Caucasus	——————
Sumerian	3200-2360 B.C.	Mesopotamia	Ur, Nippur

Canadian Provinces and Territories

Provinces and Territories	Capitals
Alberta	Edmonton
British Columbia	Victoria
Manitoba	Winnipeg
New Brunswick	Fredericton
Newfoundland	Saint John's
Northwest Territories	Yellowknife
Nova Scotia	Halifax
Ontario	Toronto
Prince Edward Island	Charlottetown
Quebec	Quebec
Saskatchewan	Regina
Yukon Territory	Whitehorse

Continents of the World

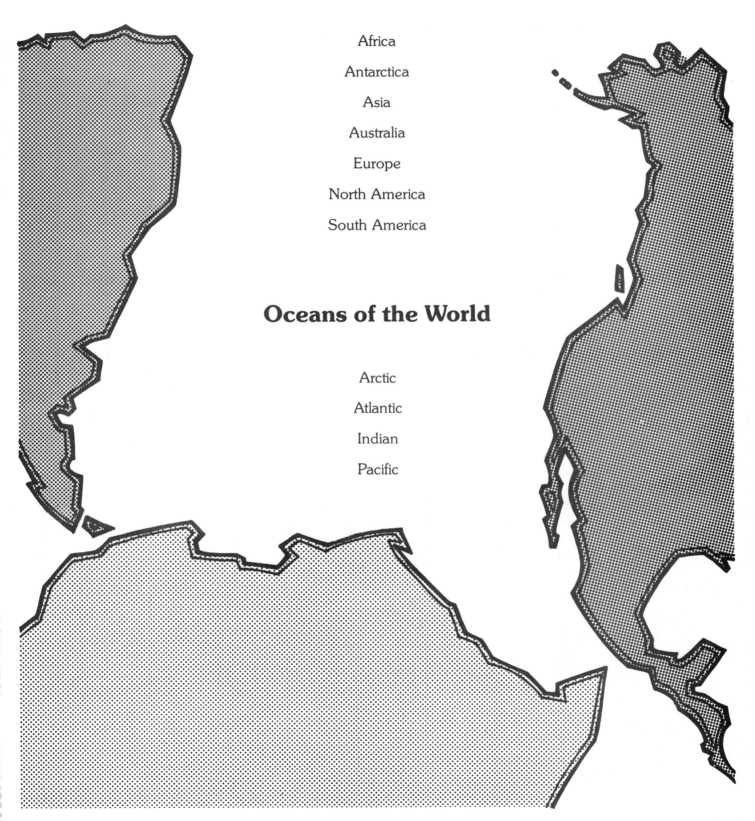

Africa

Antarctica

Asia

Australia

Europe

North America

South America

Oceans of the World

Arctic

Atlantic

Indian

Pacific

Deserts of the World

A **desert** is a region that experiences little rainfall, grows sparse vegetation, and is incapable of supporting a population of any size without an artificial water supply.

Africa
Arabian (Eastern)
Kalahari
Libyan
Namib
Nubian
Sahara

Asia
Gobi
Kara Kum
Kavir (Dasht-i-Kavir)
Kyzyl Kum
Lut (Dasht-i-Lut)
Nafud (An Nafud)
Negev
Rub al-Khali (Empty Quarter)
Syrian
Taklamakan
Thar (Great Indian)

Australia
Gibson
Great Sandy
Great Victoria
Simpson

North America
Black Rock
Colorado Desert
Death Valley
Mojave
Painted Desert
Sonoran

South America
Atacama
Sechura

1. Locate each one of these deserts on a regional or world map.

2. Do research to discover the differences among tropical deserts, polar deserts, and middle latitude deserts.

3. Select a desert from this list. Do research to find out what kinds of plant and animal life are found there.

Islands of North America

Alcatraz	Manitoulin Islands
Aleutian Islands	Martha's Vineyard
Anticosti	Mount Desert Island
Bermuda	Nantucket
Cape Breton Island	Newfoundland
Dry Tortugas	Padre Island
Ellis Island	Pribilof Islands
Florida Keys	Prince Edward Island
Governors Island	Queen Charlotte Islands
Isle Royale National Park	Sable Island
Liberty Island	Saint Pierre and Miquelon
Long Island	Southampton Island
Mackinac Island	Staten Island
Magdalen Islands	Thousand Islands
Manhattan Island	Vancouver Island

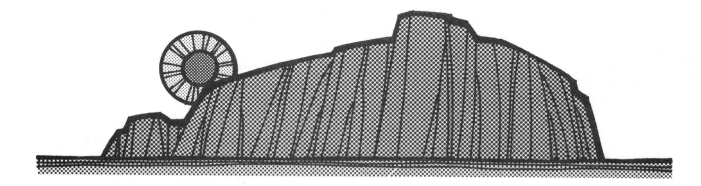

This is a partial listing and includes only some of the islands of North America. Many islands, such as Santa Catalina off the coast of California and both Camano and Whidbey in Puget Sound, have been omitted. Look up the names of some of the omitted islands in your area and add them to this list.

Landmarks of the World

Europe

The Alhambra (Red Castle)	Spain
The Colosseum	Rome
Dome of the Rock	Israel
Eiffel Tower	France
The Grand Canal	Italy
The Iron Bridge	England
Kapellbrucke (Chapel Bridge)	Switzerland
Leaning Tower of Pisa	Italy
Meteora Monasteries	Greece
Neuschwanstein Castle	Germany
Newgrange	Ireland
The Parliament Building	Hungary
The Parthenon	Greece
Pompidou Center	France
Sacré-Coeur	France
The Sagrada Familia	Spain
St. Peter's Basilica	Italy
Stonehenge	England
Versailles	France
Wailing Wall	Israel
Windsor Castle	England

South America

The Inca Trails	Bolivia
Itaipu Dam	Brazil
The Nazca Lines	Peru
Statue of Christ the Redeemer	Brazil
Valley of the Statues	Columbia

Africa

Carthage	Tunisia
The Great Pyramid	Egypt
Suez Canal	Egypt
Temple of Karnak	Egypt

Asia

Angkor Wat	Cambodia
The Blue Mosque	Turkey
The Forbidden City	China
The Great Palace	Russia
Great Wall of China	China
Hall of the Great Buddha	Japan

Asia (continued)

Itsukushima Shrine	Japan
The Kremlin	Russia
Persepolis	Iran
Potala Palace of the Dalai Lamas	Tibet
The Red Fort	India
Taj Mahal	India
The Terra-Cotta Warriors	China
Topkapi Palace	Turkey

North America

C.N. Tower	Canada
The Empire State Building	New York, NY
Gateway Arch	St. Louis, MO
Golden Gate Bridge	San Francisco, CA
Hearst Castle	San Simeon, CA
Hoover Dam	near Las Vegas, NV
Jefferson Memorial	Washington, DC
Lincoln Memorial	Washington, DC
Mormon Temple	Salt Lake City, UT
Mount Rushmore	near Rapid City, SD
Statue of Liberty	New York City, NY
Washington Memorial	Washington, DC

Central America

Church of Our Lady of Guadalupe	Mexico
Maya Temple-Cities	jungle of Yucantan Peninsula
Panama Canal	Panama
Pyramid of the Sun	Mexico
Quetzalcoatl (Chichen Itza)	Mexico

Australia and the Pacific

Borobudur	Java
Easter Island statues	Easter Island
Nan Madol	Caroline Islands
Rotorua	New Zealand
Sydney Opera House	Australia

Longest Rivers

Name	Location	Length in Miles
Nile	Africa	4,145
Amazon	South America	4,000
Yangtze	Asia	3,915
Huang Ho	Asia	2,903
Congo	Africa	2,900
Amur	Asia	2,744
Lena	Asia	2,734
Irtysh	Asia	2,640
Mackenzie	North America	2,635
Mekong	Asia	2,600
Niger	Africa	2,590
Yenisey	Asia	2,543
Paraná	South America	2,485
Mississippi	North America	2,348
Missouri	North America	2,315
Murray-Darling	Australia	2,310
St. Lawrence	North America	2,280
Ob	Asia	2,268
Volga	Europe	2,194
Purús	South America	2,100
Madeira	South America	2,013
São Francisco	South America	1,988
Yukon	North America	1,979
Rio Grande	North America	1,885
Brahmaputra	Asia	1,800
Indus	Asia	1,800
Danube	Europe	1,777
Japurá	South America	1,750
Euphrates	Asia	1,700
Zambezi	Africa	1,700
Tocantins	South America	1,677

Missions of California
(in the order of their founding)

Name	Year Founded	Location
1. San Diego de Alcalá	1769	San Diego
2. San Carlos Borromeo del Carmelo	1770	Monterey
3. San Antonio de Padua	1771	near King City
4. San Gabriel Arcángel	1771	San Gabriel
5. San Luis Obispo de Tolosa	1772	San Luis Obispo
6. San Francisco de Asís	1776	San Francisco
7. San Juan Capistrano	1776	San Juan Capistrano
8. Santa Clara de Asís	1777	Santa Clara
9. San Buenaventura	1782	Ventura
10. Santa Barbara Virgen y Mártir	1786	Santa Barbara
11. La Purísima Concepción	1787	near Lompoc
12. Santa Cruz	1791	Santa Cruz
13. Nuestra Senora de la Soledad	1791	Soledad
14. San José de Guadalupe	1797	near San Jose
15. San Juan Bautista	1797	San Juan Bautista
16. San Miguel Arcángel	1797	San Miguel
17. San Fernando Rey de España	1797	San Fernando
18. San Luis Rey de Francia	1798	Oceanside
19. Santa Inés Virgen y Mártir	1804	Solvang
20. San Rafael Arcángel	1817	San Rafael
21. San Francisco Solano	1823	Sonoma

Mountains of the World

Africa
Atlas Mountains
Kilimanjaro
Mount Kenya

Asia
Altai Mountains
Annapurna
Ararat
Himalaya
Hindu Kush
Khyber Pass
Krakatoa
Lebanon Mountains
Mount Apo
Mount Carmel
Mount Everest
Mount Fuji
Mount Godwin Austen
Mount Kanchenjunga
Mount Makalu
Mount of Olives
Stanovoy Mountains
Tien Shan
Ural Mountains
Yablonovyy Mountains

Australia and New Zealand
Mount Cook
Mount Kosciusko
Owen-Stanley Mountains

Canada
Canadian Shield
Coast Range
Mount Logan
Rocky Mountains
Saint Elias Mountains
Selkirk Mountains

Europe
Alps
Apennines
Ardennes Mountains
Ben Nevis
Black Forest
Carpathian Mountains
Caucasus Mountains
Jungfrau
Matterhorn
Mont Blanc
Montserrat
Mount Elbrus
Mount Etna
Olympus
Parnassus
Pyrenees
Stromboli
Vesuvius

Mexico
Ixtacihuatl
Orizaba
Parícutin
Popocatepetl
Sierra Madre

Mountains of the World
(continued)

South America

Aconcagua
Andes Mountains
Chimborazo

Pichincha

Cotopaxi
El Misti
Ojos del Salado

United States

Adirondack Mountains
Allegheny Mountains
Appalachian Mountains
Blue Ridge Mountains
Cascade Range
Catskill Mountains
Cumberland Mountains
Diamond Head
Great Smoky Mountains
Green Mountains
Kilauea
Lassen Peak
Mauna Kea
Mauna Loa
Mesabi Range
Mount Hood
Mount McKinley

Mount Mitchell
Mount Rainier
Mount Rushmore
Mount St. Helens
Mount Shasta
Mount Washington
Mount Whitney
Olympic Mountains
Ozark Mountains
Pikes Peak
Rocky Mountains
Sierra Madre
Sierra Nevada
Stone Mountains
Teton Range
Wasatch Range
White Mountains

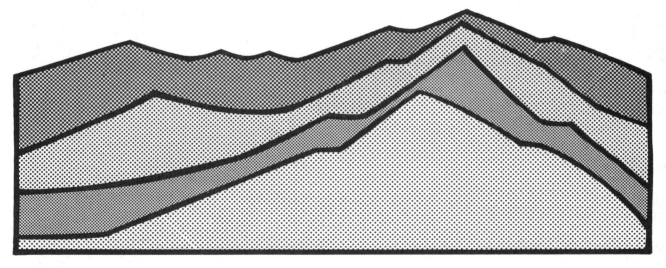

1. Select ten mountains from this list and use a bar graph to compare their heights.

2. Pretend that you are climbing one of the mountains on this list. Write a story telling about your preparations for the climb, your reasons for attempting to scale this peak, the things you see and feel as you ascend, and/or your adventures and misadventures along the way.

Nations of the World

North America

Nation	Capital
The Bahamas	Nassau
Barbados	Bridgetown
Belize	Belmopan
Canada	Ottawa
Costa Rica	San José
Cuba	Havana
Dominica	Roseau
Dominican Republic	Santo Domingo
El Salvador	San Salvador
Grenada	Saint George's
Guatemala	Guatemala City
Haiti	Port-au-Prince
Honduras	Tegucigalpa
Jamaica	Kingston
Mexico	Mexico City
Nicaragua	Managua
Panama	Panama City
Saint Kitts and Nevis	Basseterre
Saint Lucia	Castries
Saint Vincent and the Grenadines	Kingstown
Trinidad and Tobago	Port of Spain
United States of America	Washington, DC

South America

Nation	Capital
Argentina	Buenos Aires
Bolivia	Sucre (legal), La Paz (de facto)
Brazil	Brasilia
Chile	Santiago
Colombia	Bogotá
Ecuador	Quito
Guyana	Georgetown
Paraguay	Asuncíon
Peru	Lima
Suriname	Paramaribo
Uruguay	Montevideo
Venezuela	Caracas

Nations of the World
(continued)

Africa

Nation	Capital	Nation	Capital
Algeria	Algiers	Libya	Tripoli
Angola	Luanda	Madagascar	Antananarivo
Benin	Porto-Novo	Malawi	Lilongwe
Botswana	Gaborone	Mali	Bamako
Burkina Faso		Mauritania	Nouakchott
(formerly Upper Volta)	Ouagadougou	Mauritius	Port Louis
Burundi	Bujumbura	Morocco	Rabat
Cameroon	Yaoundé	Mozambique	Maputo
Central African		Namibia	Windhoek
Republic	Bangui	Niger	Niamey
Chad	N'djamena	Nigeria	Abuja
Comoros	Moroni	Rwanda	Kigali
Congo	Brazzaville	São Tomé and	
Cote d'Ivoire		Príncipe	São Tomé
(Ivory Coast)	Yamoussoukro	Senegal	Dakar
Djibouti	Djibouti	Sierra Leone	Freetown
Egypt	Cairo	Somalia	Mogadishu
Equatorial Guinea	Malabo	South Africa	Cape Town
Eritrea	Asmera	Sudan	Khartoum
Gabon	Libreville	Swaziland	Mbabane
The Gambia	Banjul	Tanzania	Dar-es-Salaam
Ghana	Accra	Togo	Lomé
Guinea	Conakry	Tunisia	Tunis
Guinea-Bissau	Bissau	Uganda	Kampala
Kenya	Nairobi	Zaire	Kinshasa
Lesotho	Maseru	Zambia	Lusaka
Liberia	Monrovia	Zimbabwe	Harare

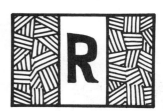

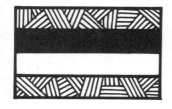

Nations of the World
(continued)

Asia

Nation	Capital	Nation	Capital
Afghanistan	Kabul	Lebanon	Beirut
Armenia	Yerevan	Malaysia	Kuala Lumpur
Azerbaijan	Baku	Maldives	Male
Bahrain	Manama	Marshall Islands	Majuro
Bangladesh	Dhaka	Micronesia	Palikir
Belarus	Minsk	Myanmar (formerly	
Bhutan	Thimphu	Burma)	Yangôn
Bosnia and Herzegovina	Sarajevo	Nauru	Yaren
Brunei	Bandar Seri	Nepal	Kathmandu
	Begawan	Oman	Muscat
Cambodia		Pakistan	Islamabad
(Kampuchea)	Phnom Penh	Papua New Guinea	Port Moresby
China	Beijing	Philippines	Manila
Cyprus	Nicosia	Qatar	Doha
Estonia	Tallinn	Russia	Moscow
Georgia	Tbilisi	Saudi Arabia	Riyadh
India	New Delhi	Singapore	Singapore
Indonesia	Jakarta	Solomon Islands	Honiara
Iran	Teheran	Sri Lanka	Colombo
Iraq	Baghdad	Syria	Damacus
Israel	Jerusalem	Tajikistan	Dushanbe
Japan	Tokyo	Thailand	Bangkok
Jordan	Amman	Tonga	Nuku'alofa
Kazakhstan	Almaty	Turkey	Ankara
	(Alma-Ata)	Turkmenistan	Ashgabat
Kiribati	Tarawa	Ukraine	Kiev
North Korea	Pyongyang	United Arab Emirates	Abu Dhabi
South Korea	Seoul	Uzbekistan	Tashkent
Kuwait	Kuwait City	Vietnam	Hanoi
Kyrgyzstan	Bishkek	Western Samoa	Apia
Laos	Vientiane	Yemen	Sanaa

Nations of the World
(continued)

Europe

Nation	Capital	Nation	Capital
Albania	Tirana	Malta	Valletta
Andorra	Andorra la Vella	Moldova	Chisinau
Austria	Vienna	Monaco	Monaco
Belgium	Brussels	Netherlands	Amsterdam
Bulgaria	Sofia	Norway	Oslo
Croatia	Zagreb	Poland	Warsaw
Czech Republic	Prague	Portugal	Lisbon
Denmark	Copenhagen	Romania	Bucharest
Finland	Helsinki	San Marino	San Marino
France	Paris	Slovakia	Bratislava
Germany	Berlin	Slovenia	Ljubljana
Greece	Athens	Spain	Madrid
Hungary	Budapest	Sweden	Stockholm
Ireland	Dublin	Switzerland	Bern
Italy	Rome	United Kingdom of	
Latvia	Riga	Great Britain and	
Liechtenstein	Vaduz	Northern Ireland	London
Lithuania	Vilnius	Vatican City	(in Rome, Italy)
Luxembourg	Luxembourg	Yugoslavia	Belgrade
Macedonia	Skopje		

Other

Antigua and Barbuda	St. John's	
Australia	Canberra	
Cape Verde	Praia	
Fiji	Suva	
Greenland (Kalaallit Nunaat)	Nuuk	
Iceland	Reykjavik	
New Zealand	Wellington	
Seychelles	Victoria	
Vanuatu	Vila	

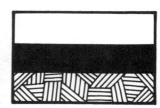

Natural Wonders of the World

Africa

Kilimanjaro	highest mountain in Africa
Nile River	longest river in the world

Asia

Caspian Sea	largest inland sea in the world
Dead Sea	the lowest body of water in the world
Fujiyama	tallest mountain in Japan; focus of poets, painters, and tourists
Ganges Delta	the largest delta in the world
Himalayas	the highest mountain range in the world
Krakatoa	Indonesian island formed by volcanic eruptions, largest in 1883
Mount Ararat	once believed to be the landing place of Noah's ark
Mount Everest	highest point on Earth, formed by the collision of continents
Yangtze River	China's longest river and most important waterway

Australia and Pacific

Ayers Rock	one of the world's largest monoliths, made of golden-red sandstone
Mauna Loa (Hawaii)	the world's largest active volcano

Antarctica

Mount Erebus	only active volcano in Antarctica; hurls lava "bombs" from its summit daily

Europe

Greenland	the largest island in the world
Matterhorn	one of the world's best-known mountains; recognized for its pyramid-like shape
Mount Blanc	the highest mountain in Western Europe
Mount Elbrus	highest peak in Europe, known for its double-cone summit
Mount Etna	the highest and one of the oldest active volcanoes in Europe
Mount Vesuvius	one of the world's most celebrated volcanoes; known for its destruction of Pompeii in A.D. 79
Olympus	highest peak in Greece; thought by the ancient Greeks to be the home of the gods
Sogne Fjord	Norway's longest and deepest fjord
Volga River	Europe's longest river
Zugspitze	highest summit in the Bavarian Alps

Natural Wonders of the World
(continued)

North America

The Badlands	an ever-changing, eroded plateau found in South Dakota; site of many prehistoric fossil finds
Carlsbad Caverns	New Mexico's popular tourist attraction; made up of more than 60 caves
Crater Lake	deepest lake in the United States; formed by volcanic activity
Death Valley	lowest, hottest, and driest spot in North America
Devils Tower	tallest monolith in the United States; featured in the movie *Close Encounters of the Third Kind*
The Everglades	Florida's "river of grass" is part prairie, part jungle, and part flowing water; home to more than 300 species of birds
Grand Canyon	the grandest of all canyons at 277 miles long, 18 miles wide, and 1 mile deep; carved by the Colorado River
Grand Tetons	Wyoming's majestic sawtooth summits, which seem to rise from the valley floor; admired for their natural beauty
Great Salt Lake	largest salt lake in the Western Hemisphere
Mammoth Cave	longest cave in the world, with 200 miles having been surveyed
Meteor Crater	Arizona's colossal saucer-shaped depression, which was created when a huge meteorite crashed to earth
Mount McKinley	highest peak in North America
Mount Rainier	highest peak in the Cascade Range; the most famous landmark in the Pacific Northwest
Niagara Falls	most famous waterfall in North America
Old Faithful	one of the best-known geysers in the world; named for the regularity of its eruptions, which occur about every 72 minutes
Petrified Forest	largest collection of fossilized wood in the world
Rainbow Bridge	world's largest natural bridge, spanning a distance of 275 feet
Stone Mountain	one of North America's largest exposed masses of granite

South America

Amazon River	largest river in the world
Andes Mountains	longest mountain system in the world at 5,500 miles
Angel Falls	tallest waterfall in the world, with a total drop of 3,212 feet
Cape Horn	located at the southern tip of Chile, known for its fierce storms, violent seas, and gale-force winds; site of countless shipwrecks
Lake Titicaca	highest navigable lake in the world; birthplace of the Incan people

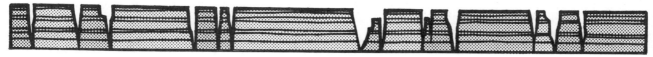

Places of Interest to Visit

airport	mission
animal shelter	movie
aquarium	national park
art gallery	natural history museum
art museum	packing plant
bakery	park
bank	pet shop
beach	photography studio
botanical gardens	planetarium
bus station	post office
circus	printing company
college	radio station
computer store	repair shop
concert	restaurant
construction site	science museum
courthouse	sports event
dairy	supermarket
factory	telephone company
farm	television station
government building	theater
grocery store	theme park
historical site	train station
hospital	university
hotel	veterinarian's office
library	zoo

States, Their Capitals, and Their Abbreviations

State Name	Capital	Standard Abbreviation	Two-Letter Abbreviation
Alabama	Montgomery	Ala.	AL
Alaska	Juneau	Alaska	AK
Arizona	Phoenix	Ariz.	AZ
Arkansas	Little Rock	Ark.	AR
California	Sacramento	Calif.	CA
Colorado	Denver	Colo.	CO
Connecticut	Hartford	Conn.	CT
Delaware	Dover	Del.	DE
Florida	Tallahassee	Fla.	FL
Georgia	Atlanta	Ga.	GA
Hawaii	Honolulu	Hawaii	HI
Idaho	Boise	Idaho	ID
Illinois	Springfield	Ill.	IL
Indiana	Indianapolis	Ind.	IN
Iowa	Des Moines	Iowa	IA
Kansas	Topeka	Kans.	KS
Kentucky	Frankfort	Ky.	KY
Louisiana	Baton Rouge	La.	LA
Maine	Augusta	Maine	ME
Maryland	Annapolis	Md.	MD
Massachusetts	Boston	Mass.	MA
Michigan	Lansing	Mich.	MI
Minnesota	Saint Paul	Minn.	MN
Mississippi	Jackson	Miss.	MS
Missouri	Jefferson City	Mo.	MO
Montana	Helena	Mont.	MT
Nebraska	Lincoln	Nebr.	NE
Nevada	Carson City	Nev.	NV
New Hampshire	Concord	N.H.	NH
New Jersey	Trenton	N.J.	NJ
New Mexico	Santa Fe	N.Mex.	NM
New York	Albany	N.Y.	NY
North Carolina	Raleigh	N.C.	NC
North Dakota	Bismarck	N.Dak.	ND
Ohio	Columbus	Ohio	OH
Oklahoma	Oklahoma City	Okla.	OK
Oregon	Salem	Oreg.	OR
Pennsylvania	Harrisburg	Pa.	PA
Rhode Island	Providence	R.I.	RI
South Carolina	Columbia	S.C.	SC
South Dakota	Pierre	S.Dak.	SD
Tennessee	Nashville	Tenn.	TN
Texas	Austin	Tex.	TX
Utah	Salt Lake City	Utah	UT
Vermont	Montpelier	Vt.	VT
Virginia	Richmond	Va.	VA
Washington	Olympia	Wash.	WA
West Virginia	Charleston	W.Va.	WV
Wisconsin	Madison	Wis.	WI
Wyoming	Cheyenne	Wyo.	WY

Thirteen Original Colonies
(in order of their adoption of the Constitution)

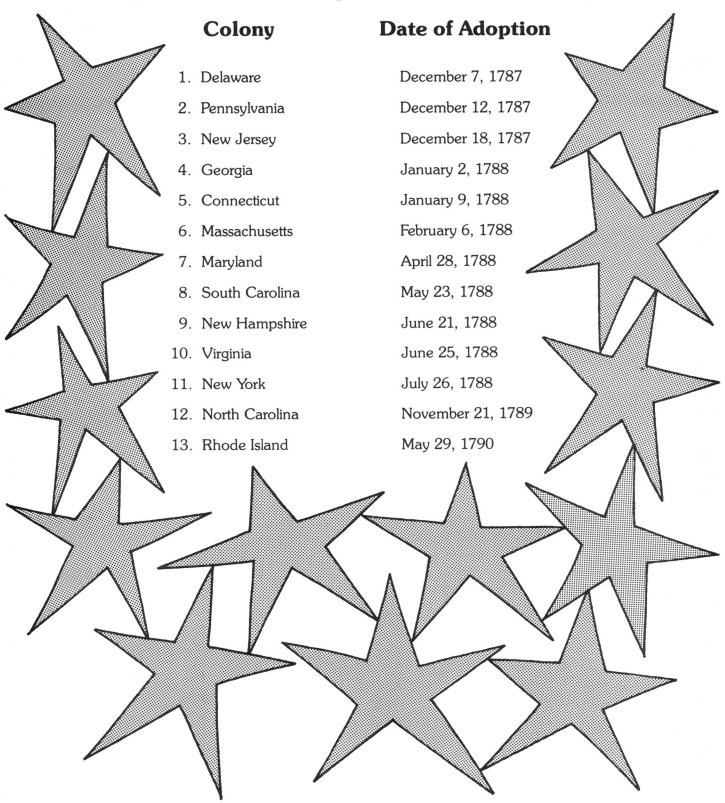

Colony	Date of Adoption
1. Delaware	December 7, 1787
2. Pennsylvania	December 12, 1787
3. New Jersey	December 18, 1787
4. Georgia	January 2, 1788
5. Connecticut	January 9, 1788
6. Massachusetts	February 6, 1788
7. Maryland	April 28, 1788
8. South Carolina	May 23, 1788
9. New Hampshire	June 21, 1788
10. Virginia	June 25, 1788
11. New York	July 26, 1788
12. North Carolina	November 21, 1789
13. Rhode Island	May 29, 1790

Volcanic Eruptions

A **volcano** is an opening in the earth's surface through which rock fragments, hot gasses, and lava *erupt*, or burst forth. Volcanoes occur when melted rock from within the earth blasts through the surface. This list contains only the largest eruptions, or those causing the most destruction.

Date	Name	Place
1400 B.C.	Thera	Santorini, Greece
August 24, A.D. 79	Mount Vesuvius	Pompeii, Italy
First century A.D.	Stromboli	Lipari Islands, Italy
1169	Mount Etna	Sicily, Italy
1631	Mount Vesuvius	Italy
1669	Mount Etna	Sicily
1772	Mount Papandayan	Java
1792	Mount Unzen-Dake	Japan
April 1815	Mount Tambora	Sumbawa, Indonesia
1832	Mauna Loa	Hawaii, United States
1877	Cotopaxi	near Quito, Ecuador
August 26, 1883	Krakatoa	Sunda Strait, Indonesia
April 8, 1902	Santa Maria	Guatemala
1911	Mount Taal	Philippines
May 8, 1902	Mount Pelee	Martinique, West Indies
June 6, 1912	Mount Katmai	Alaska, United States
1919	Mount Kelud	Java, Indonesia
February 20, 1943	Parícutin	Michoacan, Mexico
January 18, 1951	Mount Lamington	Papua, New Guinea
1951	Hibokhibok	Northern Mindanao, Philippines
March 1963	Mount Agung	Bali, Indonesia
November 1963	Surtsey	Surtsey, Iceland
September 28, 1965	Mount Taal	Luzon, Philippines
April 28, 1966	Mount Kelud	Java, Indonesia
July 29, 1968	Mount Arenal	Costa Rica
February 20, 1979	Mount Sinila	Java, Indonesia
September 12, 1979	Mount Etna	Sicily, Italy
May 18, 1980	Mount St. Helens	Washington, United States
March 28, 1982	El Chichon	Pichucalco, Mexico
April 9, 1982	Galunggung	Java, Indonesia
November 13, 1985	Nevado del Ruiz	Columbia
August 24, 1986	NW Cameroon	Cameroon
1992	Pinatubo	Philippines
March 4, 1995	Fogo	Cape Verde

Careers

accountant
actor
adjuster
administrator
advertising executive
advocate
archaeologist
architect
artist
assembler
astronaut
attorney
author
bailiff
baker
banker
barber
beautician
biochemist
biologist
bookkeeper
broadcaster
builder
bus driver
butcher

buyer
carpenter
cartographer
cashier
chauffeur
chef
chemist
choreographer
cinematographer
clergymember
coach
collector
composer
comptroller
computer analyst
computer graphic artist
computer programmer
construction worker
consultant
copywriter
critic
dancer
data entry clerk
database manager
delivery person

dental assistant
dental hygienist
dentist
designer
developer
director
economist
editor
electrician
engineer
entertainer
environmental specialist
equipment analyst
exporter
farmer
financial advisor
fire fighter
florist
foreign correspondent
gardener
geneologist
geographer
geologist
grocer
hazardous waste technician

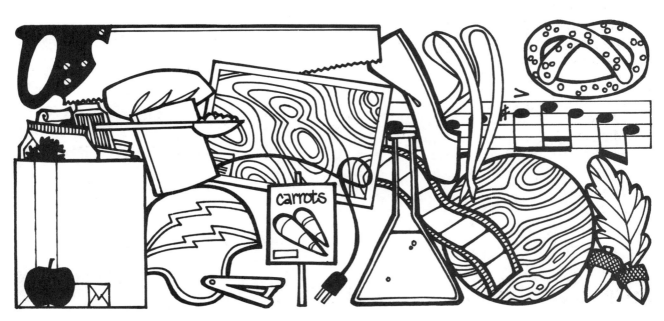

Careers
(continued)

historian	nurse	realtor
human resources manager	oceanographer	receptionist
illustrator	optometrist	recreation worker
immigration official	painter	recruiter
importer	paramedic	reporter
information clerk	park ranger	retail clerk
insurance agent	pharmacist	salesperson
interior decorator	photographer	scuba diver
interpreter	physical therapist	sculptor
inventor	physician	seamstress
investigator	physicist	secretary
janitor	pilot	social worker
jeweler	plumber	soldier
journalist	poet	surgeon
judge	police officer	taxi driver
librarian	politician	teacher
linguist	principal	therapist
locksmith	probation officer	travel agent
longshoreman	professional athlete	truck driver
mail carrier	professor	typesetter
marketing manager	project manager	undertaker
mechanic	psychologist	urban planner
meteorologist	public relations manager	veterinarian
musician	publisher	welder
nuclear specialist	rancher	zookeeper

From this list, select a career that interests you. Find out more about the educational requirements, the working conditions, the salary, the advantages and disadvantages, and the employment outlook for people who choose to pursue this career.

Coins of the United States

Coin	Portrait
Cent	Abraham Lincoln
Nickel	Thomas Jefferson
Dime	Franklin D. Roosevelt
Quarter	George Washington
Half Dollar	John F. Kennedy
Dollar	Dwight D. Eisenhower

Currency of the United States

Denomination	Portrait	Design on Back
$1	George Washington	Great Seal of the United States
$2	Thomas Jefferson	Declaration of Independence
$5	Abraham Lincoln	Lincoln Memorial
$10	Alexander Hamilton	U.S. Treasury Building
$20	Andrew Jackson	The White House
$50	Ulysses S. Grant	U.S. Capitol
$100	Benjamin Franklin	Independence Hall
$500	William McKinley	large $500 sign
$1,000	Grover Cleveland	large $1,000 sign
$5,000	James Madison	large $5,000 sign
$10,000	Salmon P. Chase	large $10,000 sign
$100,000	Woodrow Wilson	large $100,000 sign

Colonial Terms

batten	meeting house
bayberry	minuet
blacksmith	musket
breeches	New England Primer
candles	pewter
cards	pillory
colonists	plague
common house	plantation
dame schools	powder horn
dasher	Puritans
doublet	ruff
fiddler	rushlight
flax	Quakers
flint	quilting bee
gristmill	sconce
hatchet	smock
heddles	snuffer
hornbook	spinning wheel
house-raising	tallow
indigo	tankard
lantern	tinder
loom	town crier
lye	venison
mansion	

Communication

Communication is a process by which information is exchanged between individuals or groups by means of a mutually understood system of symbols, signs, or actions. Below are listed some means of communication.

art
banners
body language
braille
brochures
bumper stickers
buttons
cable
carrier pigeon
clothing
coat of arms
code
computer
costumes
dance
drums
facial expressions
flags
gestures
hieroglyphics
letters
logos

magazines
mail
masks
Morse code
music
newspapers
pennants
pictographs
postcards
posters
radio
satellite
semaphore
sign language
signs
sky writing
smoke signals
symbols
telegrams
telegraph
telephone
television

Constitution of the United States

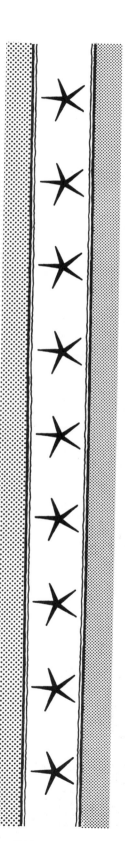

Original Constitution

Preamble

Article
1. The Legislature
2. The Executive Departments
3. The Judicial Departments
4. Relations Among States
5. Amending the Constitution
6. Role of the National Government
7. Ratification

Bill of Rights

Amendment
1. Religious and Political Freedoms
2. Right to Bear Arms
3. Quartering Troops
4. Search and Seizure
5. Rights of Accused Persons
6. Right to a Speedy, Public Trial
7. Trial by Jury in Civil Cases
8. Limits of Fines and Punishments
9. Rights of the People
10. Powers of the States and People

Additional Amendments

11. Lawsuits Against States
12. Election of Executives
13. Abolition of Slavery
14. Civil Rights
15. Right to Vote
16. Income Tax
17. Direct Election of Senators
18. Prohibition
19. Women's Suffrage
20. "Lame Duck" Session
21. Repeal of Prohibition
22. Limit on Presidential Terms
23. Voting in District of Columbia
24. Abolition of Poll Taxes
25. Presidential Succession
26. Voting Age Lowered to Eighteen

Famous Airplanes

Air Force One   dedicated to transporting the president of the United States

Albany Flyer   first plane to take-off and land on a warship

Arc-en-Ciel   plane which provided the first mail service between France and the United States

Bockscar   dropped the atomic bomb on Nagasaki, Japan, ending WWII

Bremen   plane flown for first east-to-west crossing of the north Atlantic

Columbus   plane flown during first non-stop, east-to-west transatlantic crossing

Concorde   high-speed French plane used for transatlantic crossing

Electra   Amelia Earhart's plane, in which she attempted to fly around the world; Earhart and her plane were lost somewhere over the Pacific

Enola Gay   dropped the atomic bomb on Hiroshima, Japan, ending WWII

Floyd Bennett   first plane flown over the South Pole

Flyer   name given to the Wright Brothers' plane flown at Kill Devil Hills

Josephine Ford   first plane flown over the North Pole

Memphis Belle   famous for its many bombing missions over Germany in WWII

Nungesser-Coli   plane used on first non-stop, south-Atlantic flight

Southern Cross   first plane flown across the Pacific from the United States to Australia

Spirit of St. Louis   plane flown by Charles Lindbergh on his first solo flight across the Atlantic

Spruce Goose   millionaire Howard Hughes' plane, which was too heavy to fly

Winnie Mae   first plane to fly around the world

Famous American Trials

The John Peter Zenger Trial   1735   New York, NY

Defendant: Newspaperman John Peter Zenger
Charged with seditious libel
Decision: Not guilty, because he wrote "the truth" regarding an elected official
(trial laid foundations for freedom-of-the-press portion of the Constitution)

The Aaron Burr Trial   1807   Richmond, VA

Defendant: Former Vice-President Aaron Burr
Charged with treason
Decision: Not guilty (but his political career was destroyed)

Dred Scott Decision   1856   Washington, DC

Appellant: Dred Scott
Defendant: John F.A. Sanford
Appellant's claim: Scott, who was a slave, became free when his owner took him to a free state, Missouri.
Decision: Scott is still a slave, no matter where his owner takes him.
(trial hardened the political rivalry between the North and South, paving the way for the Civil War)

Famous American Trials
(continued)

John Thomas Scopes Trial   1925   Dayton, TN

(also known as the "Monkey Trial")
Defendant: John Thomas Scopes
Charged with teaching evolution
Decision: Guilty; neither side really won, decision was reversed on a technicality
Sentence: $100 fine

The Tokyo Rose Trial   1949   San Fransisco, CA

Defendant: Iva Ikuko Togrui (Tokyo Rose)
Charged with treason for providing pro-Japanese radio propoganda to U.S. troops during
World War II
Decision: Guilty
Sentence: 10 years in prison and $10,000 fine
(pardoned in 1977 by President Ford and U.S. citizenship restored)

Brown v. Board of Education   1954   Washington, DC

Appellants: parents of African-American elementary school-age children
Defendant: Topeka, KS Board of Education
Appellants' claim: Segregation is unconstitutional.
Decision: Segregated schools are unconstitutional.
(essentially, the impetus for demolishing segregated public school systems)

Famous American Trials
(continued)

Miranda v. Arizona   1966

Decision: Before questioning an accused person, the police must inform him or her of his or her rights. An accused person has the right to remain silent and to be represented by a lawyer.

Roe and others v. Wade   1973   Washington, DC

Plantiff: Norma McCorvey (using Roe as an alias), representing all pregnant women in a class-action suit

Defendant: Texas District Attorney Henry B. Wade

Plantiff's claim: Texas abortion laws are in violation of an individual's constitutional rights

Decision: Overturned individual state's abortion laws because of individual's implied "right to privacy"

Silkwood v. Kerr-McGee   1979   Oklahoma City, OK

Plantiff: Estate of Karen Silkwood

Defendant: Kerr-McGee Nuclear Company

Plantiff's claim: Damages for negligence leading to the plutonium contamination of Karen Silkwood

Decision: Defendant found negligent; ordered to pay $505,000 actual and $10 million punitive damages

(case brought to national attention issues of safety around nuclear facilities)

Famous American Trials
(continued)

Ryan White v. Board of Education   1984   Kokomo, IN

Plantiff: Ryan White
Defendant: Kokomo, IN Board of Education
Plantiff's claim: That he had the right to attend public schools, though he was ill with AIDS
Decision: Ryan White has a constitutional right to attend public schools
(Ryan White became a national spokesperson for children with HIV and AIDS.)

Clara and Daniel Schmidt v.
Jan and Roberta DeBoer   1991, 1992, 1993   Michigan

Plantiffs: Clara and Daniel Schmidt, Jessica's biological parents
Defendants: Jan and Roberta DeBoer, Jessica's adoptive parents
Plantiff's claim: Seeking permanent custody of their biological daughter, "Baby Jessica"
Decision: That the child should be in the custody of her biological parents; father did not give up custody

Shannon Faulkner v. The Citadel   1993   Charleston, SC

Plantiff: Shannon Faulkner
Defendant: The Citadel (an all-male military school)
Plantiff's claim: That she had a constitutional right to attend the public school of her choice
Decision: That Shannon Faulkner could attend classes at The Citadel

Famous Ships

Matthew	first European ship to reach North America, 1497
Discoverie	Henry Hudson's ship in which he discovered Hudson Bay
Mayflower	brought the first Pilgrims to America in 1620
Bonhomme Richard	John Paul Jones' flagship, an American man-of-war
Empress of China	first American vessel to travel to the coast of China
Columbia	first American ship to sail around the world
Constitution	frigate commissioned to protect U.S. commerce from pirates; known for her involvement in the War of 1812; popular name is "Old Ironsides"
Dreadnaught	made the fastest packet-ship passage across the Atlantic, 1859
Britannia	inaugurated the Cunard Line service
Savannah	first steamship to cross the Atlantic, 1819
Monitor & Merrimac	two "ironclads" known for their famous Civil War battle, 1862
Flying Cloud	fastest long-voyage American clipper ship
Bismarck	powerful German battleship; sunk in one of the most important naval actions of World War II, 1941
Titanic	British steamer considered unsinkable; in 1912, sank in the North Atlantic after striking an iceberg; 1,500 people died
Lusitania	British passenger ship sunk near Ireland by a German submarine (U-boat) during World War I; 1,198 people died
Arizona	U.S. battleship sunk in the Japanese attack on Pearl Harbor, December 7, 1941; more than 1,000 men are buried in her hull
PT 109	John F. Kennedy's boat during World War II; after it was struck by Japanese forces near the Solomon Islands, he saved the lives of several crew members, for which he received medals honoring his heroism
Nina, Pinta, & Santa Maria	ships used by Christopher Columbus and his crewmembers to travel from Spain to the New World

Famous Ships
(continued)

Queen Mary	luxury ocean liner; now moored in Long Beach, CA as a floating museum
Pueblo	U.S. electronics surveillance ship which was captured by North Korea in 1968
Globtik Tokyo	one of the largest tankers afloat; weighs 477,000 tons; built in Japan
Enterprise	longest (but not the largest) aircraft carrier in the world
Campbell's Bluebird	first boat to obtain a speed of 200 miles per hour
Pen Duik IV	French ship which broke the record for crossing the Atlantic by sail
Flying Dutchman	fictional ship condemned to wander the seas forever
Bounty	1932 British ship upon which the book *Mutiny on the Bounty* is based
Maine	U.S. battleship which was sunk in 1898, an event that helped start the Spanish-American War; "Remember the *Maine!*" became a popular patriotic slogan
Clermont	first commercially-successful steamboat; designed by Robert Fulton; provided passenger service on the Hudson River beginning in 1807
Graf Spee	one of three German pocket battleships which preyed on British merchant ships in the Atlantic during early World War II; Hitler ordered it scuttled rather than have the enemy learn the secrets obtained by its crew
Alabama	most famous of the Confederate cruisers that preyed on Union merchant ships and whalers during the Civil War
Constellation	first U.S. Navy ship to capture a foreign warship, 1799

Geographical Jargon

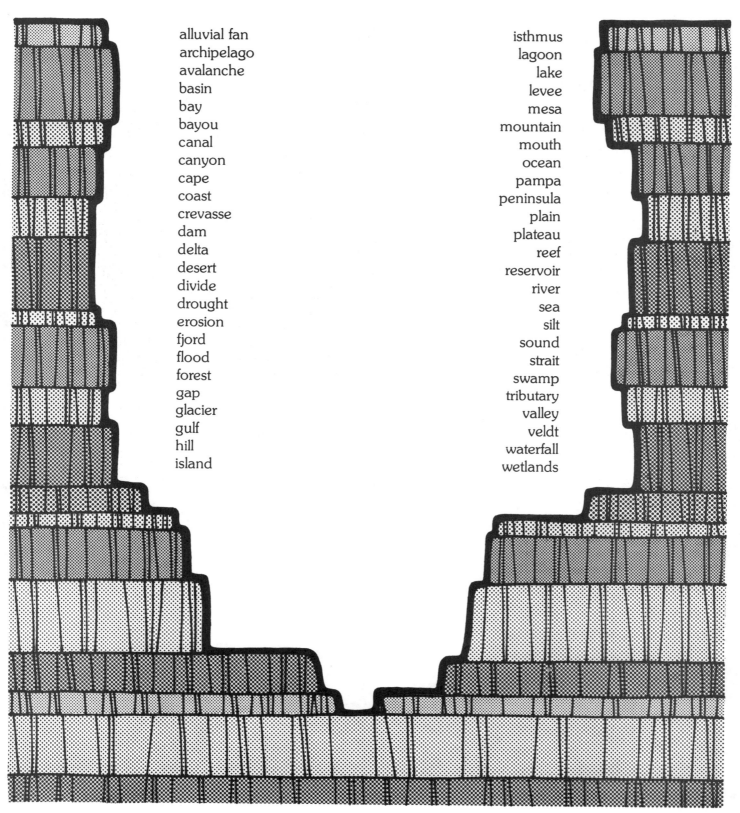

alluvial fan
archipelago
avalanche
basin
bay
bayou
canal
canyon
cape
coast
crevasse
dam
delta
desert
divide
drought
erosion
fjord
flood
forest
gap
glacier
gulf
hill
island

isthmus
lagoon
lake
levee
mesa
mountain
mouth
ocean
pampa
peninsula
plain
plateau
reef
reservoir
river
sea
silt
sound
strait
swamp
tributary
valley
veldt
waterfall
wetlands

Government Addresses

Central Intelligence Agency (CIA)
Washington, D.C.   20505

Council on Environmental Quality
722 Jackson Place, N.W.
Washington, D.C.   20006

Department of Defense
The Pentagon
Washington, D.C.   20301

Department of the Interior
18th and C Streets, N.W.
Washington, D.C.   20240

Department of Justice
Constitution Avenue and 10th Street, N.W.
Washington, D.C.   20530

Department of the Treasury
15th Street and Pennsylvania Avenue, N.W.
Washington, D.C.   20220

Environmental Protection Agency (EPA)
401 M Street, S.W.
Washington, D.C.   20460

Federal Reserve System
20th Street and Constitution Avenue, N.W.
Washington, D.C.   20551

Office of the Vice-President
Executive Office Building
Washington, D.C   20501

The White House
1600 Pennsylvania Avenue, N.W.
Washington, D.C.   20500

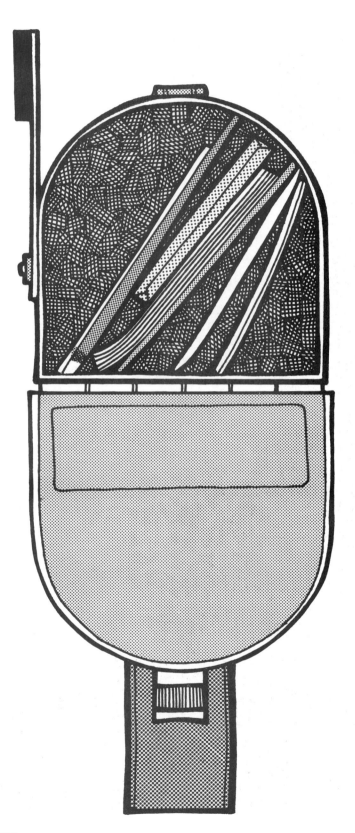

Hello, Goodbye, Please, and Thank You

German
hello	guten Tag (good day)
goodbye	auf Wiederschen!
please	bitte
thank you	danke

French
hello	bonjour
goodbye	au revoir
please	s'il vous plaît
thank you	merci

Italian
hello	ciao
goodbye	arrivederci
please	por favore
thank you	grazie

Spanish
hello	buenos dias (good day)
goodbye	adios
please	por favor
thank you	gracias

Vietnamese
hello	tieng chao
goodbye	gia tu
please	lam vui long
thank you	cam o

Japanese
hello	kon-ni-shi-wa
goodbye	sa-yo-na-ra
please	o-ne-gai shi-ma-su
thank you	a-ri-ga-to

Greek
hello	kaliméra
goodbye	kalí andámosi
please	parakaló
thank you	efcharistó

Hawaiian
hello	aloha
goodbye	aloha (also, a hui hou aku)
please	ho olu
thank you	mahalo

Swedish
hello	god gag
goodbye	adjø
please	behaga
thank you	tacka

Hebrew
hello	shalom (peace)
goodbye	shalom (peace)
please	b'vakasha
thank you	todah

Words in languages that do not use the Roman alphabet have been spelled phonetically.

Homes and Shelters

adobe house
A-frame house
apartment
Bedouin tent
beehive hut
bungalow
bunk house
Cape Cod house
castle
cave
condominium
duplex
Dutch Colonial house
earth lodge
English Tudor house
fort
geodesic dome
grass hut
guesthouse
houseboat
igloo

lean-to
long house
manor house
pagoda
palace
patio house
pueblo
ranch style house
saltbox house
skyscraper
solar house
split-level house
tent
tepee
townhouse
transitional house
treehouse
underground house
Victorian house
wigwam
yurt

1. Select ten of the above structures and do research to determine whether they are stationary or portable, then identify the main building materials used in their construction.

2. Some of the homes listed above were used by Native Americans. Do some research and see if you can find out which ones. (Hint: There are at least five.)

3. Choose a home from the list above that is different from the home in which you live. Write about what life is like in your "new" home. (It might be fun to choose a home that's *really* different.)

4. The homes listed above were used by people. Make a list of all the homes that you can think of that are used by animals.

Kinds of Furniture

armoire
banquette
Barcelona chair
bar stool
barrel chair
basin stand
bergere
bookcase
breakfront
bunk bed
bureau
butcher block table
butterfly table
canopied bed
card table
chaise longue
chest of drawers
Chippendale sofa
coffee table
commode
computer desk
console
corner cupboard
couch
cradle
credenza
crib
day bed
dinette
director's chair
drafting table

dresser
dressing table
drop-leaf table
easy chair
entertainment center
etagere
fautevil
folding screen
footstool
four-poster bed
futon
grandfather clock
harvest table
highboy
Hitchcock chair
hoopback chair
hutch
jewelry chest
ladder-back chair
Lawson sofa
lounge chair
love seat
lowboy
nesting tables
night stand
ottoman
oval-back chair
Parsons table
pencil-post bed
pie safe
plantation bed

printer stand
Queen Anne chair
recliner
ribbon chair
rocker
roll-away bed
rolltop desk
secretary
serving trolley
settee
settle
sideboard
slat-back chair
sleeper sofa
sling chair
slipper chair
swing-leg table
tea table
tier table
tilt-top table
trestle table
tripod table
trundle bed
tub chair
tuxedo sofa
water bed
wig stand
Windsor chair
wing chair
writing desk
writing-arm chair

1. Some of the furniture pieces listed above are from long ago. They are not produced widely today. Do some research and see if you can identify the pieces from the past eras.

2. Six of the furniture pieces listed above have a proper name as part of their name (Example: Windsor chair). Find out why, and write a brief explanation for each one.

3. Pretend that you are furnishing a home. Choose furniture pieces from the list above and put them in the appropriate rooms of your house. Be sure to include furniture for all of your rooms.

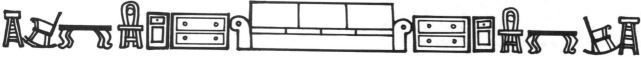

Languages of the World

A **language** is the words, their pronunciations, and the methods for combining them used and understood by a considerable community. Linguistic experts estimate that more than six hundred languages are spoken in the world today. This number does not include languages, such as Ionian, Latin, Moabite, and Phoenician, which are no longer spoken and are said to be **dead languages**. Below is a list of the twenty-nine languages of the world which have more than thirty million speakers each.

Amoy-Swatow Chinese
Arabic
Bengali
Bhojpuri
Cantonese
Eastern Hindi
English
French
German
Gujarati
Hindu with Urdu
Italian
Japanese
Javanese
Korean
Mandarin Chinese
Marathi
Panjabi
Polish
Portuguese
Russian
Spanish
Tamil
Telugu
Thai with Lao
Turkish
Ukrainian
Vietnamese
Wu [Shanghai] Chinese

Law Terms

accessory
accomplice
affidavit
alias
alibi
appeal
arraignment
arson
assault and battery
autopsy
bail
bill of attainder
bona fide
bribery
brief
burglary
complaint
confession
conspiracy
contempt
crime
curfew
deposition
Doe, John
embezzlement
equity
evidence
extortion
felony
forgery
fraud
habeas corpus

hearing
homicide
incompetence
indictment
injunction
inquest
judgment
jury
larceny
libel
malice
manslaughter
minor
misdemeanor
murder
oath
perjury
robbery
slander
smuggling
subpoena
suit
summons
testimony
treason
trial
vagrancy
vandalism
witness
writ
writ of assistance
writ of mandamus

Money of the World

A **monetary unit** is the standard unit of value of a currency. For example, the monetary unit in the United States is the dollar. All of the money used in this country is either a fraction or a multiple of one dollar. Listed below are some examples of the monetary units used in different countries around the world.

afghani	krone	peso
baht	kroner	pound
balboa	kroon	pula
birr	kwacha	punt
bolivar	kwanza	quetzal
bolivianos	kyat	rand
cedi	lei	rial
colón	lek	ringgit
cordoba	lempira	riyal
cruzeiro	leone	ruble
dalesi	leu	rufiyaa
denar	lev	rupee
dinar	lilangeni	rupiah
dirham	lira	shekel
dollar	maloti	shilling
dong	manat	sol
drachma	mark	sucre
escudo	markka	taka
forint	metical	tala
franc	naira	tolar
gourde	new kip	tughrik
guaraní	new sheqalim	vatu
guilder	new sol	won
karbovanet	ngultrum	yen
kina	ouguiya	yuan
kip	pa'anga	zaire
koruna	peseta	zloty

1. Do some research to match each of these monetary units with the country or countries in which it is used.

2. Make a chart showing the values of at least ten of these monetary units as measured in U.S. dollars.

Renaissance Terms and Topics

The word **Renaissance** means "rebirth." This word is used to name the period of European history which began during the fourteenth century and lasted about three hundred years.

Battle of Agincourt
Black Death
Giovanni Boccaccio
Anne Boleyn
Botticelli
Cervantes
château
chiaroscuro
Christendom
Manuel Chrysoloras
classics
Dante
Donatello
Don Quixote de la Mancha
Elizabeth I
exploration
Guy Fawkes
Florence, Italy
frescoes
Great Schism
El Greco
Gunpowder Plot

Johann Gutenberg
Henry VIII
Huguenots
humanism
Hundred Years' War
Joan of Arc
Leonardo da Vinci
Machiavelli
Martin Luther
Medici
Michelangelo
Mona Lisa
Petrarch
Pietà
Sir Walter Raleigh
Raphael
Reformation
Richelieu
Luca della Robbia
Savonarola
William Shakespeare
Titian

Social Studies Terms

accord	to exhibit agreement or perfect fitness in a relationship or association
agreement	harmony of opinion, action, or character
alliance	a bond or connection between groups or individuals
bias	to show an unreasonable distortion in judgment toward certain individuals or groups
common	belonging to or shared by all members of a group
confederation	the state of being united, as in a league
contrast	a person or thing that exhibits differences when compared with another
cooperation	the action of working together with a common effort
culture	the customary beliefs, social forms, and material traits of a racial, religious, or social group
discrimination	a difference in treatment or favor on a basis other than individual merit
diversity	the condition of being different or having differences
esprit de corps	the common spirit existing in the members of a group and inspiring enthusiasm, devotion, and strong regard for the honor of the group
fraternity	a group of people associated or formally organized for a common interest or purpose
harmony	a pleasing arrangement; to be together in agreement
mosaic	forming pictures or patterns by decorating or designing with small pieces or varying materials; people of different races, sizes, sexes, and cultures mixed together form a mosaic
prejudice	an irrational attitude of hostility directed against an individual, group, or race
segregation	the separation or isolation of a race, class, or ethnic group by enforced or voluntary residence in a restricted area, by barriers to social interaction, by separate educational facilities, or by other discriminatory means
union	the formation of a single unit from two or more independent units
variation	a difference in some attribute or characteristic

Use a dictionary to investigate the meanings of these additional words: attributes, characteristics, conformity, détente, differences, fusion, homogeneity, partisanship, similarities, solidarity, unique, and unison.

Social Studies Topics

advertising
American Indians
architecture
art
California missions
Canada (or any other country)
careers
castles
Civil War
colonial life
communication
Congress
Constitution
crime
Dark Ages
Declaration of Independence
early civilization
economics
Egypt
elections
Eskimos
Europe
explorers
famous men in history
famous women in history
Federal Bureau of Investigation (FBI)
Florida (or any other state)

French Revolution
geography
Hellenic Age
human rights
League of Nations
Lewis and Clark expedition
maps and map making
Middle East
national parks
Olympics
pioneers
pony express
presidents
Renaissance
Revolutionary War
stock market
Stone Age
Supreme Court
transportation
underground railroad
United Nations
voyages and discoveries
War of 1812
westward movement
White House
world neighbors
world of the future

State Tourism Agencies

Alabama
Alabama Bureau of Tourism
    and Travel
P.O. Box 4927
Montgomery, AL 36103-4927

Alaska
Alaska Division of Tourism
P.O. Box 110801
Juneau, AK 99811-0801

Arizona
Arizona Office of Tourism
1100 W. Washington Street
Phoenix, AZ 85007

Arkansas
Arkansas Dept. of Parks
    and Tourism
1 Capitol Mall
Little Rock, AR 72201

California
California Office of Tourism
1121 L Street, Suite 103
Sacramento, CA 95814

Colorado
Colorado Tourism Board
1625 Broadway, Suite 1700
Denver, CO 80202

Connecticut
Tourism Division
Connecticut Dept. of
    Economic Development
865 Brook Street
Rocky Hill, CT 06067

Delaware
State Travel Service
Delaware Development Office
99 Kings Highway,
    P.O. Box 1401
Dover, DE 19903

District of Columbia
Washington DC Convention
    and Visitors Association
1212 New York Avenue, N.W.
Washington, DC 20005

Florida
Florida Division of Tourism
126 Van Buren Street
Tallahassee, FL 32399-2000

Georgia
Georgia Tourism
P.O. Box 1776
Atlanta, GA 30301-1776

Hawaii
Hawaii Visitors Bureau
2270 Kalakaua Avenue,
    Suite 801
Honolulu, HI 96815

Idaho
Dept. of Commerce
700 West State Street
Boise, ID 83720

Illinois
Illinois Bureau of Tourism
James R. Thompson Center
100 W. Randolph Street,
    Suite 3-400
Chicago, IL 60601

Indiana
Tourism Development Division
Indiana Dept. of Commerce
1 N. Capitol, Suite 700
Indianapolis, IN 46204-2288

Iowa
Division of Tourism
Iowa Dept. of Economic
    Development
200 E. Grand Avenue
Des Moines, IA 50309

Kansas
Travel and Tourism Development
700 Southwest Harrison,
    Suite 1300
Topeka, KS 66603

Kentucky
Dept. of Travel Development
Capitol Plaza Tower, 22nd Floor
Frankfort, KY 40601

Louisiana
Louisiana Office of Tourism
P.O. Box 94291
Baton Rouge, LA 70804-9291

Maine
Maine Publicity Bureau
P.O. Box 2300
Hallowell, ME 04347

Maryland
Maryland State Office of Tourism
217 E. Redwood Street,
    9th Floor
Baltimore, MD 21202

Massachusetts
Massachusetts Office of Travel
    and Tourism
100 Cambridge Street,
    13th Floor
Boston, MA 02202

Michigan
Michigan Travel Bureau
P.O. Box 30226
Lansing, MI 48909

Minnesota
Minnesota Office of Tourism
375 Jackson Street
250 Skyway Level
St. Paul, MN 55101

Mississippi
Division of Tourism
Mississippi Dept. of Economic
    Development
1301 Walter Sillars Building
P.O. Box 849
Jackson, MS 39201

Missouri
Missouri Division of Tourism
P.O. Box 1055
Jefferson City, MO 65102

Montana
Montana Travel Promotion
1424 9th Avenue
Helena, MT 59620-0411

CO MS IL MN DC FL MI MD HI MO KS

State Tourism Agencies
(continued)

Nebraska
Nebraska Travel and Tourism
Dept. of Economic Development
P.O. Box 94666
Lincoln, NE 68509

Nevada
Nevada Commission on Tourism
Capitol Complex
Carson City, NV 89710

New Hampshire
Dept. of Resources and Economic
    Development
Division of Travel and Tourism
    Development
P.O. Box 1856
Concord, NH 03302-1856

New Jersey
New Jersey Dept. of Commerce
    and Economic Development
Division of Travel and Tourism
CN 826
Trenton, NJ 08625

New Mexico
New Mexico Dept. of Tourism
P.O. Box 20003
Santa Fe, NM 87503

New York
New York State Dept. of
    Economic Development
1 Commerce Plaza
Albany, NY 12245

North Carolina
Travel and Tourism Division
430 N. Salisbury Street
Raleigh, NC 27603

North Dakota
North Dakota Tourism Office
Liberty Memorial Building
Capital Grounds
604 East Boulevard
Bismarck, ND 58505

Ohio
Office of Travel and Tourism
P.O. Box 1001
Columbus, OH 43266-0101

Oklahoma
Oklahoma Tourism Department
P.O. Box 60789
Oklahoma City, OK 73146-0789

Oregon
Tourism Division
Oregon Economic Development
    Department
775 Aummer Street, N.E.
Salem, OR 97310

Pennsylvania
Bureau of Travel Marketing
Pennsylvania Dept. of Commerce
453 Forum Building
Harrisburg, PA 17120

Rhode Island
Rhode Island Dept. of Tourism
7 Jackson Walkway
Providence, RI 02903

South Carolina
Dept. of Parks, Recreation,
    and Tourism
1205 Pendleton Street
Edgar A. Brown Building
Columbia, SC 29201

South Dakota
South Dakota Tourism
711 E. Wells Avenue
Pierre, SD 57501-3369

Tennessee
Dept. of Tourist Development
Rachel Jackson Bldg., 5th Floor
320 6th Avenue, N.
Nashville, TN 37202

Texas
Texas Dept. of Commerce
Tourism Division
P.O. Box 12728
Austin, TX 78711-2728

Utah
Utah Travel Council
Council Hall/Capitol Hill
Salt Lake City, UT 84114

Vermont
Vermont Dept. of Travel
    and Tourism
134 State Street
Montpelier, VT 05602

Virginia
Virginia Division of Tourism
1021 E. Cary Street
Richmond, VA 23219

Washington
Washington State Tourism
    Division
P.O. Box 2500, Department 199
Olympia, WA 98504-2500

West Virginia
Dept. of Commerce
Tourism Division
State Capitol
Charleston, WV 25305

Wisconsin
Dept. of Development
Division of Tourism
123 W. Washington Avenue
Madison, WI 53702

Wyoming
Wyoming Travel Commission
Etchepare Circle
Cheyenne, WY 82002

WV NJ RI SC ND OH NM WI OK NC OR

Things That Travel on Land

ambulance	perambulator
automobile	roller skates
bicycle	scooter
bus	skateboard
camel	snowmobile
carriage	stagecoach
cart	streetcar
chariot	taxicab
coach	tractor
dogsled	train
donkey	tram
escalator	travois
horse	tricycle
jinrikisha	trolley
monorail	truck
moped	unicycle
motorcycle	wagon

Things That Travel on Water

argosy	felucca	prau
barge	ferryboat	punt
bark	float	raft
barkentine	frigate	rowboat
bireme	galleon	sailboat
brig	galliot	sampan
brigantine	gig	schooner
caïque	gondola	scow
canoe	houseboat	shallop
caravel	hovercraft	sharpie
carrack	hydrofoil	skiff
catamaran	hydroplane	sloop
clipper	junk	smack
coracle	kayak	steamship
corvette	ketch	submarine
cruiser	launch	surfboat
cutter	lifeboat	tugboat
destroyer	lugger	wherry
dhow	motorboat	xebec
dinghy	outrigger	yacht
dugout	pontoon	yawl

Make a **Water Transportation** booklet in which you describe and draw pictures of at least twenty of these vessels.

Wars

Greco-Persian War	499–478 B.C.	Greek states versus Persia
Peloponnesian War	431-404 B.C.	Sparta versus Athens
Punic Wars	264–146 B.C.	Rome versus Cathage
Norman Conquest	A.D. 1066	Normandy versus England
Crusades	1096–1291	Christianity versus Islam
Hundred Years' War	1338–1453	England versus France
French and Indian War	1755–1763	England versus France
Seven Years' War	1756–1763	Prussia versus Austria, France and Russia
Revolutionary War	1775–1783	American Colonies versus England
Napoleonic Wars	1796–1815	France versus Austria, England, Prussia, and Russia
War of 1812	1812–1815	United States versus England
Mexican War	1846–1848	United States versus Mexico
Crimean War	1854–1856	England, France, Sardinia, and Turkey versus Russia
U.S. Civil War	1861–1865	Union (North) versus Confederacy (South)
Franco-Prussian War	1870–1871	France versus Prussia
Spanish-American War	1898	United States versus Spain
Boer War	1899–1902	England versus the Transvaal Republic and the Orange Free State
Russo-Japanese War	1904–1905	Russia versus Japan
World War I	1914–1918	Allies (Belgium, England, France, Russia, and Serbia) versus Central Powers (Austria-Hungary and Germany)
World War II	1941–1945	Allies (England, France, United States, and USSR) versus Axis Powers (Germany, Italy, and Japan)
Indochinese War	1946–1954	Communists versus the French
Korean War	1950–1952	South Korea and United Nations forces versus invading forces from Communist-supported North Korea
Vietnam War	1959–1973	Communist-led soldiers from North Vietnam versus the South Vietnamese government supported by the United States
Persian Gulf War	1991	U.S. forces and U.N. allies liberated Kuwait from Saddam Hussein's invading Iraqi troops
Falklands War	1982	Argentina versus England
War in Bosnia	1992–present	Civil war centered on ethnic conflicts between the Serbs, Croats, and Muslims

Bonus Ideas for Social Studies

1. Choose a topic from one of the social studies lists, and do research on this topic. Then, use your topic as the basis for a pictorial scroll. On a long strip of butcher or shelf paper, draw a series of pictures and write a brief caption for each one. Attach each end of the paper strip to a dowel. Cut a screen-sized opening in one side of a cardboard box. Mount the dowels so that the scroll can be rolled past this opening and the pictures can be viewed through it.

2. Select a topic from one of the social studies lists and research it thoroughly. Wrap a medium-sized cube-shaped box in colored butcher, construction, or shelf paper. Paste interesting information and pictures about your topic on all sides of the box. Display your fact cube for classmates to enjoy.

3. Pick a topic from one of the social studies lists and research it thoroughly. Use cardboard, clay, papier-mâché, Popsicle sticks, soap, sugar cubes, or other appropriate media to construct a model related to this topic.

4. Select a famous woman from the list on page 81. Do research to learn more about her life and achievements. Then, design a postage stamp in her honor.

5. Using the state names and capitals on page 106, create a matching game to play with a friend.

6. Select an address of a government agency or building listed on page 123. Write a letter requesting booklets, pamphlets, and any free information they may distribute. Be sure to include your name and return address.

Name _____

Create a Social Studies List

Think of a social studies topic that interests you. On the lines below, create a list that reflects this topic. Illustrate your list and give it a title.

_____

_____

_____

_____

_____

_____

_____

_____

_____

_____

_____

Science

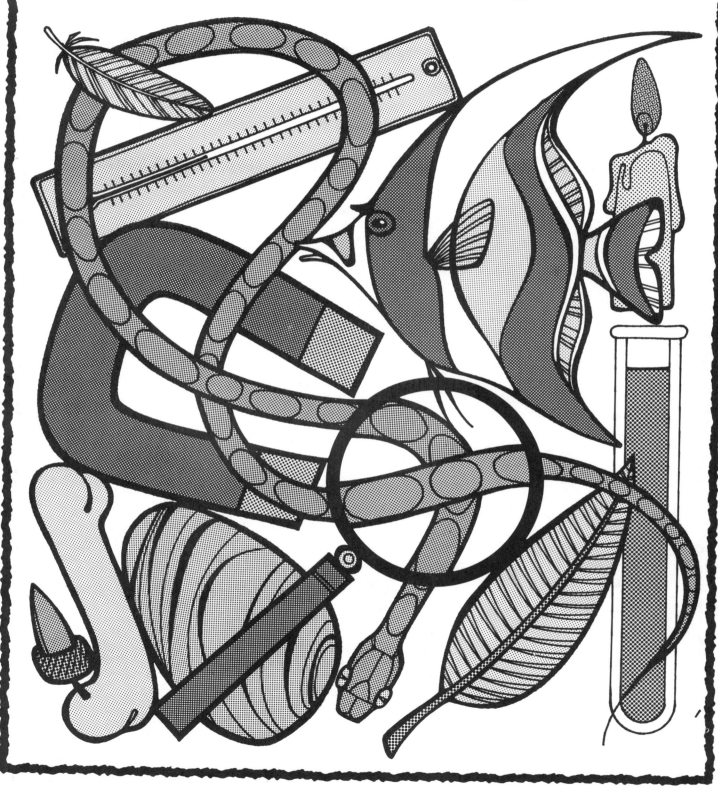

Animal Groups

a **bevy** of larks or quail

a **brood** of birds

a **cast** of hawks

a **cete** of badgers

a **clowder** of cats

a **clutch** of chicks

a **colony** of ants, beavers, or rabbits

a **covert** of coots

a **covey** of partridges or quail

a **drift** of hogs

a **drove** of pigs or sheep

a **fall** of woodcocks

a **flight** of birds

a **flock** of chickens or goats

a **gaggle** of geese

a **gam** of whales

a **gang** of buffalo or elk

a **herd** of cattle, elephants, or horses

a **hive** of bees

a **muster** of peacocks

a **nide** of pheasants

a **pack** of dogs or wolves

a **pod** of seals or whales

a **pride** of lions

a **rafter** of turkeys

a **school** of fish

a **shoal** of fish or whales

a **skulk** of foxes

a **sloth** of bears

a **sord** of mallards

a **swarm** of bees

a **troop** of kangaroos or monkeys

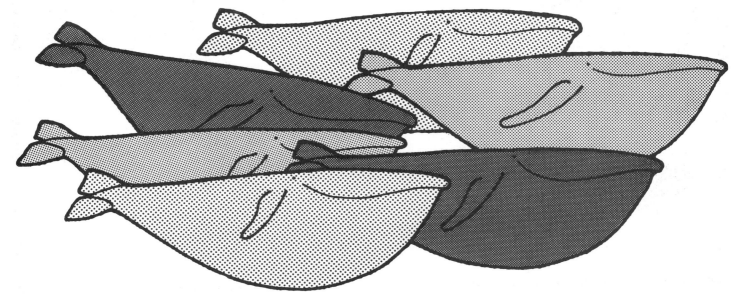

Animal Offspring

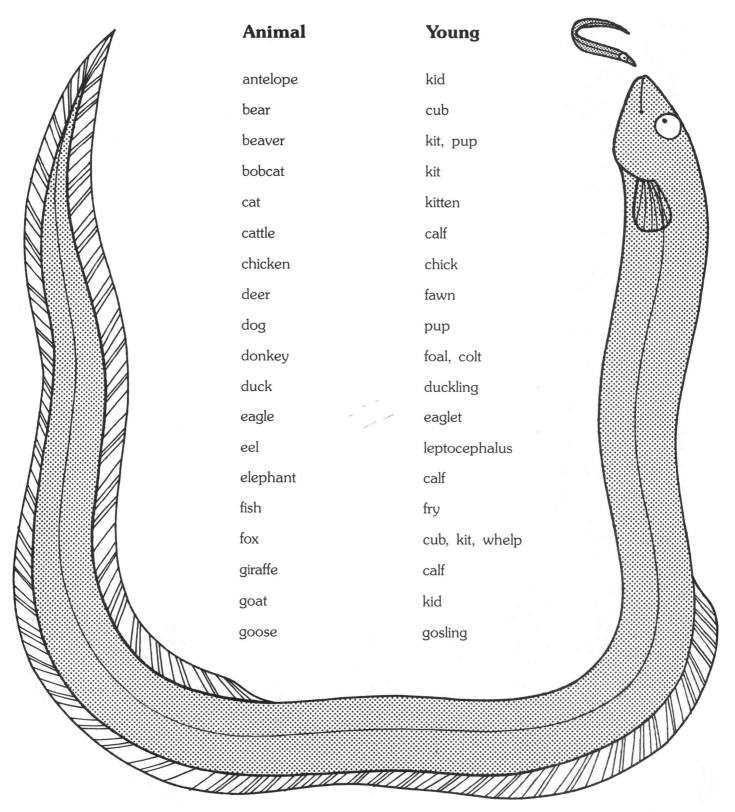

Animal	Young
antelope	kid
bear	cub
beaver	kit, pup
bobcat	kit
cat	kitten
cattle	calf
chicken	chick
deer	fawn
dog	pup
donkey	foal, colt
duck	duckling
eagle	eaglet
eel	leptocephalus
elephant	calf
fish	fry
fox	cub, kit, whelp
giraffe	calf
goat	kid
goose	gosling

Animal Offspring
(continued)

Animal	Young
hawk	eyas
hog	piglet, shoat
horse	foal, colt (male), filly (female)
kangaroo	joey
lion	cub
ostrich	chick
otter	whelp
oyster	spat
rabbit	kit, kitten
rhinoceros	calf
seal	pup, whelp
sheep	lamb, lambkin, teg
swan	cygnet
tiger	cub
turkey	poult
whale	calf
wolf	cub, whelp
zebra	colt

Birds

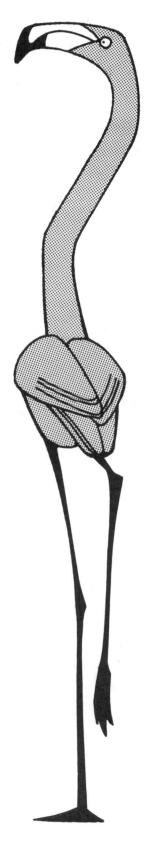

adjutant
albatross
anhinga
auk
avocet
bird of paradise
bittern
bluebird
bobolink
bobwhite
booby
bowerbird
brant
cahow
cardinal
cassowary
cedar waxwing
chat
chickadee
chicken
cockatoo
cock of the rock
coly
condor
coot
cormorant
courser
crow
cuckoo
curlew
dipper
dodo
dove
duck
eagle
egret
emu
falcon
flamingo
flicker
flycatcher
frogmouth

goldfinch
goose
goshawk
grebe
grosbeak
guinea fowl
gull
hawk
heron
honey guide
hornbill
hummingbird
ibis
jackdaw
jay
kea
kestrel
killdeer
kingfisher
kiwi
kookaburra
loon
lorikeet
lovebird
lyrebird
macaw
magpie
marabou
meadlowlark
mockingbird
myna
nightingale
nightjar
nuthatch
oriole
osprey
ostrich
ovenbird
owl
oyster catcher
parakeet
parrot
partridge

peafowl
pelican
penguin
petrel
pheasant
pigeon
puffin
quail
quetzal
rail
raven
rhea
roadrunner
robin
secretary bird
skua
skylark
sparrow
spoonbill
starling
stork
sunbird
swallow
swan
swift
tailorbird
tanager
tern
thrush
tinamou
toucan
touraco
towhee
trogon
turkey
vulture
warbler
weaverbird
whippoorwill
whydah
woodpecker
wren

Classification of Animals

Scientists classify all members of the animal kingdom using a system of seven categories: **phylum**, **subphylum**, **class**, **order**, **family**, **genus**, and **species**. The phyla are the largest groups into which the animal kingdom is divided. For example, man belongs to the phylum **Chordata**, the subphylum **Vertebrata**, the class **Mammalia**, the subclass **Eutheria**, the order **Primates**, the family **Hominidae**, the genus **Homo**, and the species **sapiens**. Below are listed some of the categories used by scientists to classify animals.

Protozoa	Simple, one-celled animals, including amebas, euglenas, malarial parasites, and paramecia.
Porifera	Sponges, the simplest of the many-celled animals.
Coelenterata	Corals, hydra, jellyfishes, and sea anemones.
Annelida	Segmented worms, including clamworms, earthworms, and leeches.
Arthropoda	Joint-footed animals.
Crustacea	Crustaceans, including crabs, lobsters, crayfishes, and sowbugs.
Chilopoda	Centipedes.
Diplopoda	Millipedes and thousand-legged worms.
Arachnoidea	Spiders, scorpions, mites, and ticks.
Insecta	Probably the largest group of animals. Includes bees and wasps, beetles, butterflies and moths, crickets and grasshoppers, flies, termites, and others.
Mollusca	Mollusks.
Gastropoda	Abalones, slugs, and snails.
Pelecypoda	Clams, mussels, oysters, and scallops.
Cephalopoda	Squids, cuttlefishes, and octopuses.
Echinodermata	Includes sand dollars, sea cucumbers, sea urchins, and starfishes.
Chordata	Chordates; bilaterally symmetrical animals with a notochord.
Vertebrata	Vertebrates; animals with a definite head, a well-developed brain, a bony support structure, and a backbone, or spine.
Cyclostomata	Cyclostomes, including lampreys and hagfishes.
Chondrichthyses	Cartilaginous fishes, including rays, sharks, and skates.
Osteichthys	Bony fishes, including garpike, herring, mackerel, and sturgeon.
Amphibia	Amphibians, including frogs, newts, salamanders, and toads.
Reptilia	Reptiles, including alligators, crocodiles, lizards, snakes, and turtles.
Aves	Birds, the only animals that have feathers.
Mammalia	Mammals, the only animals that have true hair.
Eutheria	Placental mammals.
Primates	Lemurs, tarsiers, monkeys, apes, and man.

Dog Breeds

The American Kennel Club (AKC) is the main organization of dog breeders in the United States. It recognizes more than one hundred breeds in six groups. The following list includes some examples from each category.

Sporting Group

American Water Spaniel
Cocker Spaniel
Curly-Coated Retriever
English Setter
Golden Retriever
Irish Setter
Labrador Retriever
Pointer
Sussex Spaniel
Vizsla

Hound Group

Afghan Hound
Basenji
Basset Hound
Beagle
Bloodhound
Borzoi
Dachshund
Greyhound
Irish Wolfhound
Whippet

Toy Group

Chihuahua
English Toy Spaniel
Italian Greyhound
Japanese Chin
Maltese
Miniature Pinscher
Papillon
Pekingese
Shih Tzu
Yorkshire Terrier

Working Group

Akita
Alaskan Malamute
Bearded Collie
Boxer
Bullmastiff
Collie
Doberman Pinscher
German Shepherd
Great Dane
Samoyed

Terrier Group

Airedale Terrier
Australian Terrier
Bull Terrier
Cairn Terrier
Fox Terrier
Irish Terrier
Scottish Terrier
Skye Terrier
Welsh Terrier
West Highland White Terrier

Nonsporting Group

Bichon Frise
Boston Terrier
Bulldog
Chow Chow
Dalmation
French Bulldog
Keeshond
Lhasa Apso
Poodle
Schipperke

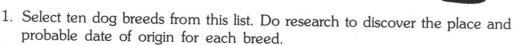

1. Select ten dog breeds from this list. Do research to discover the place and probable date of origin for each breed.
2. Select one dog group listed above and do research to add more breed names to that list.

Fishes

alewife	dolphin	marlin	sawfish
amber jack	drum	menhaden	sculpin
anableps	eel	minnow	scup
anchovy	electric fish	molly	sea bat
anemone	flatfish	mosquito fish	sea horse
angelfish	flounder	mudskipper	shad
archerfish	flying fish	mullet	shark
barracuda	garfish	oarfish	skate
bass	goldfish	paddlefish	smelt
blackfish	grayling	perch	snapper
blindfish	grouper	pickerel	sole
bluefish	grunion	pike	spot
bocaccio	grunt	pilot fish	sprat
bonefish	guppy	pipefish	stickleback
bonito	gurnard	piranha	stingray
bowfin	haddock	pollack	sturgeon
buffalo fish	hagfish	pompano	sunfish
bullhead	hake	porcupine fish	swordfish
butterfish	halibut	porgy	tarpon
candlefish	herring	puffer	tilefish
carp	jewfish	pupfish	toadfish
catfish	kingfish	ray	torpedo
chub	lamprey	redfish	trout
cod	lanternfish	remora	tuna
coelacanth	leaf fish	roach	turbot
cutlass fish	lionfish	rosefish	wahoo
darter	lumpfish	sailfish	weakfish
discus	lungfish	salmon	whitefish
doctorfish	mackerel	sardine	wolf fish
dogfish			

1. Classify these fishes as either freshwater fishes or saltwater fishes.

2. Create an entirely new fish by combining the head of one of the fishes on this list with the body of another and the tail of a third. Draw a picture of your new fish, and write a paragraph or two in which you describe how big your fish is, where it lives, what it eats, what distinguishing coloration and markings it has, and any unusual habits of which you may be aware. Don't forget to give your fish a name.

Habitats

Because different kinds of animals have different needs, they thrive in different kinds of places. An animal's **habitat** is the type of place where that animal naturally lives and grows.

coniferous woodlands

deciduous woodlands

deserts

fields and meadows

lakes

mountains

polar regions

ponds

prairies and grasslands

rivers

rocky shores

sandy shores

seas and oceans

shrubland and chaparral

streams

swamps, marshes, and wetlands

tropical rain forests

tundra

Give three or more examples of animals that live in each of the habitats listed above. Then, draw a picture or make a shoe box diorama of one of these habitats and some of the animals that are indigenous to it.

Horses

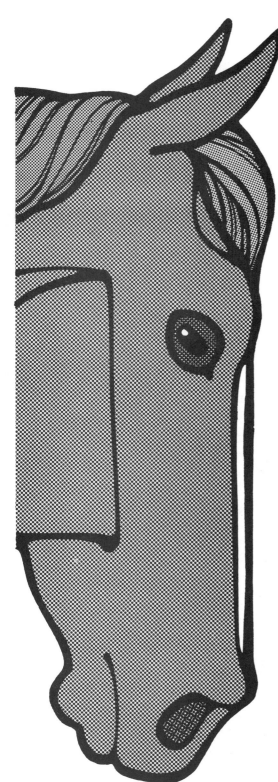
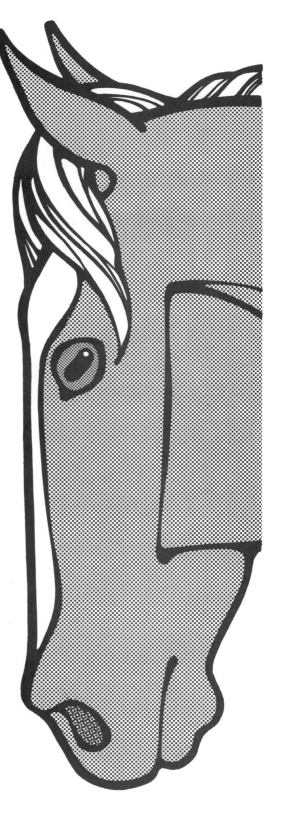

American saddle horse
Andalusian
Appaloosa
Arab
Barb
Belgian
Camargue
Chincoteague pony
Clydesdale
Connemara pony
Falabella (miniature horse)
Hackney
Iceland pony
Lippizaner
Morgan
palomino
Paso Fino
Percheron
Peruvian Paso
pinto
Pony of the Americas (POA)
Przewalski's horse
quarter horse
Shetland Pony
Shire
Standardbred
Suffolk
Tennessee Walking Horse
Thoroughbred
Welsh Mountain pony

Mammals

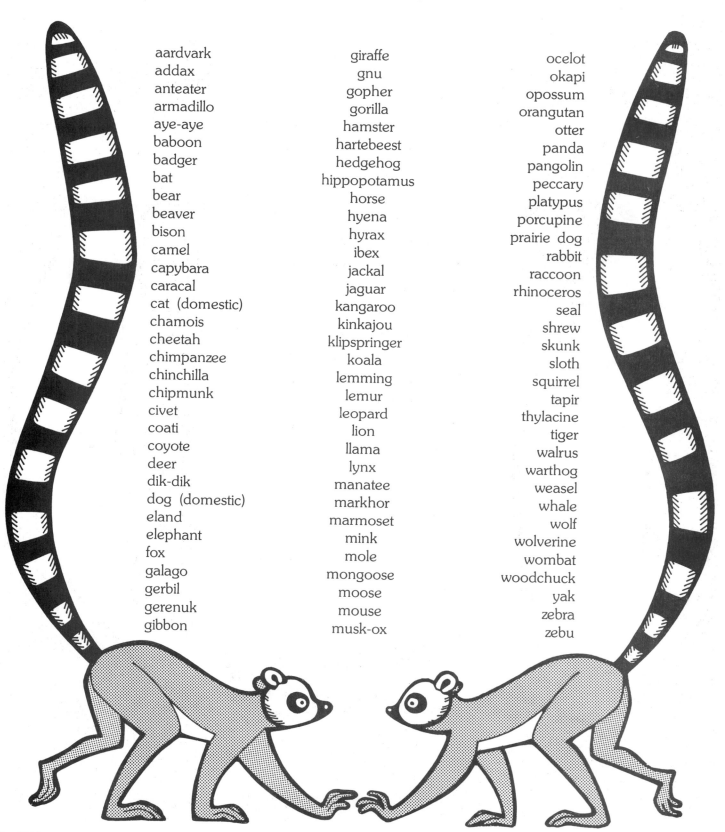

aardvark
addax
anteater
armadillo
aye-aye
baboon
badger
bat
bear
beaver
bison
camel
capybara
caracal
cat (domestic)
chamois
cheetah
chimpanzee
chinchilla
chipmunk
civet
coati
coyote
deer
dik-dik
dog (domestic)
eland
elephant
fox
galago
gerbil
gerenuk
gibbon

giraffe
gnu
gopher
gorilla
hamster
hartebeest
hedgehog
hippopotamus
horse
hyena
hyrax
ibex
jackal
jaguar
kangaroo
kinkajou
klipspringer
koala
lemming
lemur
leopard
lion
llama
lynx
manatee
markhor
marmoset
mink
mole
mongoose
moose
mouse
musk-ox

ocelot
okapi
opossum
orangutan
otter
panda
pangolin
peccary
platypus
porcupine
prairie dog
rabbit
raccoon
rhinoceros
seal
shrew
skunk
sloth
squirrel
tapir
thylacine
tiger
walrus
warthog
weasel
whale
wolf
wolverine
wombat
woodchuck
yak
zebra
zebu

Prehistoric Animals

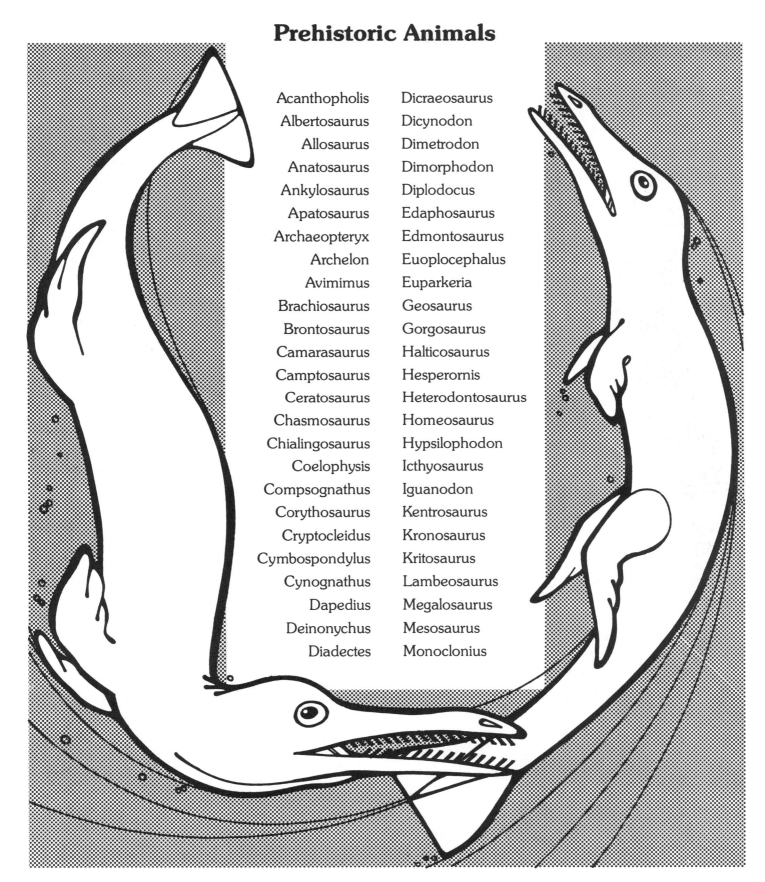

Acanthopholis
Albertosaurus
Allosaurus
Anatosaurus
Ankylosaurus
Apatosaurus
Archaeopteryx
Archelon
Avimimus
Brachiosaurus
Brontosaurus
Camarasaurus
Camptosaurus
Ceratosaurus
Chasmosaurus
Chialingosaurus
Coelophysis
Compsognathus
Corythosaurus
Cryptocleidus
Cymbospondylus
Cynognathus
Dapedius
Deinonychus
Diadectes

Dicraeosaurus
Dicynodon
Dimetrodon
Dimorphodon
Diplodocus
Edaphosaurus
Edmontosaurus
Euoplocephalus
Euparkeria
Geosaurus
Gorgosaurus
Halticosaurus
Hesperornis
Heterodontosaurus
Homeosaurus
Hypsilophodon
Icthyosaurus
Iguanodon
Kentrosaurus
Kronosaurus
Kritosaurus
Lambeosaurus
Megalosaurus
Mesosaurus
Monoclonius

Prehistoric Animals
(continued)

Moschops	Psittacosaurus
Mystriosaurus	Pteranodon
Nemegtosaurus	Pterodactylus
Nodosaurus	Quetzalcoatlus
Nothosaurus	Rhamphorhynchus
Nyctosaurus	Scelidosaurus
Omosaurus	Spinosaurus
Ophiacodon	Stegosaurus
Ornitholestes	Struthiosaurus
Ornithomimus	Styracosaurus
Pachycephalosaurus	Teratosaurus
Pachyophis	Thecodontosaurus
Paleoscincus	Theriosuchus
Parasaurolophus	Titanosaurus
Pentaceratops	Torosaurus
Phobosuchus	Trachodon
Pinacosaurus	Triceratops
Placodus	Trilophosaurus
Plateosaurus	Tylosaurus
Polacanthus	Tyrannosaurus
Polyodontosaurus	Velociraptor
Proganochelys	Yaverlandia
Protoceratops	Zephyrosaurus
Protorosaurus	

Prehistoric Dig

The activities on this page are for use with the list of Prehistoric Animals.

1. Make a time line showing which ones of these animals lived during the following geologic periods and systems:

   Carboniferous   310-280 million years ago
   Permian   280-230 million years ago
   Triassic   230-190 million years ago
   Jurassic   190-135 million years ago
   Cretaceous   135-63 million years ago
   Tertiary   63-1 million years ago
   Quaternary   1 million years ago

2. Do research to discover the diet of at least ten of these prehistoric animals. From what you learn, classify each one as either **herbivorous**, or plant-eating; **carnivorous**, or meat-eating; or **omnivorous**, both plant- and meat-eating.

3. Using a globe or map of the world, show where the fossil remains of at least ten of these prehistoric animals were found.

4. Represent the lengths of at least ten of these prehistoric animals on a bar graph.

5. Make a chart on which you compare the dimensions and/or weight of ten prehistoric animals with the dimensions and/or weight of familiar present-day animals or objects.

Prehistoric Plants and Animals That Still Exist Today

Australian Lungfish On the earth 200 million years ago; discovered alive in 1869

Bristlecone Pine (tree) This tree was on Earth in 6200 B.C.; one specimen, known as Methuselah, is 4,600 years old and can be seen at an elevation of 9,000 feet on one of the White Mountains in California

Coelacanth (fish) A six-foot fish discovered alive in 1939 off the coast of South Africa in the Indian Ocean; previously thought to have become extinct 70 million years ago

Crocodile Found throughout the world; twenty-one species known today are from 160 to 195 million years old

Dawn Redwood Found in China in 1946 and later cultivated in California; dates back 100 million years; also known as Metasequoia

Duckbill Platypus (aquatic mammal) At least 150 million years old; first seen in Australia in 1797; found in Australia and Tasmania

Ginkgo (tree) Dates back to the time of the dinosaurs; still found in the U.S., China, and elsewhere; Charles Darwin called it a "living fossil"

Horseshoe Crab Unchanged after 500 million years

Lingula (marine animal) Has been in existence half a billion years; longest lived of all animals; member of the phylum Brachiopoda

Okapi (African mammal) Related to the giraffe; dates back 30 million years and remains almost unchanged

Peripatus (worm) Found in the tropics; dates back 500 million years

Stephens Island Frog Believed to be the frog from which all living frogs have descended; from 170 to 275 million years old; first found in 1917 in its present home, New Zealand; differs from most frogs in that it does not have webbed toes

Tuatara (reptile) Found on islands near New Zealand; unchanged for 200 million years

Turtle About 275 million years old; from 200 to 250 species can be found in most parts of the world; earliest species called Proganochelys

Welwitschia (desert plant) Can still be found in southwest Africa; on the earth millions of years ago

Wollemi Pine Discovered in 1994 in Australia; thought to have become extinct during the Jurassic Period; name means "look around you;" largest found was 130 feet tall and 10 feet in diameter; bark is waxy and said to resemble melting chocolate

Reptiles

Snakes

anaconda
ball python
boa constrictor
boomslang
bull snake
bushmaster
carpet snake
copperhead
coral snake
corn snake
cottonmouth
death adder
diamondback rattlesnake
emerald tree boa
fer-de-lance
gaboon viper
garter snake
hognose snake
horned viper
Indian cobra
indigo snake
king cobra
king snake

krait
mamba
mangrove snake
massasauga
milk snake
puff adder
rainbow boa
rat snake
reticulated python
rhinoceros viper
ring-necked snake
rock python
rosy boa
rubber boa
sea snake
sidewinder
spitting cobra
tiger snake
vine snake
wart snake
water snake
whip snake
worm snake

Lizards

agama
alligator lizard
anole
blue-tongued skink
chuckwalla
collared lizard
flying lizard
frilled lizard
gila monster
glass snake
goanna
green iguana
horned toad
Komodo dragon
marine iguana
moloch
Nile monitor
plumed basilisk
sand skink
slowworm
sungazer
three-horned chameleon
tokay gecko

Turtles

Adalbra giant tortoise
big-headed turtle
box turtle
cooter
desert tortoise
diamondback terrapin
Galápagos giant tortoise
gopher tortoise
hawksbill turtle

hinged-back tortoise
leatherback turtle
leopard tortoise
loggerhead turtle
map turtle
marginated tortoise
matamata
painted turtle
pancake tortoise

red-eared turtle
side-necked turtle
slider turtle
snapping turtle
soft-shelled turtle
spotted turtle
star tortoise
stinkpot
wood turtle

Alligators and Crocodiles

American alligator
black caiman
Chinese alligator
dwarf crocodile

estuarine crocodile
gavial
Nile crocodile
spectacled caiman

Bones in the Human Body

The entire human skeleton consists of two hundred distinct bones. These bones are distributed as follows:

Skull		22
Cranium	8	
Face	14	
Spine		26
Hyoid bone, sternum, ribs		26
Upper extremities		64
Lower extremities		62

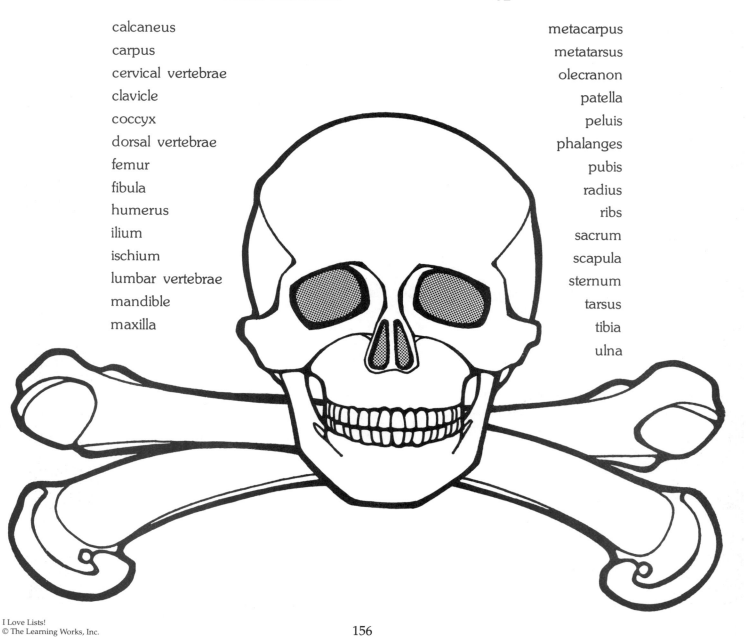

calcaneus	metacarpus
carpus	metatarsus
cervical vertebrae	olecranon
clavicle	patella
coccyx	peluis
dorsal vertebrae	phalanges
femur	pubis
fibula	radius
humerus	ribs
ilium	sacrum
ischium	scapula
lumbar vertebrae	sternum
mandible	tarsus
maxilla	tibia
	ulna

Itises

Words ending in **-itis** usually name an inflammation. In the list below, the description following each *-itis* tells what part of the human body is inflamed.

appendicitis	appendix
arthritis	joint
bronchitis	bronchi, or tubes branching off at the lower part of the trachea
bursitis	bursa, a fluid-filled sac in a joint
colitis	colon, or large intestine
conjunctivitis	conjunctiva, or transparent membrane lining the front of the eyeball
cystitis	bladder
dermatitis	skin
diverticulitis	diverticula, or abnormal pouches or soft-walled cavities that form along the walls of the intestines
encephalitis	brain
enteritis	intestines
gastritis	stomach
gastroenteritis	mucous membranes of the intestines and stomach
gingivitis	gums
hepatitis	liver
laryngitis	larynx
mastoiditus	mastoid cells
myringitis	the tympanic membrane, or eardrum

Itises
(continued)

nephritis	kidney
neuritis	nerve
omphalitis	navel
ophthalmitis	eye
osteochondritis	bone and cartilage
osteomyelitis	bone and marrow
pancarditis	structures of the heart
pancreatitis	pancreas
pericarditis	pericardium, or tissue covering the heart
periodontitis	periodontal membrane, or connective tissue covering the cement layer of a tooth
peritonitis	peritoneum, or membrane that lines the abdominal organs
pharyngitis	pharynx, or tube that connects the mouth and nasal passages and becomes continuous with the esophagus
phlebitis	vein
pneumonitis	lung tissue
rhinitis	mucous membrane of the nose
sinusitis	sinus
stomatitis	soft tissues of the mouth
tendinitis	tendon
tonsillitis	tonsils
tracheitis	trachea

Phobias

A **phobia** (fō′ - bē - ə) is an intense abnormal or unreasonable fear of a particular class or type of people, places, things, or situations. Below is a list of words that name phobias. Beside each word is a brief description of the thing feared by a person suffering from this phobia.

acrophobia	heights	**hypnophobia**	sleep
agoraphobia	open spaces	**lalophobia**	speech or speaking
ailurophobia	cats	**mysophobia**	uncleanliness or contamination
amaxophobia	being or riding in vehicles	**necrophobia**	death or dead bodies
androphobia	men		
apeirophobia	that which is unlimited or indeterminate	**nyctophobia**	night, darkness
		ophidiophobia	reptiles, especially snakes
astrophobia	stars	**pedophobia**	infants or children
autophobia	being alone with oneself	**phagophobia**	eating
		phonophobia	sounds or noise
bathophobia	depths	**psychrophobia**	cold
chionophobia	snow	**pyrophobia**	flames or fire
claustrophobia	narrow or closed spaces	**thalassophobia**	ocean or sea
		thanatophobia	death
cynophobia	dogs	**toxicophobia**	drugs or poison
demophobia	people, crowds	**triskaidekaphobia**	the number 13
entomophobia	insects	**xenophobia**	foreigners or strangers, or anything that is foreign or strange
erythrophobia	the color red		
gamophobia	marriage		
gynophobia	women	**zoophobia**	animals
hemophobia	blood		
hydrophobia	water		

Pioneers in Medicine

Name	Achievements
Christiaan N. Barnard	in 1967, performed the first successful human heart transplant.
Albert C. T. Billroth	made important contributions in the areas of histology and pathology, and advanced military surgery by citing bacteria as the cause of infection in wounds.
Elizabeth Blackwell	in 1849, became the first woman doctor of medicine in modern times.
Gerhard Domagk	in 1934, discovered and performed experimental work with "prontosil," forerunner of sulfanilamide, the first sulfa drug.
Charles Richard Drew	in 1940, developed a safe and efficient way to store blood plasma in blood banks.
John Franklin Enders	in 1954, developed a vaccine for measles and later made important discoveries concerning the poliomyelitis virus.
Sir Alexander Fleming	in 1928, discovered and later developed penicillin.
Sigmund Freud	developed psychoanalysis as one way of treating mental illness.
Joseph Goldberger	between 1913 and 1925, discovered the nature of and cure for pellagra.
Stephen Hales	invented many mechanical devices, including artificial ventilators and, in 1727, inaugurated the science of plant physiology.
William Harvey	discovered circulation of the blood, a theory which he first expounded in lectures delivered between 1628 and 1651.
Hippocrates	lived between *ca.* 460 and *ca.* 377 B.C.; called the "father of medicine"; is said to have devised for his students the code of medical ethics which today is administered as an oath to persons seeking to enter medical practice.

Pioneers in Medicine
(continued)

Name	Achievements
Carl Gustav Jung	developed analytic psychology as a way of treating mental illness.
Anton von Leeuwenhoek	made simple microscopes which enabled him to become the first to give an accurate description of red blood corpuscles and to describe bacteria in 1676.
Sir Joseph Lister	influenced by the discoveries of Pasteur, used carbolic acid to prevent septic infection and, thus, became the founder of antiseptic surgery.
Crawford Williamson Long	in 1842, became the first to use ether as an anesthetic during surgery.
George Richards Minot	an authority on blood diseases; in 1934, won the Nobel prize in medicine for research on liver treatment of anemias.
Florence Nightingale	in 1860, founded an institution for training nurses and, thus, established nursing as a profession.
Louis Pasteur	was the first to prove that fermentation is caused by minute organisms and to use heating (pasteurization) as a means of killing the organisms and preventing spoilage; also was the first to prove that bacteria cause disease; developed a vaccine for rabies.
Walter Reed	helped to prove that yellow fever is transmitted by a mosquito, which made it possible to eradicate this disease by eliminating its carriers.
Albert Sabin	in 1955, developed an oral poliomyelitis vaccine.
Jonas Salk	in 1953, developed the first successful vaccine for poliomyelitis.
Mary Edwards Walker	pioneer woman physician who served as a nurse with the Union army during the Civil War and received the Congressional Medal of Honor.

Specialty Fields in Medicine

allergy and immunology	concerned with altered and/or abnormally severe body reactivity to substances or situations
anesthesiology	study and practice of using drugs or other means to induce a controlled loss of sensation with or without a loss of consciousness
dermatology	medical and surgical treatment of skin disorders
emergency medicine	immediate recognition and treatment of acute illnesses and injuries
endocrinology	diagnosis and treatment of disorders of the endocrine glands, which regulate the complex metabolic process by which the body's cells are nourished, repaired, and/or replaced
family or general practice	supervision of the total health care of individual adults and/or of family groups
gastroenterology	diseases and pathology of the stomach and intestines
gynecology	diseases and disorders of the female reproductive organs
hematology	diseases and disorders of the blood and blood-forming organs
internal medicine	complete nonsurgical care of adults
neurology	diseases and disorders of the nervous system
nuclear medicine	use of radioactive substances to diagnose and treat disease
obstetrics	care of women during pregnancy and childbirth
ophthalmology	diagnosis and treatment of eye and vision disorders using surgery and other corrective techniques
otolaryngology	medical and surgical treatment of ear, nose, and throat disorders
pathology	analysis of the causes and effects of disease by examination of visible changes in cells, fluids, tissues, and life processes
pediatrics	medical care of children from birth through adolescence
preventive medicine	prevention of disease and disability with an emphasis on analyzing present health services and planning ways to meet future health care needs
psychiatry	diagnosis and treatment of persons with mental, emotional, or behavioral disorders
radiology	use of X-rays, ultrasound, nuclear medicine, computer axial tomography (CAT), and magnetic resonance imaging (MRI) for the diagnosis and treatment of disease
surgery	correction of diseased or injured parts of the body by means of operative treatment
urology	diagnosis and treatment of abnormalities and diseases of the urinary tract of men, women, and children and of disorders affecting the male reproductive system

Astronauts

Thomas D. Akers

Edwin E. Aldrin, Jr.

Andrew M. Allen

Joseph Allen

William A. Anders

Jay Apt

Neil A. Armstrong

Patrick Baudry

Alan L. Bean

John Blaha

Guion Bluford

Karol J. Bobko

Charles F. Bolden, Jr.

Frank Borman

Kenneth D. Bowersox

Vance Brand

Daniel Brandenstein

Curtis L. Brown, Jr.

James F. Buchli

Robert D. Cabana

Kenneth D. Cameron

M. Scott Carpenter

Gerald P. Carr

John H. Casper

Robert J. Cenker

Eugene A. Cernan

Roger B. Chaffee

Franklin R. Chang-Diaz

Leroy Chiao

Kevin C. Chilton

Mary L. Cleave

Michael R. Cliffordn

Michael L. Coats

Kenneth D. Cockrell

Michael Collins

Charles Conrad, Jr.

L. Gordon Cooper, Jr.

Richard O. Covey

John O. Creighton

Robert L. Crippen

R. Walter Cunningham

N. Jan Davis

Charles M. Duke, Jr.

Bonnie J. Dunbar

Donn F. Eisele

Joe Engle

Ronald E. Evans

John Fabian

Martin J. Fettman

Dr. Anna L. Fisher

C. Michael Foale

C. Gordon Fullerton

Richard Furrer

Dale Gardner

Jake Garn

Marc Garneau

Astronauts
(continued)

Owen K. Garriott	David C. Leestma
Charles D. Gemar	William Lenoir
Edward G. Gibson	Byron Lichtenberg
Robert Gibson	John M. Lounge
John H. Glenn, Jr.	Jack R. Lousma
Linda Godwin	James A. Lovell, Jr.
Richard F. Gordon, Jr.	Shannon W. Lucid
Ronald J. Grabe	Thomas K. Mattingly, II
S. David Griggs	William S. McArthur, Jr.
Virgil I. Grissom	Christa McAuliffe
Sidney M. Guiterrez	Jon A. McBride
Fred W. Haise, Jr.	Bruce McCandless
James D. Halsell, Jr.	James A. McDivitt
Terry J. Har	Ronald McNair
Henry Hartsfield, Jr.	Bruce E. Melnick
Frederick Hauck	Ulf Merbold
Steven A. Hawley	Ernst Messerschmid
Richard J. Hieb	Edgar D. Mitchell
David C. Hilmers	Mamoru Mohri
Jeffrey A. Hoffman	Richard M. Mullane
James B. Irwin	Story Musgrave
Marsha S. Ivins	Steven R. Nagel
Gregory P. Jarvis	Chiaki Naito-Mukai
Mae Carol Jemison	Bill Nelson
Thomas D. Jones	George D. Nelson
Joseph P. Kerwin	Rodolfo Neri
Sergei K. Krikalev	Claude Nicollier
Mark Lee	Ellen Ochoa

Astronauts
(continued)

Wubbo J. Ockels	Alan B. Shepard, Jr.
Bryan D. O'Conner	Loren J. Shriver
Ellison S. Onizuka	Donald K. Slayton
Stephen S. Oswald	Michael J. Smith
Robert Overmyer	Sherwood C. Spring
William A. Pailes	Thomas P. Stafford
Robert Parker	Robert Stewart
Donald Peterson	Kathryn D. Sullivan
William Pogue	John L. Swigart, Jr.
Kenneth S. Reightier, Jr.	Norman Thagard
Judith A. Resnik	Donald A. Thomas
Sally K. Ride	Karen Thornton
Stuart A. Roosa	William Thornton
Jerry L. Ross	Pierre J. Thuot
Prince Sultan Salman al-Saud	Richard Truly
Walter M. Schirra	James D. Van Hoften
Harrison H. Schmitt	Charles D. Walker
Russel L. Schweickart	David M. Walker
Francis R. Scobee	Carl E. Walz
David R. Scott	Paul J. Weitz
Paul D. Scully-Power	Edward H. White, II
Richard A. Searfoss	Donald E. Williams
M. Rhea Seddon	David A. Wolf
Ronald M. Sega	Alfred M. Worden
Brewster Shaw, Jr.	John W. Young

Comets

A **comet** is a heavenly body that looks like a fuzzy star and travels around the sun in an elliptical orbit. A comet has three parts: a center, which is called the **nucleus**; a hazy cloud around this center, which is called the **coma**; and a stream of dust particles and gas molecules, which always points away from the sun and is called the **tail**. Although some comets appear to be very bright, they do not produce any light of their own. Instead, like our moon, they reflect light from the sun.

Name	Year in Which It Was First Seen	Name	Year in Which It Was First Seen
Halley's Comet	Before 240 B.C.	Comet Morehouse	1908
Tycho Brahe's Comet	1577	Comet Schwassmann-Wachmann I	1927
Biela's Comet	1772	Comet Humason	1961
Encke's Comet	1786	Comet Ikeya-Seki	1965
Comet Flaugergues	1811	Comet Tago-Sato-Kosaka	1969
Comet Pons-Winnecke	1819	Comet Bennett	1969
Great Comet of 1843	1843	Comet Kohoutek	1973
Donati's Comet	1858	Comet West	1976

1. Halley's Comet was named for English astronomer Edmond Halley. Do some research to learn where five other comets on this list got their names.

2. The time it takes a comet to make one complete orbit is termed its **period**. Edmond Halley was the first person to recognize that the period for Halley's Comet is approximately seventy-seven years. Using this figure, predict the years in which the next ten sightings of this comet will take place.

3. Because the orbits of comets often take them across the paths of other celestial bodies in the solar system, it would be possible for a comet and a planet to collide. In fact, in 1910, the earth passed unharmed through the edge of Halley's Comet's tail. What would have happened if, instead of passing through the tail, the earth had gone into the coma and collided with the nucleus? Write a science fiction story about how the earth faces the threat of a collision with a comet's nucleus.

Constellations

A **constellation** is any one of eighty-eight arbitrary groups of stars recognized by astronomers. Ancient observers named forty-eight of these groups according to the pictures made by the stars they contained. All eighty-eight constellations—both ancient and modern—are listed below. Those marked with an asterisk (*) are not visible from midnorthern latitudes.

Latin Name	English Name	Latin Name	English Name
Andromeda	Chained Maiden	Cepheus	King
Antila	Air Pump	Cetus	Whale
Apus*	Bird of Paradise	Chamaeleon*	Chameleon
Aquarius	Water Bearer	Circinus*	Compasses
Aquila	Eagle	Columba	Dove
Ara*	Altar	Coma Berenices	Berenice's Hair
Aries	Ram	Corona Australis	Southern Crown
Auriga	Charioteer	Corona Borealis	Northern Crown
Bootes	Herdsman	Corvus	Crow
Caelum	Chisel	Crater	Cup
Camelopardalis	Giraffe	Crux*	(Southern) Cross
Cancer	Crab	Cygnus	Swan
Canes Venatici	Hunting Dogs	Delphinus	Dolphin
Canis Major	Great Dog	Dorado*	Swordfish
Canis Minor	Small Dog	Draco	Dragon
Capricornus	Sea Goat	Equuleus	Little Horse
Carina*	Keel	Eridanus	River Eridanus
Cassiopeia	Lady in Chair	Fornax	Furnace
Centaurus*	Centaur	Gemini	Twins

Constellations
(continued)

Latin Name	English Name	Latin Name	English Name
Grus*	Crane	Phoenix*	Phoenix
Hercules	Hercules	Pictor*	Painter's (Easel)
Horologium*	Clock	Pisces	Fishes
Hydra	Sea Serpent	Piscis Austrinus	Southern Fish
Hydrus*	Water Snake	Puppis	Poop (Stern)
Indus*	Indian	Pyxis	Compass
Lacerta	Lizard	Reticulum*	Net
Leo	Lion	Sagitta	Arrow
Leo Minor	Small Lion	Sagittarius	Archer
Lepus	Hare	Scorpius	Scorpion
Libra	Scales	Sculptor	Sculptor
Lupus*	Wolf	Scutum	Shield
Lynx	Lynx	Serpens	Serpent
Lyra	Lyre	Sextans	Sextant
Mensa*	Table (Mountain)	Taurus	Bull
Microscopium	Microscope	Telescopium*	Telescope
Monoceros	Unicorn	Triangulum	Triangle
Musca*	Fly	Triangulum Australe*	Southern Triangle
Norma*	Square	Tucana*	Toucan
Octans*	Octant	Ursa Major	Great Bear
Ophiuchus	Serpent Bearer	Ursa Minor	Small Bear
Orion	Hunter	Vela*	Sails
Pavo*	Peacock	Virgo	Virgin
Pegasus	Pegasus	Volans*	Flying Fish
Perseus	Champion	Vulpecula	Fox

Moons

A **moon** is a celestial body that orbits another celestial body of larger size. Thus, moons are **satellites**. They are sometimes called **natural satellites** to distinguish them from the **man-made satellites** that have been put into orbit in recent years. As you can see from the list below, most of the planets in our solar system have moons.

Planet	Moons	
	Number	**Names**
Mercury	0	
Venus	0	
Earth	1	Moon (Luna)
Mars	2	Phobos, Deimos
Jupiter	16	Metis, Adrastea, Amalthea, Thebe, Io, Europa, Ganymede, Callisto, Leda, Himalia, Lysithea, Elara, Ananke, Carme, Pasiphae, Sinope
Saturn	23	Titan, Iapetus, Rhea, Dione, Tethys, Enceladus, Mimas, Hyperion, Phoebe, Janus, Epimetheus, 1980 S-6, Telesto, Calypso, Pandora, Prometheus, Atlas, 1980 S-34, 1981 S-7, 1981 S-8, 1981 S-9, 1981 S-10, 1981 S-11
Uranus	15	Oberon, Titania, Umbriel, Ariel, Miranda, 1985 U-1, 1986 U-1, 1986 U-2, 1986 U-3, 1986 U-4, 1986 U-5, 1986 U-6, 1986 U-7, 1986 U-8, 1986 U-9
Neptune	2	Triton, Nereid
Pluto	1	Charon

1. As you can see from the designations given them, nine of the moons that orbit Uranus were discovered in 1986. Do some research to learn why so many moons were discovered in a single year. What event or events made their discovery possible?

2. Many of the moons on this list were named for figures in Greek or Roman mythology. Charon, for example, was the Greek ferryman of the lower world. Do some pleasure reading to learn about the identities and exploits of the deities and creatures for whom moons have been named.

Planets
(in order from the sun)

Planet Name	Diameter, miles	Average Distance from the Sun, miles	Period of Revolution		Known Moons
Mercury	3,100	35,960,000	88	days	0
Venus	7,600	67,200,000	225	days	0
Earth	7,913	93,000,000	365¼	days	1
Mars	4,200	141,500,000	687	days	2
Jupiter	88,000	483,400,000	11.86	years	16
Saturn	71,500	886,200,000	29.5	years	23
Uranus	32,000	1,783,000,000	84	years	15
Neptune	31,000	2,794,000,000	165	years	2
Pluto	1,900	3,670,000,000	248	years	1

Recent Spaceflights

Mission Name	Date(s)	Crew Members
Soyuz T-9	6/27/83	Vladimir A. Lyakhov
Challenger	8/30-9/5/83	Richard Truly Daniel Brandenstein William Thornton Guion Bluford Dale Gardner
Columbia	11/28-12/8/83	John W. Young Brewster Shaw, Jr. Robert Parker Owen K. Garriott Byron Lichtenberg Ulf Merbold
Challenger	2/3-2/11-84	Vance Brand Robert Gibson Ronald McNair Bruce McCandless Robert Stewart
Soyuz T-10	2/8-10/2/84	Leonid Kizim Vladmir Solovyov Oleg Atkov
Challenger	4/6-4/13/84	Robert L. Crippen Francis R. Scobee George D. Nelson Terry J. Har James D. Van Hoften
Soyuz T-12	7/17/84	Vladimir A. Dzhanibekov Svetlana Y. Savitskaya Igor P. Volk

Recent Spaceflights
(continued)

Mission Name	Date(s)	Crew Members
Discovery	8/30-9/5/84	Henry Hartsfield, Jr. Michael L. Coats Steven A. Hawley Judith A. Resnick Richard M. Mullane Charles D. Walker
Challenger	10/5-10/13/84	Robert L. Crippen Jon A. McBride Kathryn D. Sullivan Sally K. Ride Marc Garneau David C. Leestma Paul D. Scully-Power
Discovery	11/8-11/16/84	Frederick Hauck David M. Walker Dr. Anna L. Fisher Joseph Allen Dale Gardner
Discovery	4/12-4/19/85	Karol J. Bobko Donald E. Williams Jake Garn Charles D. Walker Jeffrey A. Hoffman S. David Griggs M. Rhea Seddon
Discovery	6/17-6/24/85	Daniel Brandenstein John O. Creighton Shannon W. Lucid Steven R. Nagel John Fabian Prince Sultan Salman al-Saud Patrick Baudry

Recent Spaceflights
(continued)

Mission Name	Date(s)	Crew Members
Atlantis	10/3/85	Karol J. Bobko Ronald J. Grabe David C. Hilmers Robert Stewart William A. Pailes
Challenger	10/30/85	Henry Hartsfield, Jr. Steven R. Nagel James F. Buchli Guion Bluford Bonnie J. Dunbar Wubbo J. Ockels Richard Furrer Ernst Messerschmid
Atlantis	11/26/85	Brewster Shaw, Jr. Bryan D. O'Conner Sherwood C. Spring Mary L. Cleave Jerry L. Ross Charles D. Walker Rodolfo Neri
Columbia	1/12/86	Robert Gibson Charles F. Bolden, Jr. Steven A. Hawley George D. Nelson Franklin R. Chang-Diaz Robert J. Cenker Bill Nelson
Challenger	1/28/86	Francis R. Scobee Michael J. Smith Judith A. Resnick Ellison S. Onizuka Ronald E. McNair Gregory P. Jarvis Christa McAuliffe

Recent Spaceflights
(continued)

Mission Name	Date(s)	Crew Members
Mir	2/20/86	(Space station with six docking ports)
Soyuz T-15	3/13/86	Leonid Kizim Vladmir Solovyov
Soyuz TM-2	2/5-12/29/87	Yuri V. Romanenko Aleksandr I. Laveikin
Soyuz TM-4	12/21/87-12/21/88	Vladimir Titov Muso Manarov Anatoly Levchenko
Discovery	9/29-10/3/88	Frederick Hauck Richard O. Covey David C. Hilmers George D. Nelson John M. Lounge
Discovery	4/24-4/29/90	Bruce McCandless Kathryn D. Sullivan Loren J. Shriver Charles F. Bolden, Jr. Steven A. Hawley
Endeavour	5/7-5/16/92	Daniel Brandenstein Kevin C. Chilton Bruce E. Melnick Pierre J. Thuot Richard J. Hieb Karen Thornton Thomas D. Akers

Recent Spaceflights
(continued)

Mission Name	Date(s)	Crew Members
Endeavour	9/12-9/21/92	Robert Gibson Curtis L. Brown, Jr. Mark Lee Jay Apt N. Jan Davis Mae Carol Jemison Mamoru Mohri
Discovery	4/8-4/17/93	Kenneth D. Cameron Stephen S. Oswald C. Michael Foale Ellen Ochoa Kenneth D. Cockrell
Columbia	10/18-11/1/93	John Blaha Richard A. Searfoss William S. McArthur, Jr. David A. Wolf M. Rhea Seddon Shannon W. Lucid Martin J. Fettman
Endeavour	12/2-12/13/93	Richard O. Covey Kenneth D. Bowersox Claude Nicollier Story Musgrave Thomas D. Akers Karen Thornton Jeffrey A. Hoffman
Discovery	2/3-2/11/94	Charles F. Bolden, Jr. Kenneth S. Reightier, Jr. N. Jan Davis Franklin R. Chang-Diaz Ronald M. Sega Sergei K. Krikalev

Recent Spaceflights
(continued)

Mission Name	Date(s)	Crew Members
Columbia	3/4-3/18/94	John H. Casper Andrew M. Allen Pierre J. Thuot Charles D. Gemar Marsha S. Ivins
Endeavour	4/9-4/20/94	Sidney M. Guiterrez Kevin C. Chilton Michael R. Cliffordn Linda Godwin Jay Apt Thomas D. Jones
Columbia	7/8-7/23/94	Robert D. Cabana James D. Halsell, Jr. Richard J. Hieb Carl E. Walz Leroy Chiao Donald A. Thomas Chiaki Naito-Mukai

Solar System Terms

aberration
airglow
albedo
altitude
apex
aphelion
apogee
aspects
asteroid
astronomy
aurora
axis
azimuth
black hole
chromatic aberration
chromosphere
comet
conjunction
constellation
Coriolis effect
corona
craters

cusps
declination
dispersion
diurnal motion
Doppler effect
dwarf
eccentricity
eclipse
ecliptic
ellipse
emission
ephemeris
equinox
galaxy
inclination
light-year
lunar
magnitude
mass
mean solar time
meteor

meteorite
moon
nadir
nebula
nodes
nova
nutation
oblateness
occultations
orbit
parabola
parallax
penumbra
perihelion
phases
photosphere
planet
polarity
precession
prominences
rays

reflection
refraction
regression
resolving power
retrograde motions
right ascension
revolution
rotation
satellite
scintillation
sidereal time
solar time
solstices
spectroheliogram
spectrum
stars
sun
sunspots
supernova
telescope
umbra
zenith

Become familiar with the meanings of at least twenty-five of these words, and use them correctly in a space adventure story.

Chemical Elements and Compounds

Elements are the basic chemical substances from which everything in the universe is made. There are more than one hundred of them. Each element consists of only one kind of atom. Here are the names and symbols for some common elements.

aluminum	Al	gold	Au	nickel	Ni
barium	Ba	helium	He	nitrogen	N
boron	B	hydrogen	H	oxygen	O
bromine	Br	iodine	I	potassium	K
calcium	Ca	iron	Fe	radium	Ra
carbon	C	krypton	Kr	silver	Ag
chlorine	Cl	lead	Pb	sodium	Na
cobalt	Co	magnesium	Mg	tin	Sn
copper	Cu	manganese	Mn	uranium	U
fluorine	F	mercury	Hg	zinc	Zn

A **compound** is a substance made of two or more elements joined into molecules.

Compound	Common Name	Molecular Formula
sodium chloride	table salt	NaCl
sucrose	table sugar	$C_{12}H_{22}O_{11}$
water	water	H_2O
_____	_____	_____
_____	_____	_____
_____	_____	_____

1. Write a short story about a super hero who uses at least one of the elements on this list to make himself even stronger.

2. Do some research so that you can add three compounds, their common names, and their chemical formulas to this list.

Computer Terms

access	to place data on, and retrieve data from, a computer's storage devices
application	a computer program that does a particular job
back-up (verb)	to copy data in case original data is lost
back-up (noun)	a copy of the original that has been stored
bit	the smallest unit of information stored in a computer
boot	short for bootstrap; it means to start up the computer
byte	a group of bits
CD-ROM	short for Compact Disc-Read Only Memory; an optical disc read by a laser beam, used for storing large amounts of information on the computer
chip	a tiny integrated electrical circuit used to build the processing and memory units of computers
computer	a programmable machine that accepts, processes, and displays data
cursor	the lighted or blinking shape on the monitor which shows where the data will appear if a key on the keyboard is pressed
data	information stored in a computer
database	a large amount of information stored in a format that allows ready access
desktop publishing	the production of printed matter using a computer with programs that integrate text and graphics
electronic mail	the transmission of memos and messages over a computer network; frequently called "e-mail"
file	any collection of data that is treated as a single unit
file server	a computer that stores data and programs shared by network users
floppy disk	a small, inexpensive, removable disk used to store and/or transfer information
graphics	pictures displayed on a computer's monitor and/or created with a computer
hard copy	printed computer output

Computer Terms
(continued)

hardware — the working mechanical and electrical parts of a computer, including the monitor, central processing unit, keyboard, mouse, modem, and printer

interactive — a type of computing in which the operator may interrupt the program and make choices that affect the outcome of the program

joystick — a handheld lever that can be tilted in different directions to control the movement of the cursor on the display screen

keyboard — the piece of computer hardware that resembles a typewriter's keys, and is used to input information into a computer

log on/log off — to connect to, or disconnect from, another computer system or file server

memory — the capacity of a computer to store information

menu — programs, functions, and other choices usually displayed as a list on the screen from which the user can make selections

modem — a device that enables data to be transmitted between computers, usually over telephone lines

mouse — a handheld input device that is rolled across a flat surface to move the cursor

network — a set of computers and terminals linked together and able to interact with one another

PC — an abbreviation for personal computer

printer — a device that converts computer output into printed images

processing — the operating step during which a computer examines, rearranges, and stores data

program — a sequence of detailed, coded instructions that tell a computer how to perform a specific function

programmer — a person who knows a computer's language and uses it to give instructions to the computer

software — all of the programs or sets of instructions that tell the computer what to do

user-friendly — easy to learn and use

window — a separate viewing area on the display screen of the monitor

Flowers

anemone
apple blossom
aster
azalea
begonia
black-eyed Susan
bluebell
buttercup
camellia
carnation
chrysanthemum
coneflower
cowslip
crocus
daffodil
daisy
dandelion
dogwood
edelweiss
forget-me-not
forsythia
foxglove
freesia
fuchsia
gardenia
geranium
gladiolus
goldenrod
heather
hibiscus
hollyhock

hyacinth
hydrangea
iris
jasmine
jonquil
lady's slipper
lantana
larkspur
lilac
lily of the valley
marigold
narcissus
nasturtium
orchid
pansy
peach blossom
peony
petunia
poppy
ranunculus
rhododendron
rose
snapdragon
sunflower
sweet pea
thistle
tulip
violet
wisteria
yucca
zinnia

Food Guide Pyramid

A Guide to Daily Food Choices

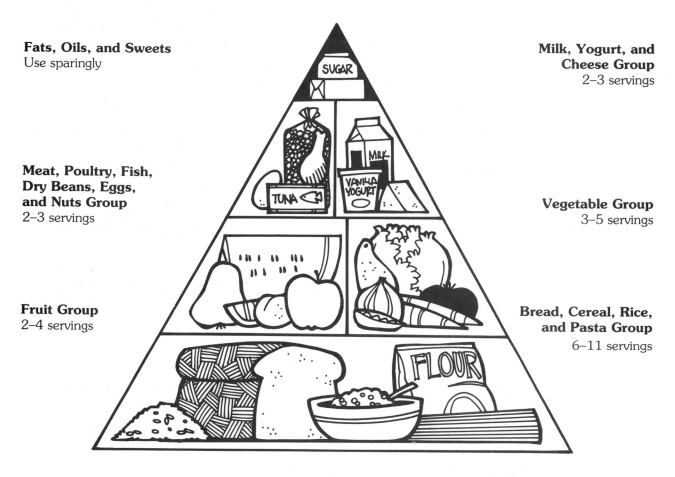

Fats, Oils, and Sweets
Use sparingly

**Milk, Yogurt, and
Cheese Group**
2–3 servings

**Meat, Poultry, Fish,
Dry Beans, Eggs,
and Nuts Group**
2–3 servings

Vegetable Group
3–5 servings

Fruit Group
2–4 servings

**Bread, Cereal, Rice,
and Pasta Group**
6–11 servings

Source: U.S. Department of Agriculture/U.S. Department of Health and Human Services

The Food Guide Pyramid has been recognized as the basic guide for building a healthy diet since its approval by the United States Department of Agriculture in 1992. The pyramid is divided into six major food groups, each with a recommended number of daily servings. This number varies on an individual basis according to age, stage of growth, and activity level.

Internet Words

address resolution	converting an internet address to a real physical address
ASCII	standard coding of characters used widely in computer industry; pronounced *ask-key* (short for American Standard Code for Information Interchange)
BBS	(Bulletin Board System);a computer that people can connect to, usually over the phone lines.
bounced	e-mail being returned because it is not deliverable
browser	a program that runs on an Internet-connected computer and provides access to the World Wide Web
cyberspace	the virtual space created by computer systems; cyberspace involves technology as complex as virtual reality and as relatively simple as electronic mail
e-mail (electronic mail)	messages sent to and from individual users over a computer network.
FAQ	(Frequently Asked Questions); generally refers to a file that contains a list of frequently-asked questions along with answers.
header	the portion of an electronic mail message which preceeds the body of the message; it contains the message originator, date, and time
home page	the document displayed when a user first accesses a Website
Internet	a worldwide network of government, educational, and private computer systems
netiquette	refers to proper behavior on the network
posting	a message sent to a person or group of people on a mailing list or bulletin board
ROFL	short for "rolling on the floor laughing"
search engine	a computer program that searches the network for information requested by the user
Website	a group of interrelated documents accessible through the World Wide Web
World Wide Web	(also know as WWW or The Web); a multimedia hypertext system built into the Internet
URL	(Universal Resource Locator); an "address" of a certain document on a certain computer system on the Web

Inventors

Name	Birth and Death Dates	Nationality	Invention
John Bardeen	1908-	American	transistor
Alexander Graham Bell	1847-1922	Scottish-American	telephone
Vincent Bendix	1882-1945	American	electric self-starter for the automobile
Emile Berliner	1851-1929	German-American	loose-contact teletransmitter, or microphone
Clarence Birdseye	1886-1956	American	preserving food by freezing
Louis Braille	1809-1852	French	system of raised-point writing for literature and music
William Seward Burroughs	1857-1898	American	key-set recording and adding machine
Edmund Cartwright	1743-1823	English	power loom
George Washington Carver	1864-1943	American	agricultural research on the industrial uses of peanuts
Samuel Colt	1814-1862	American	revolver
Peter Cooper	1791-1883	American	first American locomotive
Glenn Curtiss	1878-1930	American	hydroplane
Gottlieb Daimler	1834-1900	German	high-speed internal combustion automobile engine
Lee De Forest	1873-1961	American	radio amplifier and radio transmission
George Eastman	1854-1932	American	the Kodak camera
Thomas Alva Edison	1847-1931	American	phonograph, incandescent electric lamp, and alkaline rechargeable storage battery
Gabriel Daniel Fahrenheit	1686-1736	German	mercury thermometer and Fahrenheit scale
Alexander Fleming	1881-1955	British	penicillin
Benjamin Franklin	1706-1790	American	bifocal lens, heating stove, and lightning rod
Robert Fulton	1765-1815	American	steamboat
Charles Goodyear	1800-1860	American	vulcanization process used to manufacture rubber
Johann Gutenberg	ca. 1400-1468	German	printing from movable type
Elias Howe	1819-1867	American	sewing machine

Inventors
(continued)

Name	Birth and Death Dates	Nationality	Invention
Guglielmo Marconi	1874-1937	Italian	wireless high-frequency telegraph
Ottmar Mergenthaler	1854-1899	German-American	Linotype typesetting machine
Samuel F. B. Morse	1791-1872	American	magnetic telegraph and Morse code
Elisha Otis	1811-1861	American	steam elevator and elevator brake
Blaise Pascal	1623-1662	French	adding machine
Louis Pasteur	1822-1895	French	rabies vaccine and the pasteurization process
George Pullman	1831-1897	American	Pullman railroad sleeping car with pull-down berths
Igor Sikorsky	1889-1972	Russian-American	helicopter
James Starley	1830-1881	English	modern bicycle
Edward Teller	1908-	Hungarian-American	hydrogen bomb
George Westinghouse	1846-1914	American	air brake
Schuyler S. Wheeler	1860-1923	American	electric fan
Eli Whitney	1765-1825	American	cotton gin
Orville Wright	1871-1948	American }	first successful flight in a motor-powered heavier-than-air craft
Wilbur Wright	1867-1912	American	
Linus Yale, Jr.	1821-1868	American	cylinder lock
Ferdinand von Zeppelin	1838-1917	German	rigid dirigible

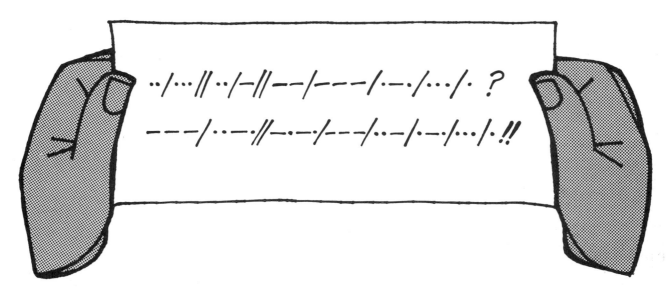

1. Become an inventor. First, straighten a wire coat hanger. Then, bend it into something entirely different. Finally, name your invention and draw a picture or diagram showing how it works or what it can be used to do.

2. Use recycled materials from home to create a unique invention. Display and demonstrate your creation at a classroom **Invention Convention**.

3. Do some research to create a time line on which you show pictures and patent dates for at least ten of these inventions.

Machines

In physics, **work** is defined as exerting enough force to overcome the resistance of friction, gravity, or inertia so that a mass can be moved through a distance. Strictly speaking, if no movement takes place, no work has been done no matter how much effort or energy has been expended. A **machine** is a device that transmits force so that work can be done. Often, a machine transmits force so as to gain a **mechanical advantage**, meaning that the force which is available for doing the work is greater than the force that was originally applied to the machine. The inclined plane, lever, screw, wedge, and wheel and axle are **simple machines** which offer a mechanical advantage. All complex machines include among their elements one or more of these simple machines.

Archimedes' screw	pump
battering ram	screw
block and tackle	steam shovel
catapult	treadmill
crane	trip-hammer
derrick	turbine
electric generator	waterwheel
engine	wedge
inclined plane	wheel and axle
lever	windlass
machine tool	windmill
pulley	

1. Select three machines from this list. Draw and label diagrams of these machines to show how they work.

2. Do some research to discover who Archimedes was and why one of these machines is named after him.

3. Archimedes said that he would use a lever to move the earth if someone would give him a place to stand while doing so. Explain what he meant.

Minerals

A **mineral** is a solid homogenous crystalline chemical element or compound that results from inorganic processes.

almandite	greenockite	sard
bauxite	hafnium	scandium
bentonite	heulandite	smithsonite
berkelium	hiddenite	sperrylite
boson	holmium	spessartite
bronze	idocrase	taconite
brookite	iridium	tantalum
cairngorm	itacolumite	tanzanite
calaverite	kernite	thenardite
carnotite	kunzite	titanium
chalcedony	lawrencium	tobernite
colemanite	magnesia	travertine
copper	mendelevium	tremolite
cordierite	mercury	troostite
covellite	millerite	turquoise
dolomite	monzonite	uranium
dumortierite	morganite	uvarovite
franklinite	niobium	vanadium
gadolinite	palladium	willemite
gallium	plutonium	witherite
garnierite	polonium	wollastonite
goethite	promethium	zoisite
	samarskite	

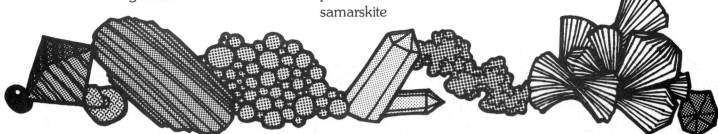

1. **Brookite** was named for the English mineralogist Henry James Brooke, who described thirteen mineral species and first introduced the groups commonly used to classify forms of crystals. **Calaverite** was named for Calaveras County in California, where this mineral was discovered. Select twelve minerals from this list. Do research to discover the origins of their names.

2. Some of the minerals on this list are magnetic, and some of them are radioactive. Choose one of the minerals on the list and pretend that it has unusual characteristics and/or special powers. Write a story set in the future. Have the hero or heroine of the story use these characteristics or powers to rescue someone in distress.

Nutrition Terms

absorption
alimentary canal
amino acids
assimilation
balanced diet
beriberi
bile
calcium
calorie
carbohydrates
carbon
carnivore
cell
cereals
chew
cholesterol
citrus
complete proteins
dairy products
deficiency
dehydration
diabetes
diet
digestion
empty calories
energy
enzyme

esophagus
fats (or lipids)
fatty acids
fiber
food groups
fruits
gall bladder
glands
glucose
glycerol
glycogen
goiter
grains
gram
herbivore
hormone
hydrogen
hydrolizing enzyme
incomplete proteins
insulin
iodine
iron
lecithin
liver
malnutrition
meats
metabolism
mouth

nitrogen
nourishment
nutrients
nutrition
omnivore
oxygen
pancreas
peristalsis
phosphorus
potassium
proteins
protoplasm
rickets
saliva
salivary amylase
salts
scurvy
small intestine
sphincter muscle
starches
stomach
sugars
swallow
teeth
vegetables
vitamins
water

First, select six of these terms. Next, do some research to learn what each one means. Then, write a paragraph in which you show what these terms have to do with nutrition and how they are related to one another. For example, you might choose **balanced diet**, **carbohydrates**, **fats**, **minerals**, **proteins**, and **water** and show that the latter five are components of the first.

Plant and Flower Words

acerate	pedate
annual	pedicel
anther	peltate
axil	perennial
blade	petal
blossom	phloem
bud	photosynthesis
bulb	pinnate
chlorophyll	pistil
chloroplast	plumule
corm	pollen
cotyledons	pollination
cross-pollination	quinquefoliolate
cutting	respiration
dormant	rhizome
embryo	root
endosperm	root hairs
epicotyl	root stock
exfoliate	runcinate
fern	seed
filament	sepal
foliage	serrate
fruit	spore
germination	stalk
graft	stamen
herbaceous	stem
hypocotyl	stigma
leaf	style
lobation	succulent
lobe	thorn
lobule	transpiration
megasporangium	trifoliolate
megaspore	tuber
osmosis	vein
ovary	whorl
ovules	xylem
palmate	

Rain Forest Words

Amazon
anaconda
antelope
angwantibo
army ant
babirusa
balsa
bellbird
Brazil nut
boa
bromeliad
buttress
cacao
caiman
camouflage
canopy
capuchin
capybara
cashew
cassia
cassowary
centipede
chameleon
chimpanzee
cichlid
cinchona
coati
duiker
durian
ecosystem
epiphyte
equator
evergreen
fer-de-lance
fern
flying frog

gecko
gibbon
gorilla
harpy eagle
hoatzin
honeycreeper
hornbill
humidity
hummingbird
humus
iguana
ironwood
jaguar
kinkajou
Komodo dragon
lemur
liana
macaque
macaw
mahogany
mandrill
mangosteen
mantis
marmoset
millipede
mist
motmot
myna
ocelot
okapi
orangutan
orchid
paca
pandanus
parrot
pavilion

philodendron
piranha
pitcher plant
pit viper
pollination
python
rafflesia
rainfall
rubber tree
salamander
saprophyte
scorpion
shrew
sloth
soft-shelled turtle
spider monkey
spoonbill
strangler fig
sunbird
sunlight
swallowtail
tamandua
tapir
tarantula
teak
termite
tiger
tortoise beetle
toucan
transpiration
tree frog
Tropic of Cancer
Tropic of Capricorn
understory
vampire bat
yapok

Rocks

Rocks are classified into three major groups according to the way in which they were formed. **Igneous** rocks are volcanic in origin and are formed by the cooling and solidifying of magma. **Metamorphic** rocks are rocks that have been changed by the action of pressure, heat, and/or water to be more compact and more highly crystalline than they were originally. **Sedimentary** rocks are formed of mechanical, chemical, or organic deposits.

Igneous	Metamorphic	Sedimentary
basalt	gneiss	breccia
gabbro	marble	clay
granite	quartzite	coal
obsidian	schist	conglomerate
peridotite	slate	flint
pumice		limestone
rhyolite		sandstone
scoria		shale
svenite		

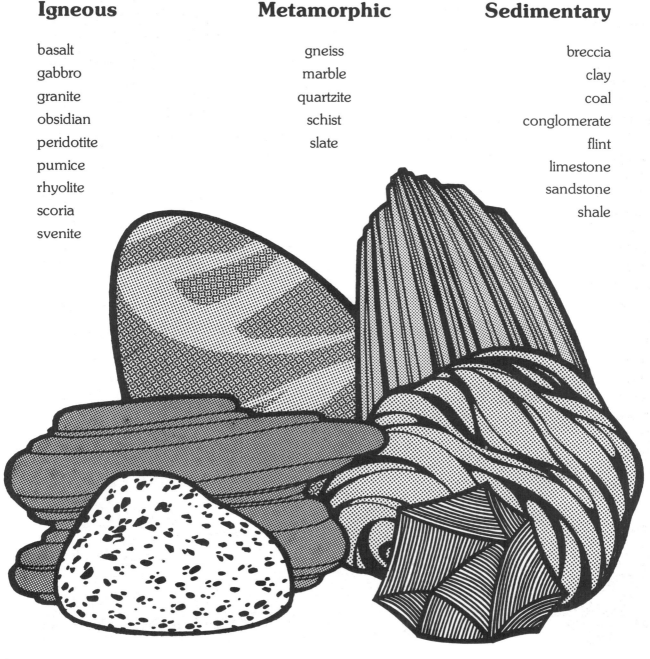

Science Topics

aerodynamics
AIDS
airplanes
allergies
amphibians
anatomy
animal behavior
astronomy
atomic energy
atoms
automation
bacteria
birds
boats
botany
brain
cells
chemistry
circulatory system
color
comets
computer axial tomography
computers
conservation
constellations
digestion

dinosaurs
disease
drugs
earth
earthquakes
ecology
electricity
endangered animals
endocrine system
energy
engines
fingerprints
first aid
fishes
flight
flowers
fossils
fruits
gardening
genetics
geodes
geology
gravity
habitats
heart
heat

hibernation
horses
human body
hurricanes
immunity
insects
inventions
invertebrates
joints
kaleidoscopes
light
lizards
lungs
machines
magnetism
mammals
man-made satellites
marine life
matter
metabolism
meteors
microscopes
migration
minerals
molecules
muscular system

Science Topics
(continued)

natural satellites
nervous system
nutrition
oceanography
optical illusions
osmosis
parasites
pest control
photosynthesis
physics
planets
plants
pollution
prehistoric life
public health
quasars

rain forests
recycling
reptiles
respiratory system
robots
rockets
rocks
seeds
senses
shells
snakes
solar energy
solar system
sound
spores
symbiosis

telescopes
terrariums
tides
tornadoes
trees
ultrasound
vaccines
vertebrates
vitamins
volcanoes
water
weather
wetlands
whales
X-rays
zoology

Select a topic from the list for independent study. Decorate the outside of a file folder to go with your topic. Inside the file folder, place the following items: (1) a title page, (2) a table of contents, (3) five pages of information about your topic, (4) illustrations to go with this information, (5) fifteen quiz questions covering your information, (6) a sheet of answers for the questions, and (7) a puzzle, maze, word search, or game based on your topic.

Trees

ailanthus	lime
alder	linden
almond	locust
apple	magnolia
ash	mahogany
aspen	maple
beech	myrtle
birch	oak
cedar	olive
cherry	orange
chestnut	palm
cycad	palmetto
cypress	peach
deodar	pear
elm	pecan
eucalyptus	pine
fig	poplar
fir	sequoia
grapefruit	spruce
hazel	sycamore
hemlock	walnut
hickory	willow
lemon	yew

Weather Words

altocumulus
altostratus
barometric pressure
Beaufort scale
blizzard
chinook
cirrocumulus
cirrostratus
cirrus
cloud
cloudburst
cold front
cumulocirrus
cumulonimbus
cumulostratus
cumulus
cyclone
dew
drizzle
false cirrus
foehn
fog
front
frost
hail
hailstone
haze
hoarfrost
humidity
hurricane

ice
icicle
lightning
mist
moisture
monsoon
nimbostratus
precipitation
rain
rime
Santa Ana
sleet
smog
snow
snowflakes
snowstorm
squall
stationary front
stratocumulus
stratus
temperature
thunder
thunderbolt
thunderstorm
thunderstorm cirrus
tornado
typhoon
warm front
wind
windstorm

Bonus Ideas for Science

1. Pick a topic from one of the science lists. Do research on this topic. Make a shoe box diorama depicting your topic, and write a one-page summary of your most important findings.

2. Choose a topic from one of the science lists and research it thoroughly. Wrap a grocery box with colored butcher, construction, or shelf paper. Paste interesting information and pictures about your topic on all six sides of the box.

3. Pick a topic from one of the science lists and research it thoroughly. Use cardboard, clay, papier-mâché, Popsicle sticks, soap, sugar cubes, or other appropriate media to construct a model related to the topic.

4. Choose two dinosaurs from the lists on pages 151 and 152. Do research to learn more about them. Make lists showing ways in which they were alike and ways in which they were different.

5. Select a reptile from the list on page 155. Design a postage stamp in honor of this reptile.

6. After referring to the list on pages 157 and 158, create a new "itis." Describe its symptoms and tell how doctors will cure it.

7. Pick three constellations from the list on pages 167 and 168. Using gummed stars (available in stationery stores), make the patterns of these constellations on black construction paper and label each one.

Name _____

Create a Science List

Think of a science-related topic that interests you. On the lines below, create a list that reflects this topic. Illustrate your list, and give it a title.

_____

_____

_____

_____

_____

_____

_____

_____

_____

_____

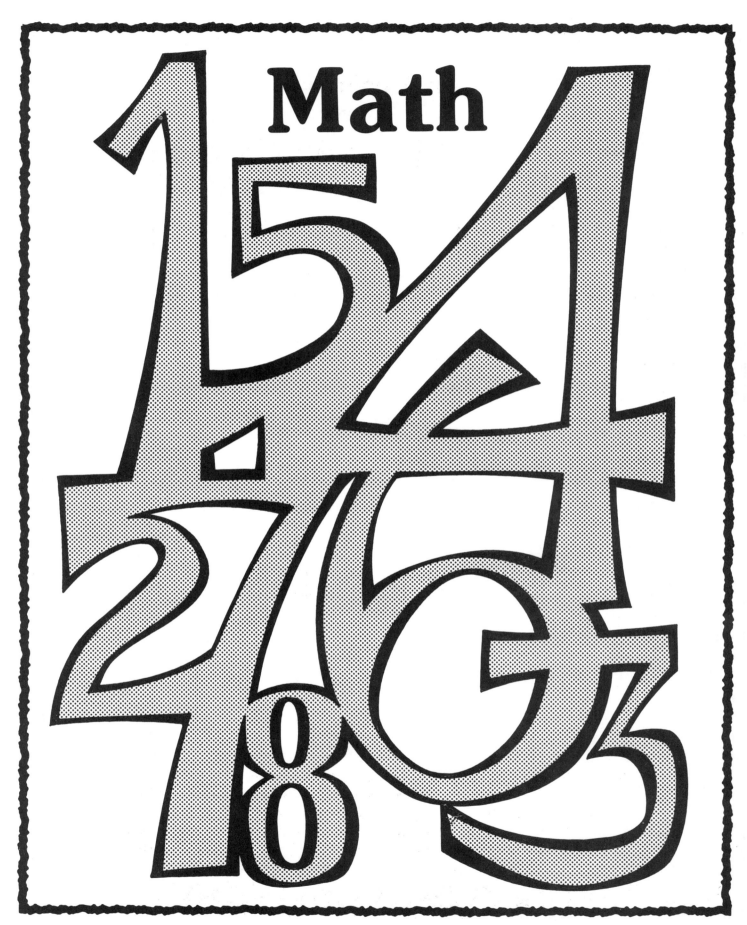

Math

I Love Lists!
© The Learning Works, Inc.

Big Numbers

Name	Value in Powers of Ten	Number of Zeros	Number of Periods of Zeros After 1,000*
million	10^6	6	1
billion	10^9	9	2
trillion	10^{12}	12	3
quadrillion	10^{15}	15	4
quintillion	10^{18}	18	5
sextillion	10^{21}	21	6
septillion	10^{24}	24	7
octillion	10^{27}	27	8
nonillion	10^{30}	30	9
decillion	10^{33}	33	10
undecillion	10^{36}	36	11
duodecillion	10^{39}	39	12
tredecillion	10^{42}	42	13
quattuordecillion	10^{45}	45	14
quindecillion	10^{48}	48	15
sexdecillion	10^{51}	51	16
septendecillion	10^{54}	54	17
octodecillion	10^{57}	57	18
novemdecillion	10^{60}	60	19
vigintillion	10^{63}	63	20
centillion	10^{303}	303	100

* In mathematics, a **period of zeros** is a group of three zeros which is set off by a comma. For example, in the number one million, which is written 1,000,000, there are two periods of zeros. The names of these big numbers are derived from the numbers of periods of zeros after 1,000 which are used in writing them. For example, the prefix *tri-* means "three," and three periods of zeros after 1,000 are used to write the number one trillion.

1,000,000,000,000

Math Signs and Symbols

+	addition; plus		<	less than
∠	angle		—	line segment
⌒	arc		×	multiplication
∷	as, equal		#	number
@	at		‖	parallel
¢	cent		%	percent
△	change		⊥	perpendicular
≅	congruent		π	pi
•	decimal point		→	ray
°	degree		⌐	right angle
÷	division		{ }	set
$	dollar		√	square root
Ø	empty set		–	subtraction
=	equal		Σ	summation
≈	equivalent		∴	therefore
>	greater than		≠	unequal
ƒ	function		≉	unequivalent
∞	infinity		∪	union (of sets)
∩	intersection (of sets)		⇀	vector
⋮	is to			

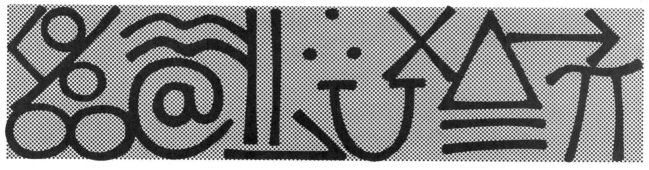

Math Terms

acute
addend
addition
algebra
angle
apothem
arc
area
array
bi
binomial
bisect
bisector
calculus
cardinal number
chord
circumference
coefficient
concurrent line
decimal
diameter
divided
division
element
equal
equidistant
equivalent
expanded notation

exponent
factor
finite
formula
fraction
geodesic
geometry
graph
grid
hypotenuse
hypothesis
imaginary number
infinite
integer
intercept
intersection
interval
inverse
line
matrix
minuend
multiplication
negative number
numeral
obtuse
operation
ordinal number
parallel
percent

percentile
perpendicular lines
place value
plane
point
polynomial
prime factor
prime number
probability
quotient
radius
ratio
real number
reciprocal
remainder
root
secant
set
sine
square root
subset
subtraction
symbol
tangent
theorem
union
vector
vertices

Metric Measurement

The metric system is a system of weights and measures that proceeds by tens and is based on the meter and the kilogram. In this system, length is measured in meters, weight is measured in grams, and capacity is measured in liters.

Length
(number of meters)

myriameter (mym)	=	10,000
kilometer (km)	=	1,000
hectometer (hm)	=	100
dekameter (dam)	=	10
meter (m)	=	1
decimeter (dm)	=	0.1
centimeter (cm)	=	0.01
millimeter (mm)	=	0.001

Mass and Weight
(number of grams)

metric ton (MT)	=	1,000,000
quintal (q)	=	100,000
kilogram (kg)	=	1,000
hectogram (hg)	=	100
dekagram (dg)	=	10
gram (g or gm)	=	1
decigram (dg)	=	0.1
centigram (cg)	=	0.01
milligram (mg)	=	0.001

Capacity
(number of liters)

kiloliter (kl)	=	1,000
hectoliter (hl)	=	100
dekaliter (dal)	=	10
liter (l)	=	1
deciliter (dl)	=	0.1
centiliter (cl)	=	0.01
milliliter (ml)	=	0.001

1. Use the information given above to fill in the blanks below.

   a. There are _____ millimeters in one centimeter.

   b. There are _____ centimeters in one meter.

   c. There are _____ millimeters in one meter.

   d. There are _____ deciliters in one liter.

   e. There are _____ milliliters in one liter.

2. For the system of weights and measures commonly used in England and the United States, length is measured in feet, yards, and miles; weight is measured in ounces and pounds; and capacity is measured in pints, quarts, and gallons. Make a table of equivalents that will help you convert measurements made in the units of one system to the units of the other system. For example, you might show how meters are related to yards.

Roman Numerals

1	I
2	II
3	III
4	IV *or* IIII
5	V
6	VI
7	VII
8	VIII
9	IX
10	X
11	XI
12	XII
13	XIII
14	XIV
15	XV
16	XVI
17	XVII
18	XVIII
19	XIX
20	XX
30	XXX
40	XL *or* XXXX
50	L
60	LX
70	LXX
80	LXXX
90	XC *or* LXXXX
100	C
150	CL
400	CD *or* CCCC
500	D
900	CM
1000	M

1. Write the year of your birth and the current year in roman numerals.

2. The copyright years for motion pictures are usually written in roman numerals. The next time you watch a movie at home or in a theater, see if you can read this year when it appears on the screen at the beginning or end of the film.

Shapes

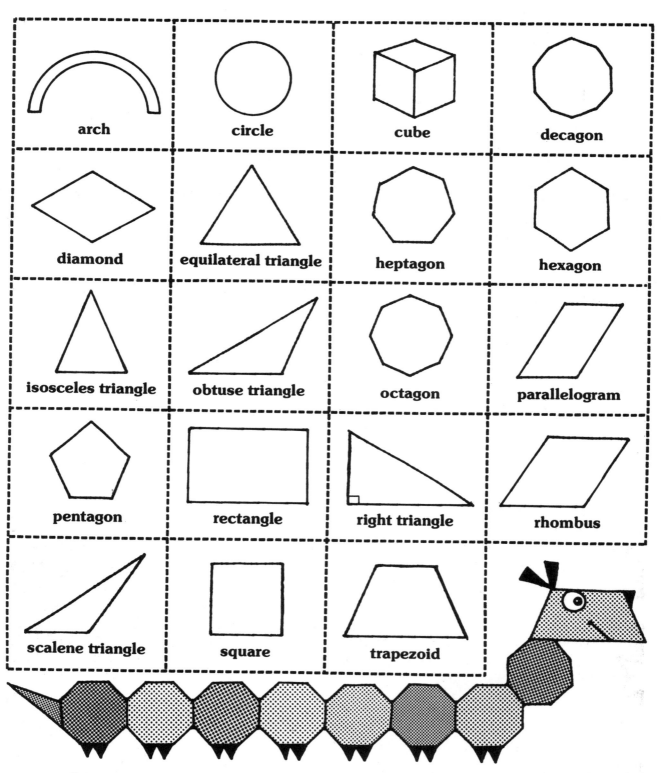

arch	circle	cube	decagon
diamond	equilateral triangle	heptagon	hexagon
isosceles triangle	obtuse triangle	octagon	parallelogram
pentagon	rectangle	right triangle	rhombus
scalene triangle	square	trapezoid	

Create a creature using some of the shapes from the list. Add other features such as a mouth, eyes, ears, and a nose.

Times Tables

1 × 1 = 1	2 × 1 = 2	3 × 1 = 3
1 × 2 = 2	2 × 2 = 4	3 × 2 = 6
1 × 3 = 3	2 × 3 = 6	3 × 3 = 9
1 × 4 = 4	2 × 4 = 8	3 × 4 = 12
1 × 5 = 5	2 × 5 = 10	3 × 5 = 15
1 × 6 = 6	2 × 6 = 12	3 × 6 = 18
1 × 7 = 7	2 × 7 = 14	3 × 7 = 21
1 × 8 = 8	2 × 8 = 16	3 × 8 = 24
1 × 9 = 9	2 × 9 = 18	3 × 9 = 27
1 × 10 = 10	2 × 10 = 20	3 × 10 = 30
1 × 11 = 11	2 × 11 = 22	3 × 11 = 33
1 × 12 = 12	2 × 12 = 24	3 × 12 = 36

4 × 1 = 4	5 × 1 = 5	6 × 1 = 6
4 × 2 = 8	5 × 2 = 10	6 × 2 = 12
4 × 3 = 12	5 × 3 = 15	6 × 3 = 18
4 × 4 = 16	5 × 4 = 20	6 × 4 = 24
4 × 5 = 20	5 × 5 = 25	6 × 5 = 30
4 × 6 = 24	5 × 6 = 30	6 × 6 = 36
4 × 7 = 28	5 × 7 = 35	6 × 7 = 42
4 × 8 = 32	5 × 8 = 40	6 × 8 = 48
4 × 9 = 36	5 × 9 = 45	6 × 9 = 54
4 × 10 = 40	5 × 10 = 50	6 × 10 = 60
4 × 11 = 44	5 × 11 = 55	6 × 11 = 66
4 × 12 = 48	5 × 12 = 60	6 × 12 = 72

I Love Lists!
© The Learning Works, Inc.

Times Tables
(continued)

7 × 1 = 7	8 × 1 = 8	9 × 1 = 9
7 × 2 = 14	8 × 2 = 16	9 × 2 = 18
7 × 3 = 21	8 × 3 = 24	9 × 3 = 27
7 × 4 = 28	8 × 4 = 32	9 × 4 = 36
7 × 5 = 35	8 × 5 = 40	9 × 5 = 45
7 × 6 = 42	8 × 6 = 48	9 × 6 = 54
7 × 7 = 49	8 × 7 = 56	9 × 7 = 63
7 × 8 = 56	8 × 8 = 64	9 × 8 = 72
7 × 9 = 63	8 × 9 = 72	9 × 9 = 81
7 × 10 = 70	8 × 10 = 80	9 × 10 = 90
7 × 11 = 77	8 × 11 = 88	9 × 11 = 99
7 × 12 = 84	8 × 12 = 96	9 × 12 = 108

10 × 1 = 10	11 × 1 = 11	12 × 1 = 12
10 × 2 = 20	11 × 2 = 22	12 × 2 = 24
10 × 3 = 30	11 × 3 = 33	12 × 3 = 36
10 × 4 = 40	11 × 4 = 44	12 × 4 = 48
10 × 5 = 50	11 × 5 = 55	12 × 5 = 60
10 × 6 = 60	11 × 6 = 66	12 × 6 = 72
10 × 7 = 70	11 × 7 = 77	12 × 7 = 84
10 × 8 = 80	11 × 8 = 88	12 × 8 = 96
10 × 9 = 90	11 × 9 = 99	12 × 9 = 108
10 × 10 = 100	11 × 10 = 110	12 × 10 = 120
10 × 11 = 110	11 × 11 = 121	12 × 11 = 132
10 × 12 = 120	11 × 12 = 132	12 × 12 = 144

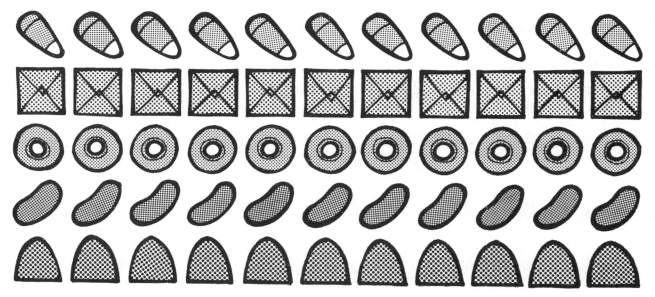

Units of Measure

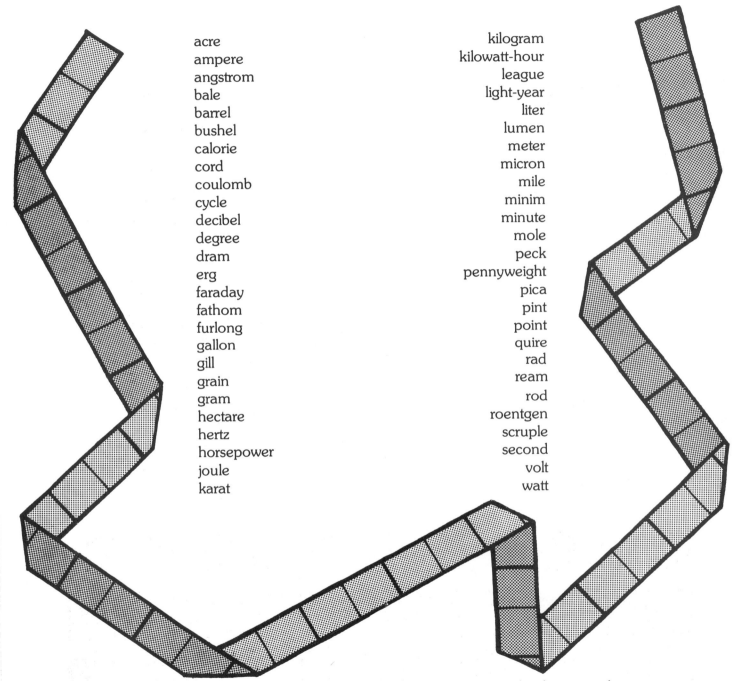

acre	kilogram
ampere	kilowatt-hour
angstrom	league
bale	light-year
barrel	liter
bushel	lumen
calorie	meter
cord	micron
coulomb	mile
cycle	minim
decibel	minute
degree	mole
dram	peck
erg	pennyweight
faraday	pica
fathom	pint
furlong	point
gallon	quire
gill	rad
grain	ream
gram	rod
hectare	roentgen
hertz	scruple
horsepower	second
joule	volt
karat	watt

1. Do research to discover what each one of the units on this list is used to measure.

2. The **ampere**, which is the unit in which the intensity of an electric current is measured, is named for André M. Ampère. Ampère was a French physicist who discovered important principles in the fields of both magnetism and electricity. Many units of measure are named for scientists. Do research to find at least five units on this list that were so named.

Weight, Measurement, and Time

Linear Measure

12 inches	= 1 foot
3 feet	= 1 yard
5½ yards	= 1 rod
40 rods	= 1 furlong
8 furlongs	= 1 statute mile

Square Measure

144 square inches	= 1 square foot
9 square feet	= 1 square yard
30¼ square yards	= 1 square rod
160 square rods	= 1 acre
640 acres	= 1 square mile

Liquid Measure

3 teaspoons	= 1 tablespoon
2 tablespoons	= 1 ounce
8 ounces	= 1 cup
2 cups	= 1 pint
2 pints	= 1 quart
4 quarts	= 1 gallon

Dry Measure

2 pints	= 1 quart
8 quarts	= 1 peck
4 pecks	= 1 bushel

Time Measure

60 seconds	= 1 minute
60 minutes	= 1 hour
24 hours	= 1 day
7 days	= 1 week
4 weeks	= 1 month
(28–31 days)	
12 months	= 1 year
10 years	= 1 decade
20 years	= 1 score
100 years	= 1 century

Weight

16 ounces	= 1 pound
2,000 pounds	= 1 ton

1. Use the information given above to fill in the blanks below.

   a. There are _____ feet in a statute mile.

   b. There are _____ yards in a furlong.

   c. There are _____ yards in a statute mile.

   d. There are _____ tablespoons in a cup.

   e. There are _____ pints in a gallon.

2. While there are four weeks in a lunar month, the number of days in a calendar month varies from 28 to 31. If there are 365 days in a year and these days are divided among 12 months, what is the average number of days in a month?

   _____ days

Who's Who in Math

Niels Henrik Abel	Norwegian mathematician known for research in the theory of elliptic functions
Howard Aiken	Harvard University professor who built the first working digital computer in 1944
Archimedes	Greek mathematician and inventor who wrote treatises in which he outlined the methods of integral calculus
George Atwood	English mathematician who wrote many books about math and invented a machine for verifying the laws of acceleration of motion
Charles Babbage	English mathematician and mechanical genius whose "analytic engine" was the forerunner of present-day calculators and computers
Eugenio Beltrami	Italian mathematician and physicist known for his work in non-Euclidian geometry
János Bolyai	Hungarian mathematician who wrote a complete system of geometry at the age of twenty-two
George Boole	English mathematician and logician who helped develop modern symbolic logic
Vannevar Bush	American electrical engineer who devised a machine for solving differential equations and, in doing so, built the first modern analog computer
Georg Cantor	German mathematician known for his work on set theory and on the theory of the infinite
René Descartes	French scientist, philosopher, and mathematician who is called the "father of modern mathematics"
Euclid	Greek mathematician who devised the theorems and problems that form a logical system of geometry
Leonhard Euler	Swiss mathematician and physicist considered to be one of the founders of the science of pure mathematics
Pierre de Fermat	French mathematician considered to be the founder of the modern theory of numbers and to have invented differential calculus and the calculus of probability
Joseph Fourier	French geometrician and physicist known for research in the theory of numerical equations
David Hilbert	German mathematician who reduced geometry to a system of axioms
Howard Kasner	American mathematician who is known for his work in higher geometry and who coined the terms googol and googolplex
Pierre Simon de Laplace	French mathematician who did outstanding work in the fields of celestial mechanics, probability, differential equations, and geodesy
James Clerk Maxwell	Scottish physicist who developed a mathematical theory to explain electromagnetic activity
John Napier	Scottish mathematician who invented logarithms and pioneered in the use of the present system of decimal notation
John von Neumann	American mathematician who wrote a book on the quantum theory and won the Fermi Award for work on the theory, design, and construction of computers
Sir Isaac Newton	English mathematician credited with the invention of both differential and integral calculus
Blaise Pascal	French scientist and philosopher who originated, with Fermat, the mathematical theory of probability

Bonus Ideas for Math

1. Write a science fiction story using some of the larger numbers from the list on page 199.

2. Brainstorm with your classmates to create a list of ways in which your life would be different if there were no numbers at all. For example, there would be no clocks as we now have, our telephone dialing system would be different, and speedometers on cars would have no meaning. Use this list to write a short story entitled "The Day the Numbers Disappeared."

3. From the list on page 201, select ten math terms that are unfamiliar to you. Use a dictionary or advanced mathematics textbook to discover the meanings of these terms.

4. Referring to the list on page 203, create addition and subtraction problems for a classmate using only Roman numerals.

5. Select a famous mathematician from the list on page 209. Do research to learn more about the life and achievements of this person.

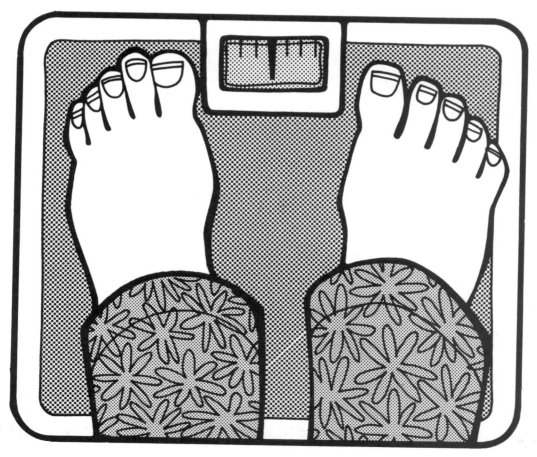

Name _____

Create a Math List

Think of a math topic that interests you. On the lines below, create a list that reflects this topic. Illustrate your list and give it a title.

_____

_____

_____

_____

_____

_____

_____

_____

_____

_____

The Arts & Sports

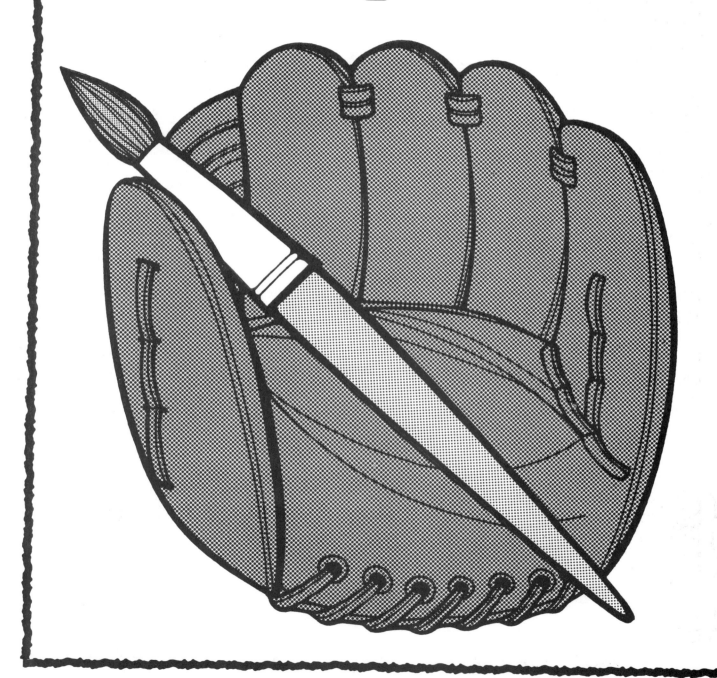

Composers

composer (kəm-pō´-zər), *n.*: a person who writes music

Baroque Period
Late 1500s to Middle 1700s

Johann Sebastian Bach (1685-1750)
Dietrich Buxtehude (*ca.* 1637-1707)
George Frederick Handel (1685-1759)
Jean Baptiste Lully (1632-1687)
Claudio Monteverdi (1567-1643)
Johann Pachelbel (1653-1706)
Henry Purcell (1659-1695)
Alessandro Scarlatti (1659-1725)
Domenico Scarlatti (1685-1757)

Rococo Period
*Last Thirty to Forty Years of the
Baroque Period*

Karl Philipp Emanuel Bach (1714-1788)
Antonio Vivaldi (*ca.* 1675-1741)

Classical Period
Middle 1700s to Early 1800s

Ludwig van Beethoven (1770-1827)
Muzio Clementi (1752-1832)
Christoph Willibald Gluck (1714-1787)
Joseph Haydn (1732-1809)
Wolfgang Amadeus Mozart (1756-1791)

Romantic Period
Early 1800s to Late 1800s

Vincenzo Bellini (1801-1835)
Hector Berlioz (1803-1869)
Georges Bizet (1838-1875)
Johannes Brahms (1833-1897)
Frédéric Chopin (1810-1849)
Gaetano Donizetti (1797-1848)
Anton Dvořák (1841-1904)
César Auguste Franck (1822-1890)
Edvard Grieg (1843-1907)
Stephen Collins Foster (1826-1864)
Ruggiero Leoncavallo (1858-1919)
Franz Liszt (1811-1886)
Edward MacDowell (1861-1908)
Felix Mendelssohn (1809-1847)
Modest Moussorgsky (1835-1881)
Jacques Offenbach (1819-1880)
Giacomo Puccini (1858-1924)
Nikolai Rimsky-Korsakov (1844-1908)
Gioacchino Rossini (1792-1868)
Camille Saint-Saens (1835-1921)
Franz Schubert (1797-1828)
Robert Schumann (1810-1856)
John Philip Sousa (1854-1932)
Johann Strauss (1825-1899)
Peter Ilyich Tchaikovsky (1840-1893)
Giuseppe Verdi (1813-1901)
Richard Wagner (1813-1886)

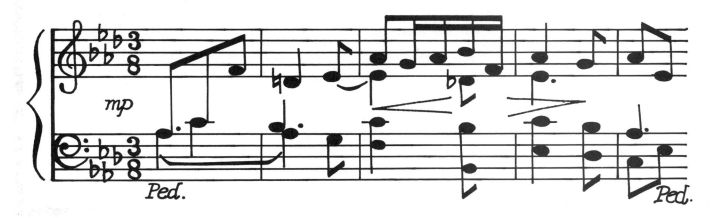

Composers
(continued)

Modern Period
Late 1800s to Middle 1900s

Béla Bartók (1881-1945)
Irving Berlin (1888-1989)
Eubie Blake (1883-1983)
Hoagy Carmichael (1899-1981)
George M. Cohan (1878-1942)
Claude Debussy (1862-1918)
Gabriel Faure (1845-1924)
Stephen Foster (1826-1964)
George Gershwin (1898-1937)
Ferde Grofe (1892-1972)
Gustav Holst (1874-1934)
Engelbert Humperdinck (1854-1921)
Charles Edward Ives (1874-1954)
Scott Joplin (1868-1917)
Jerome Kern (1885-1945)
Zoltán Kodály (1882-1967)
Carl Orff (1895-1982)
Cole Porter (1893-1964)
Sergei Prokofiev (1891-1953)
Sergei Rachmaninov (1873-1943)
Maurice Ravel (1875-1937)
Arnold Schoenberg (1874-1951)
Jean Sibelius (1865-1957)
Richard Strauss (1864-1949)
Igor Stravinsky (1882-1971)
Ralph Vaughn Williams (1872-1958)

Contemporary Period
Middle 1900s to Present

Leroy Anderson (1908-1975)
Burt Bacharach (1928-   )
Samuel Barber (1910-1981)
Leonard Bernstein (1918-1990)
Benjamin Britten (1913-1976)
Aaron Copeland (1900-1990)
Bob Dylan (1941-   )
Woodrow Wilson ("Woody") Guthrie
    (1912-1967)
Marvin Hamlisch (1944-   )
Aram Khachaturian (1903-1978)
John Lennon (1940-1980)
Frederick Loewe (1901-1988)
Henry Mancini (1924-1994)
Alan Menken (1950-   )
Gian-Carlo Menotti (1911-   )
Richard Rodgers (1902-1979)
Neil Sedaka (1939-   )
Dimitri Shostakovich (1906-1975)
Paul Simon (1942-   )
Stephen Sondheim (1930-   )
Jule Styne (1905-1994)
Fats Waller (1904-1943)
Andrew Lloyd Webber (1948-   )
Hank Williams (1923-1953)
John Towner Williams (1932-   )
Meredith Willson (1902-1984)

Use this list of composers to write a trivia puzzle for a friend. Study these examples, and then give it a try.
1. Which composer wrote the opera *Hansel and Gretel*?
2. Who wrote the music for *Oklahoma* and *Carousel*?
3. Who wrote the music for *Star Wars*?

Instruments of an Orchestra

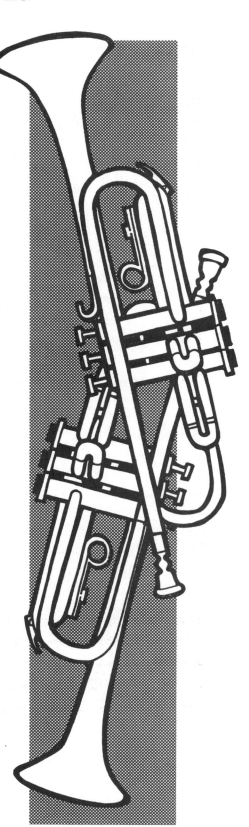

String Section

violin
viola
cello
double bass
piano
harp

Woodwind Section

piccolo
flute
oboe
English horn
clarinet
bass clarinet
bassoon
contrabassoon

Brass Section

trumpet
trombone
French horn
tuba

Percussion Section

Pitched

timpani (kettledrums)
xylophone
chimes
glockenspiel (bells)

Nonpitched

bass drum
snare drum
castanets
cymbals
gong
tambourine
triangle
woodblocks

Other Musical Instruments

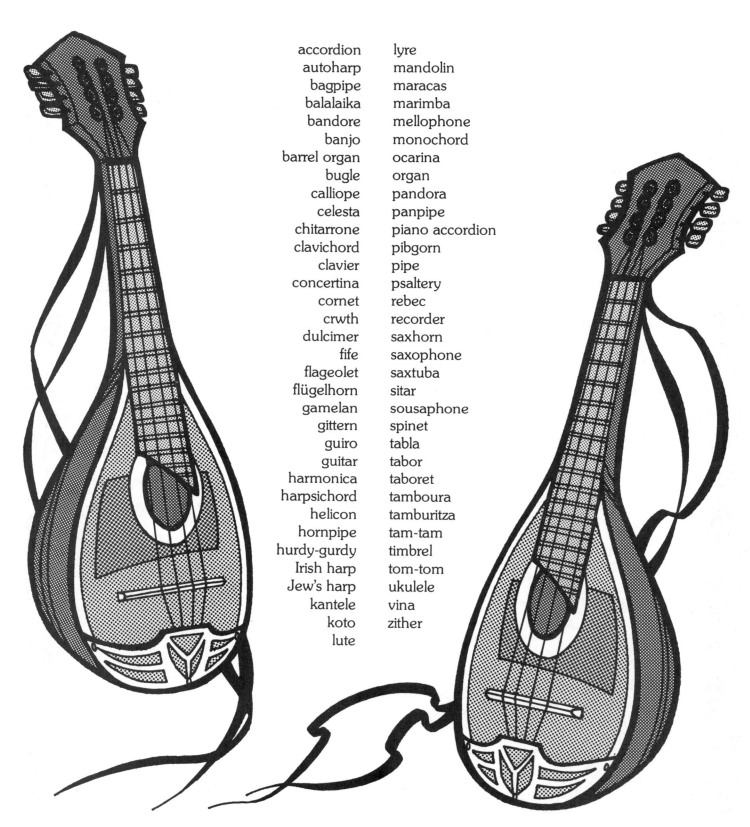

accordion
autoharp
bagpipe
balalaika
bandore
banjo
barrel organ
bugle
calliope
celesta
chitarrone
clavichord
clavier
concertina
cornet
crwth
dulcimer
fife
flageolet
flügelhorn
gamelan
gittern
guiro
guitar
harmonica
harpsichord
helicon
hornpipe
hurdy-gurdy
Irish harp
Jew's harp
kantele
koto
lute

lyre
mandolin
maracas
marimba
mellophone
monochord
ocarina
organ
pandora
panpipe
piano accordion
pibgorn
pipe
psaltery
rebec
recorder
saxhorn
saxophone
saxtuba
sitar
sousaphone
spinet
tabla
tabor
taboret
tamboura
tamburitza
tam-tam
timbrel
tom-tom
ukulele
vina
zither

Musical Symbols

whole note	o	treble clef sign	𝄞
half note	♩	bass clef sign	𝄢
quarter note	♩	staff	
eighth note	♪	bar	
sixteenth note	♬	very loud	*ff*
whole rest	▬	loud (forte)	*f*
half rest	▬	moderately loud	*mf*
quarter rest	𝄽	moderately soft	*mp*
eighth rest	𝄾	soft (piano)	*p*
sixteenth rest	𝄿	very soft	*pp*
sharp	♯	crescendo (growing louder)	<
flat	♭	decrescendo (growing softer)	>

Musical Terms

adagio	slowly; in an easy, graceful manner
allegro	in a brisk, lively manner
bass	the lower half of the whole vocal or instrumental tonal range
chord	tones that are sounded together
clef	a sign placed at the beginning of a musical staff to determine the position of the notes
dolce	in a soft, smooth, and sweet manner
downbeat	the first accented beat in a measure
forte	with strength; in a loud and forceful manner
glissando	a slide or a passing from one tone to another by a continuous change of pitch
harmony	the simultaneous combination of musical notes in a chord that is pleasing to the ear
improvise	to make up melodies while playing without a set plan
interval	the distance between the pitch of two different tones
key	scale or system of related tones which are based on, or named by, a key note
key note	the tone on which a scale or system of related tones is based
key signature	the sharps or flats placed after a clef to indicate the key in which a musical work has been written and/or is to be played
largo	in a very slow and broad manner
legato	in a manner that is smooth and connected
lento	very slowly
measure	a group of beats marked off by regularly recurring primary accents
moderato	at a medium tempo
piano	in a soft or quiet manner
pitch	the relation of one tone to another
presto	at a rapid tempo; very fast
scale	a graduated series of musical tones ascending or descending in order of pitch and according to a specified scheme of their intervals
staccato	in a manner that is short, clear-cut, and disconnected
staff	the lines and spaces on which musical notes are written
tempo	rate of speed
treble	the higher half of the whole vocal or instrumental tonal range
vivace	in a brisk and spirited manner; lively

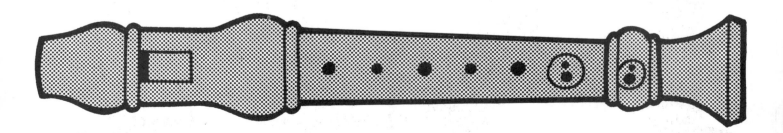

Sing It

a cappella	libretto
alto	lullaby
aria	lyric
ballad	madrigal
barbershop	march
bass	melody
bird song	minstrel
blues	note
calypso	opera
cantata	operetta
carol	oratorio
cavatina	part-song
chanson	pop
chant	popular song
chantey	quartet
chorus	quintet
country and western	recitative
croon	refrain
dirge	rhythm and blues
ditty	rock
duet	round
falsetto	scale
folk song	scat
glee	soprano
harmony	spiritual
hum	tenor
hymn	trio
jazz	troubadour
jingle	tune
lament	verse
lay	yodel

Famous Dancers

Frederick Ashton
Fred Astaire
Mikhail Baryshnikov
Michael Bennett
Ray Bolger
Irene Castle
Vernon Castle
Marian Chace
Gower Champion
Marge Champion
Cyd Charisse
Merce Cunningham
Agnes De Mille
Isadora Duncan
Katherine Dunham
Margot Fonteyn
Bob Fosse
Martha Graham
José Greco
Beryl Grey
Joel Grey
Robert Helpmann
Doris Humphrey
Gregory Hines

Danny Kaye
Gene Kelly
Gelsey Kirkland
Alicia Markova
Ann Miller
Arthur Murray
Kathryn Murray
Waslaw Nijinsky
Rudolf Nureyev
Donald O'Connor
Anna Pavlova
Marius Petipa
Juliet Prowse
Ginger Rogers
Ruth St. Denis
Moira Shearer
Michael Somes
Maria Tallchief
Helen Tamiris
Paul Taylor
Tommy Tune
Dick Van Dyke
Ben Vereen
Thommie Walsh

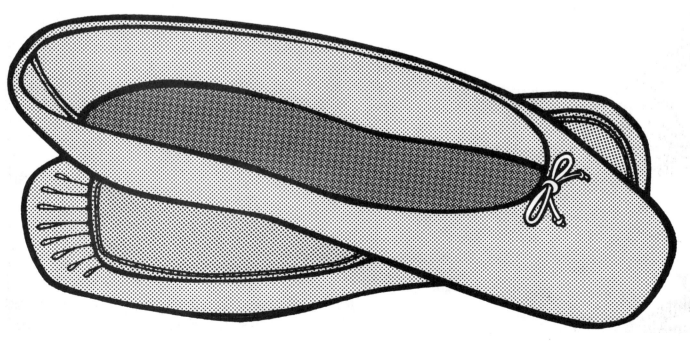

Kinds of Dances

allemande	limbo
alley cat	lindy
ballet	malagueña
ballroom dance	mambo
bolero	mazurka
bossa nova	merengue
break dance	minuet
bunny hop	modern dance
Cajun dance	morris
cancan	pavane
cha-cha	polka
Charleston	polonaise
clog dance	promenade
conga	quadrille
contra dance	rag
cotillion	reel
cotton-eyed Joe	rhumba
electric slide	rigadoon
fandango	salsa
flamenco	samba
folk dance	saraband
four corners	schottische
fox-trot	slappin' leather
galop	soft shoe
gavotte	square dance
grand march	stomp
hokey pokey	swing dance
hora	sword dance
hornpipe	tango
hula	tap dance
hustle	tarantella
jazz dance	twist
jig	two-step
jitterbug	Virginia reel
lambada	waltz

Plays by William Shakespeare

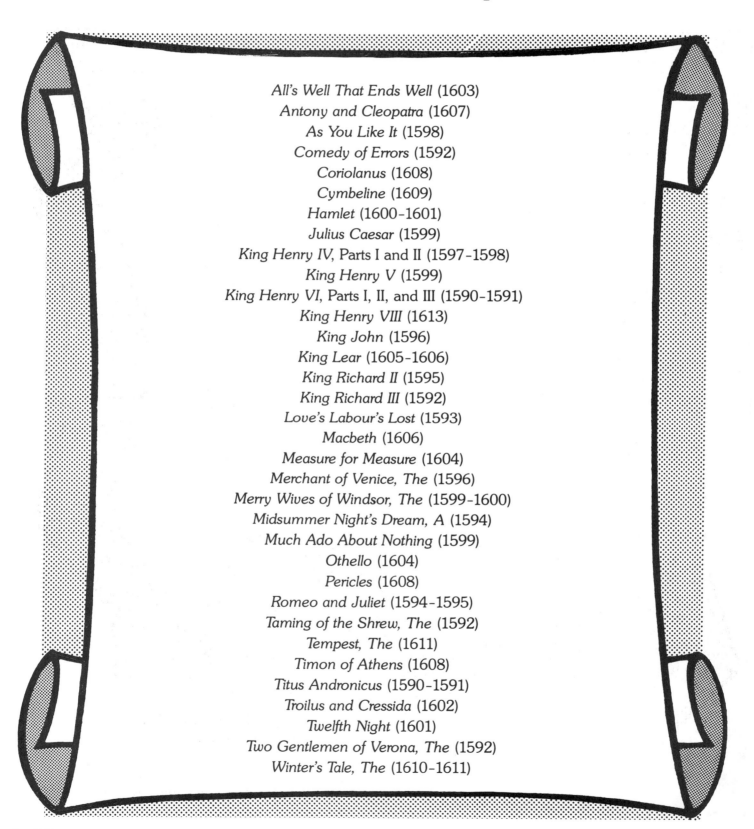

All's Well That Ends Well (1603)

Antony and Cleopatra (1607)

As You Like It (1598)

Comedy of Errors (1592)

Coriolanus (1608)

Cymbeline (1609)

Hamlet (1600–1601)

Julius Caesar (1599)

King Henry IV, Parts I and II (1597–1598)

King Henry V (1599)

King Henry VI, Parts I, II, and III (1590–1591)

King Henry VIII (1613)

King John (1596)

King Lear (1605–1606)

King Richard II (1595)

King Richard III (1592)

Love's Labour's Lost (1593)

Macbeth (1606)

Measure for Measure (1604)

Merchant of Venice, The (1596)

Merry Wives of Windsor, The (1599–1600)

Midsummer Night's Dream, A (1594)

Much Ado About Nothing (1599)

Othello (1604)

Pericles (1608)

Romeo and Juliet (1594–1595)

Taming of the Shrew, The (1592)

Tempest, The (1611)

Timon of Athens (1608)

Titus Andronicus (1590–1591)

Troilus and Cressida (1602)

Twelfth Night (1601)

Two Gentlemen of Verona, The (1592)

Winter's Tale, The (1610–1611)

Theater Terms

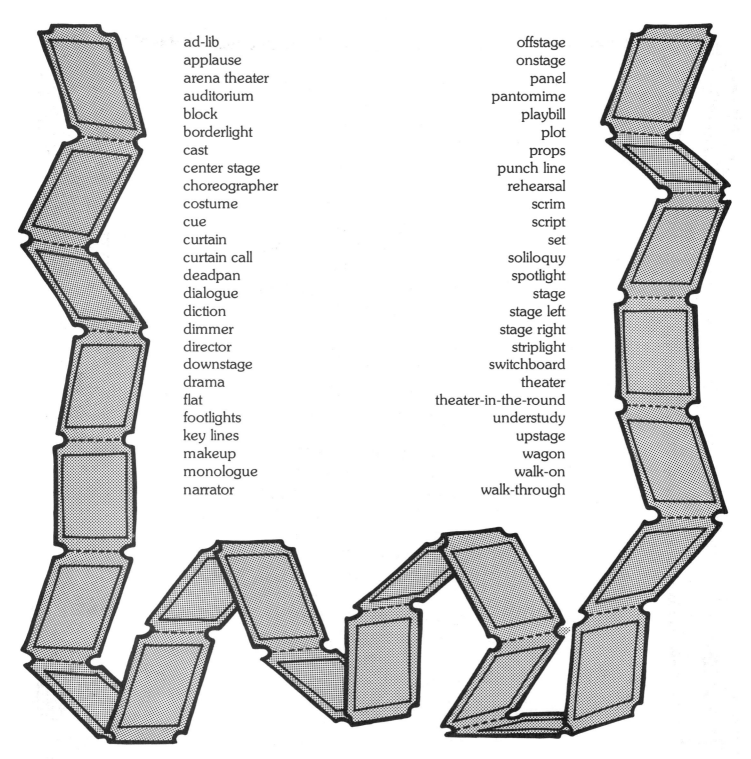

ad-lib
applause
arena theater
auditorium
block
borderlight
cast
center stage
choreographer
costume
cue
curtain
curtain call
deadpan
dialogue
diction
dimmer
director
downstage
drama
flat
footlights
key lines
makeup
monologue
narrator

offstage
onstage
panel
pantomime
playbill
plot
props
punch line
rehearsal
scrim
script
set
soliloquy
spotlight
stage
stage left
stage right
striplight
switchboard
theater
theater-in-the-round
understudy
upstage
wagon
walk-on
walk-through

Become familiar with the theater-related meanings of twenty-five of these terms. Use these terms correctly in an original one-act play for which the setting is the theater.

Architects

Names	**Achievements**
Max Abramovitz	Avery Fisher Hall, Lincoln Center, New York City
Henry Bacon	Lincoln Memorial, Washington, D.C.
Marcel Breuer	Whitney Museum of American Art, New York City
Callicrates	Collaborated with Ictinus in designing the Parthenon on the Acropolis in Athens, Greece
Alexandre Gustave Eiffel	Eiffel Tower, Paris, France
R. Buckminster Fuller	U.S. Pavilion, Expo 67, Montreal, Canada
Michael Graves	Addition to Whitney Museum of American Art, New York City; Regional Library, San Juan Capistrano, California
Walter Gropius	Pan Am Building, New York City
James Hoban	The White House, Washington, D.C.
Raymond Hood	Rockefeller Center, New York City
Ictinus	Parthenon on the Acropolis in Athens, Greece
Imhotep	Egyptian creator of the step pyramid
Philip C. Johnson	State Theater, Lincoln Center, New York City
Louis Le Vau	Parts of the Louvre and the Tuileries in Paris, France; began work on the Palace of Versailles in France
Sir Edwin L. Lutyens	New British Embassy, Washington, D.C.
Jules Hardouin-Mansart	Completed the Palace of Versailles in France
Ludwig Mies van der Rohe	Seagram Building, New York City (with Philip C. Johnson)
Robert Mills	Washington Monument, Washington, D.C.
Richard J. Neutra	Orange County Courthouse, Santa Ana, California
Gyo Obata	National Air and Space Museum, Smithsonian Institution, Washington, D.C.
Frederick L. Olmstead	Central Park, New York City
William Pereira	Transamerica Building, San Francisco, California
John Russell Pope	National Gallery, Washington, D.C.
Eero Saarinen	Gateway to the West Arch, St. Louis, Missouri
Louis H. Sullivan	Auditorium Building, Chicago, Illinois; Wainwright Building, St. Louis, Missouri
Frank Lloyd Wright	Johnson Wax Company, Racine, Wisconsin; Guggenheim Museum, New York City
William Wurster	Ghirardelli Square, San Francisco, California
Minoru Yamasaki	World Trade Center, New York City

Above are listed the names of twenty-eight architects with an example of at least one structure designed by each. Select one of these architects and do research to discover the names and locations of at least two additional buildings he designed.

Artists

Joan Miró	Raoul Dufy
Fra Angelico	Albrecht Dürer
John James Audubon	Thomas Eakins
Cicely Barker	Jan van Eyck
Max Beckmann	Jean Honoré Fragonard
George Bellows	Thomas Gainsborough
Thomas Hart Benton	Paul Gauguin
Sandro Botticelli	Giotto
Georges Braque	Vincent van Gogh
Emily Carr	Arshille Gorky
Mary Cassatt	El Greco
George Catlin	Hans Hofmann
Paul Cézanne	William Hogarth
Marc Chagall	Winslow Homer
Jules Chéret	Edward Hopper
John Singleton Copley	Jean Auguste Dominique Ingres
Gustave Courbet	James M. Ives
Henri Edmond Cross	Vasily Kandinsky
Nathaniel Currier	Paul Klee
John Steuart Curry	Oscar Kokoschka
Salvador Dali	Leonardo da Vinci
Honoré Daumier	Edouard Manet
Jacques Louis David	Reginald Marsh
Hilaire Germain Edgar Degas	Henri Matisse
Marcel Duchamp	Michelangelo Buonarroti

Artists
(continued)

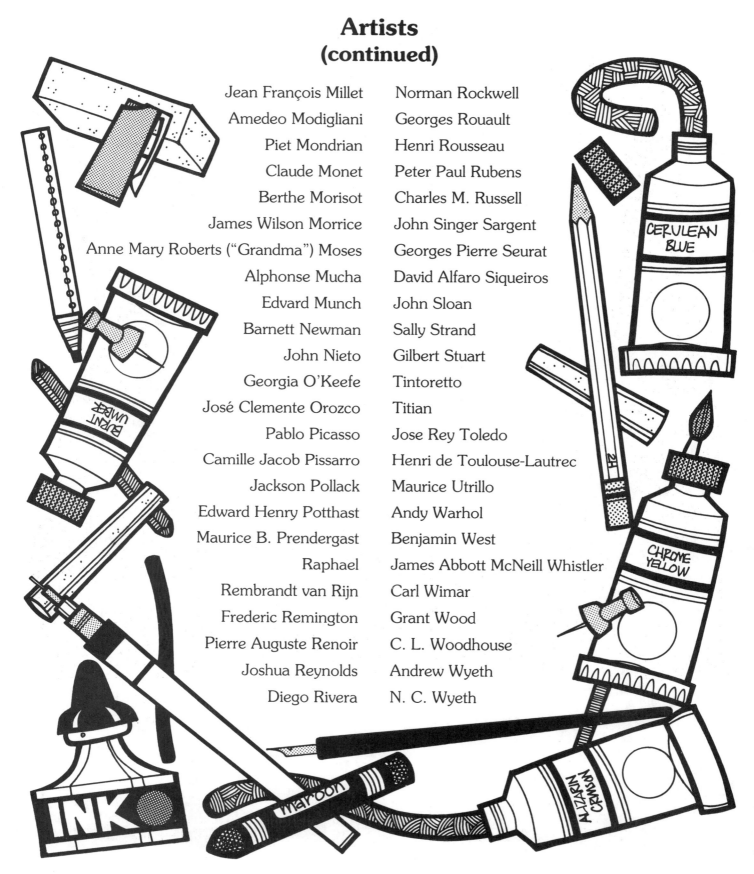

Jean François Millet

Amedeo Modigliani

Piet Mondrian

Claude Monet

Berthe Morisot

James Wilson Morrice

Anne Mary Roberts ("Grandma") Moses

Alphonse Mucha

Edvard Munch

Barnett Newman

John Nieto

Georgia O'Keefe

José Clemente Orozco

Pablo Picasso

Camille Jacob Pissarro

Jackson Pollack

Edward Henry Potthast

Maurice B. Prendergast

Raphael

Rembrandt van Rijn

Frederic Remington

Pierre Auguste Renoir

Joshua Reynolds

Diego Rivera

Norman Rockwell

Georges Rouault

Henri Rousseau

Peter Paul Rubens

Charles M. Russell

John Singer Sargent

Georges Pierre Seurat

David Alfaro Siqueiros

John Sloan

Sally Strand

Gilbert Stuart

Tintoretto

Titian

Jose Rey Toledo

Henri de Toulouse-Lautrec

Maurice Utrillo

Andy Warhol

Benjamin West

James Abbott McNeill Whistler

Carl Wimar

Grant Wood

C. L. Woodhouse

Andrew Wyeth

N. C. Wyeth

Arts and Crafts

acrylics
batik
block printing
book binding
calligraphy
candle making
carpentry
cartooning
carving
ceramics
champlevé
china painting
cloisonné
crewelwork
crocheting
decoupage
doodle art
dough art
drawing
embroidery
enameling
etching
fabric painting

fashion design
graphic design
jewelry making
knitting
macramé
model building
needlepoint
oil painting
origami
paper making
photography
printmaking
puppet making
quilting
rug making
sculpting
sewing
silk-screening
textile design
tie dying
watercolor painting
weaving
woodcraft

1. Collect pictures or actual examples of objects created or decorated by means of some of these arts or crafts and display them in a **Classroom Crafts Corner**.

2. Add books containing step-by-step instructions or patterns to this special corner.

3. Learn enough about one of these arts or crafts to demonstrate it for classmates. As a part of your demonstration, show and/or explain tools and materials that are needed, and acquaint class members with the terminology that is peculiar to this art or craft.

Famous Sculptors

Robert Aitken
Louis Amateis
Alexsandr Archipenko
Thomas Ball
Ernst Barlach
Frédéric Auguste Bartholdi
Gianlorenzo Bernini
Gutzon Borglum
Constantin Brancusi
Alexander Calder
Benvenuto Cellini
Donatello
Jean Dubuffet
John Joseph Earley
Jacob Epstein
Erté
Rudolph Evans
John Bernard Flannagan
James Earle Fraser
Daniel Chester French
Harriet Whitney Frishmuth
Lorenzo Ghiberti
Alberto Giacometti
Jean-Robert Ipousteguy
Carl Paul Jennewein
Donald Judd
Gaston Lachaise

Walter Linck
Jacques Lipchitz
William M. McVey
Aristide Maillol
Paul Manship
Michelangelo Buonarroti
Carl Milles
Clark Mills
Henry Moore
Louise Nevelson
Constantino Nivola
Brenda Putnam
Andre Ramseyer
Frederic Remington
José de Rivera
François Auguste René Rodin
Augustus Saint-Gaudens
Johann Gottfried Schadow
Henry Merwin Shrady
Franklin Simmons
David Smith
Andrea del Verrocchio
John Quincy Adams Ward
George Frederic Watts
Sidney Waugh
Adolph Alexander Weinman
Felix W. de Weldon
Ossip Zadkine

Authors

Past

Listed below are the names of some authors from the past and the title of at least one literary work by each.

Name	Birth and Death Dates	Title
Louisa May Alcott	1832-1888	*Little Women*; *Little Men*
Hans Christian Andersen	1805-1875	Fairy tales: "The Ugly Duckling"
Isaac Asimov	1920-1992	*I, Robot*
James M. Barrie	1860-1937	*Peter Pan*
L. Frank Baum	1856-1919	Wizard of Oz series
Pearl S. Buck	1892-1973	*The Good Earth*
Edgar Rice Burroughs	1875-1950	*Tarzan of the Apes*
Lewis Carroll	1832-1898	Poetry: "Jabberwocky" Short stories: *Alice's Adventures in Wonderland*
Agatha Christie	1891-1976	*Murder on the Orient Express*
James Fenimore Cooper	1789-1851	Leatherstocking series
Daniel Defoe	1660-1731	*Robinson Crusoe*
Charles Dickens	1812-1870	*A Christmas Carol*; *A Tale of Two Cities*
Arthur Conan Doyle	1859-1930	Sherlock Holmes series
Robert Frost	1874-1963	Poetry: "Mending Wall"; "The Road Not Taken"; "Stopping by Woods on a Snowy Evening"
Erle Stanley Gardner	1889-1970	Perry Mason series
Theodor Geisel (Dr. Seuss)	1904-1991	The Cat in the Hat series
Jakob Grimm	1785-1863	*Grimm's Fairy Tales*
Wilhelm Grimm	1786-1859	*Grimm's Fairy Tales*
Alex Haley	1921-1992	*Roots*; *The Autobiography of Malcolm X*
Bret Harte	1836-1902	*The Luck of Roaring Camp*
Nathaniel Hawthorne	1804-1864	*The House of Seven Gables*; *The Scarlet Letter*
O. Henry	1862-1910	Short stories: "The Gift of the Magi"; "Ransom for Red Chief"
Washington Irving	1783-1859	"The Legend of Sleepy Hollow"
Rudyard Kipling	1865-1936	*The Jungle Book*
Hugh Lofting	1886-1947	Dr. Doolittle series
Jack London	1876-1916	*Call of the Wild*
Henry Wadsworth Longfellow	1807-1882	"The Song of Hiawatha"

Authors
(continued)

Name	Birth and Death Dates	Title
Herman Melville	1819-1891	*Moby Dick*
A. A. Milne	1882-1956	*Winnie-the-Pooh*
Ogden Nash	1902-1971	Humorous verse: *I'm a Stranger Here Myself*
George Orwell	1903-1950	*Animal Farm*
Edgar Allan Poe	1809-1849	Poetry: "The Raven" Short stories: "The Fall of the House of Usher"; The Tell-Tale Heart"
Carl Sandburg	1878-1967	Poetry: "Chicago"; "Fog"
Antoine de Saint-Exupéry	1900-1944	*Le Petit Prince* (*The Little Prince*)
Richard Scarry	1920-1994	*Richard Scarry's Cars, and Trucks, and Things That Go*; *Busy, Busy World*
William Shakespeare	1564-1616	*Romeo and Juliet*
Robert Louis Stevenson	1850-1894	*Treasure Island*
Jonathan Swift	1667-1745	*Gulliver's Travels*
James Thurber	1894-1961	*The Owl in the Attic*
J. R. R. Tolkien	1892-1973	*The Hobbit*; *Lord of the Rings*
Mark Twain	1835-1910	*The Adventures of Tom Sawyer*
Jules Verne	1828-1905	*Twenty Thousand Leagues Under the Sea*
E. B. White	1899-1985	*Charlotte's Web*
Laura Ingalls Wilder	1867-1957	Little House on the Prairie series
Thornton Wilder	1897-1975	Plays: *Our Town*; *The Skin of Our Teeth*

Contemporary Authors

Avi	Jean Craighead George	Carl Sagan
Chris Van Allsburg	John Grisham	Maurice Sendak
Maya Angelou	P. D. James	Shel Silverstein
Judy Blume	Garrison Keillor	Neil Simon
Ray Bradbury	Stephen King	Isaac Bashevis Singer
Tom Clancy	Madeleine L'Engle	Theodore Taylor
Beverly Cleary	Lois Lowry	Leon Uris
Pat Conroy	Robert Ludlum	Gore Vidal
Michael Crichton	Arthur Miller	Judith Viorst
Roald Dahl	Katherine Paterson	Robert Penn Warren

Caldecott Medal Winners

The **Caldecott Medal** is awarded each year by the American Library Association to the illustrator of the most distinguished picture book for children published in the United States. This medal is named for Randolph Caldecott (1846-1886), an English artist who is famous for his charming and humorous illustrations.

Year	Title	Illustrator
1938	*Animals of the Bible*	Dorothy P. Lathrop
1939	*Mei Li*	Thomas Handforth
1940	*Abraham Lincoln*	Ingri and Edgar Parin Aulaire
1941	*They Were Strong and Good*	Robert Lawson
1942	*Make Way for Ducklings*	Robert McCloskey
1943	*The Little House*	Virginia Lee Burton
1944	*Many Moons*	Louis Slobodkin
1945	*Prayer for a Child*	Elizabeth Orton Jones
1946	*The Rooster Crows*	Maud and Miska Petersham
1947	*The Little Island*	Leonard Weisgard
1948	*White Snow, Bright Snow*	Roger Duvoisin
1949	*The Big Snow*	Berta and Elmer Hader
1950	*Song of the Swallows*	Leo Politi
1951	*The Egg Tree*	Katherine Milhous
1952	*Finders Keepers*	Nicholas Mordvinoff
1953	*The Biggest Bear*	Lynd K. Ward
1954	*Madeline's Rescue*	Ludwig Bemelmans

Caldecott Medal Winners
(continued)

Year	Title	Illustrator
1955	*Cinderella; or The Little Glass Slipper*	Marcia Brown
1956	*Frog Went A-Courtin'*	Feodor Rojankovsky
1957	*A Tree Is Nice*	Marc Simont
1958	*Time of Wonder*	Robert McCloskey
1959	*Chanticleer and the Fox*	Barbara Cooney
1960	*Nine Days to Christmas*	Marie Hall Ets
1961	*Baboushka and the Three Kings*	Nicolas Sidjakov
1962	*Once a Mouse*	Marcia Brown
1963	*The Snowy Day*	Ezra Jack Keats
1964	*Where the Wild Things Are*	Maurice Sendak
1965	*May I Bring a Friend?*	Beni Montresor
1966	*Always Room for One More*	Nonny Hogrogian
1967	*Sam, Bangs, and Moonshine*	Evaline Ness
1968	*Drummer Hoff*	Ed Emberley
1969	*The Fool of the World and the Flying Ship*	Uri Shulevitz
1970	*Sylvester and the Magic Pebble*	William Steig
1971	*A Story—A Story*	Gail E. Haley
1972	*One Fine Day*	Nonny Hogrogian
1973	*The Funny Little Woman*	Blair Lent
1974	*Duffy and the Devil*	Margot Zemach
1975	*Arrow to the Sun: A Pueblo Indian Tale*	Gerald McDermott
1976	*Why Mosquitoes Buzz in People's Ears: A West African Tale*	Leo and Diane Dillon
1977	*Ashanti to Zulu: African Traditions*	Leo and Diane Dillon

Caldecott Medal Winners
(continued)

Year	Title	Illustrator
1978	*Noah's Ark*	Peter Spier
1979	*The Girl Who Loved Wild Horses*	Paul Goble
1980	*Ox-Cart Man*	Barbara Cooney
1981	*Fables*	Arnold Lobel
1982	*Jumanji*	Chris Van Allsburg
1983	*Shadow*	Marcia Brown
1984	*The Glorious Flight Across the Channel with Louis Blériot*	Alice and Martin Provensen
1985	*Saint George and the Dragon*	Trina Schart Hyman
1986	*The Polar Express*	Chris Van Allsburg
1987	*Hey, Al*	Richard Egielski
1988	*Owl Moon*	John Schoenherr
1989	*Song and Dance Man*	Stephen Gammell
1990	*Lon Po Po: A Red Riding Hood Story from China*	Ed Young
1991	*Black and White*	David Macaulay
1992	*Tuesday*	David Wiesner
1993	*Mirette on the High Wire*	Emily Arnold McCully
1994	*Grandfather's Journey*	Allen Say
1995	*Smoky Night*	Eve Bunting
1996	*Officer Buckle and Gloria*	Peggy Rathmann

Newbery Medal Winners

The **Newbery Medal** is awarded each year by the American Library Association to the American author of the most distinguished contribution to literature for children. This medal is named for John Newbery (1713-1767), an English publisher and bookseller.

Year	Title	Author
1922	*The Story of Mankind*	Hendrik Van Loon
1923	*The Voyages of Doctor Dolittle*	Hugh Lofting
1924	*The Dark Frigate*	Charles Hawes
1925	*Tales from Silver Lands*	Charles Finger
1926	*Shen of the Sea*	Arthur Chrisman
1927	*Smoky*	Will James
1928	*Gay-Neck, the Story of a Pigeon*	Dhan Gopal Mukerji
1929	*The Trumpeter of Krakow*	Eric P. Kelly
1930	*Hitty, Her First Hundred Years*	Rachel Field
1931	*The Cat Who Went to Heaven*	Elizabeth Coatsworth
1932	*Waterless Mountain*	Laura Adams Armer
1933	*Young Fu of the Upper Yangtze*	Elizabeth Lewis
1934	*Invincible Louisa*	Cornelia Meigs
1935	*Dobry*	Monica Shannon
1936	*Caddie Woodlawn*	Carol Brink
1937	*Roller Skates*	Ruth Sawyer
1938	*The White Stag*	Kate Seredy
1939	*Thimble Summer*	Elizabeth Enright
1940	*Daniel Boone*	James Daugherty
1941	*Call It Courage*	Armstrong Sperry
1942	*The Matchlock Gun*	Walter D. Edmonds
1943	*Adam of the Road*	Elizabeth Janet Gray
1944	*Johnny Tremain*	Esther Forbes
1945	*Rabbit Hill*	Robert Lawson
1946	*Strawberry Girl*	Lois Lenski
1947	*Miss Hickory*	Carolyn Sherwin Bailey

Newbery Medal Winners
(continued)

Year	Title	Author
1948	*The Twenty-One Balloons*	William Pene du Bois
1949	*King of the Wind*	Marguerite Henry
1950	*The Door in the Wall*	Marguerite de Angeli
1951	*Amos Fortune, Free Man*	Elizabeth Yates
1952	*Ginger Pye*	Eleanor Estes
1953	*Secret of the Andes*	Ann Nolan Clark
1954	*. . . And Now Miguel*	Joseph Krumgold
1955	*The Wheel on the School*	Meindert DeJong
1956	*Carry On, Mr. Bowditch*	Jean Lee Latham
1957	*Miracles on Maple Hill*	Virginia Sorensen
1958	*Rifles for Watie*	Harold V. Keith
1959	*The Witch of Blackbird Pond*	Elizabeth George Speare
1960	*Onion John*	Joseph Krumgold
1961	*Island of the Blue Dolphins*	Scott O'Dell
1962	*The Bronze Bow*	Elizabeth George Speare
1963	*A Wrinkle in Time*	Madeleine L'Engle
1964	*It's Like This, Cat*	Emily Neville
1965	*Shadow of a Bull*	Maia Wojciechowska
1966	*I, Juan de Pareja*	Elizabeth Borton de Treviño
1967	*Up a Road Slowly*	Irene Hunt
1968	*From the Mixed-Up Files of Mrs. Basil E. Frankweiler*	Elaine Konigsburg
1969	*The High King*	Lloyd Alexander
1970	*Sounder*	William H. Armstrong
1971	*The Summer of the Swans*	Betsy Byars

Newbery Medal Winners
(continued)

Year	Title	Author
1972	Mrs. Frisby and the Rats of NIMH	Robert C. O'Brien
1973	Julie of the Wolves	Jean Craighead George
1974	The Slave Dancer	Paula Fox
1975	M. C. Higgins, the Great	Virginia Hamilton
1976	The Grey King	Susan Cooper
1977	Roll of Thunder, Hear My Cry	Mildred D. Taylor
1978	Bridge to Terabithia	Katherine Paterson
1979	The Westing Game	Ellen Raskin
1980	A Gathering of Days: A New England Girl's Journal	Joan Blos
1981	Jacob Have I Loved	Katherine Paterson
1982	A Visit to William Blake's Inn	Nancy Willard
1983	Dicey's Song	Cynthia Voigt
1984	Dear Mr. Henshaw	Beverly Cleary
1985	The Hero and the Crown	Robin McKinley
1986	Sara, Plain and Tall	Patricia MacLachlan
1987	The Whipping Boy	Sid Fleischman
1988	Lincoln: A Photo-Biography	Russell Freedman
1989	Joyful Noise: Poems for Two Voices	Paul Fleischman
1990	Number the Stars	Lois Lowry
1991	Maniac Magee	Jerry Spinelli
1992	Shiloh	Phyllis Naylor
1993	Missing May	Cynthia Rylant
1994	The Giver	Lois Lowry
1995	Walk Two Moons	Sharon Creech
1996	The Midwife's Apprentice	Karen Cushman

Men in Sports

Henry Aaron	Roberto Clemente	Paul Hornung
Kareem Abdul-Jabbar	Ty Cobb	Gordie Howe
Muhammad Ali	Sebastian Coe	Bobby Hull
Lance Alworth	Jimmy Connors	Reggie Jackson
Mario Andretti	Robin Cousins	Dan Jansen
Eddie Arcaro	Angel Cordero	Bruce Jenner
Arthur Ashe	Pete Dawkins	Earvin "Magic" Johnson
Ernie Banks	Dizzy Dean	Jimmy Johnson
Roger Bannister	Jack Dempsey	Rafer Johnson
Elgin Baylor	Joe DiMaggio	Michael Jordan
Bob Beamon	Julius Erving	Duke Kahanamoku
Boris Becker	Nick Faldo	Jean-Claude Killy
Johnny Bench	Whitey Ford	Johann Koss
Yogi Berra	George Foreman	Sandy Koufax
Matt Biondi	Dick Fosbury	Tom Landry
Larry Bird	A. J. Foyt	Rod Laver
George Blanda	Joe Frazier	Ivan Lendl
Brian Boitano	Mitch Gaylord	Sugar Ray Leonard
Bjorn Borg	Lou Gehrig	Carl Lewis
Terry Bradshaw	Bob Gibson	Vince Lombardi
Paul "Bear" Bryant	Dwight Gooden	Greg Louganis
Andrei Bukin	Wayne Gretzky	Joe Louis
Dick Butkus	George Halas	Phil Mahre
Dick Button	Scott Hamilton	Mickey Mantle
Roy Campanella	John Havlicek	Juan Marichal
Billy Casper	Eric Heiden	Rocky Marciano
Wilt Chamberlain	Ben Hogan	Roger Maris

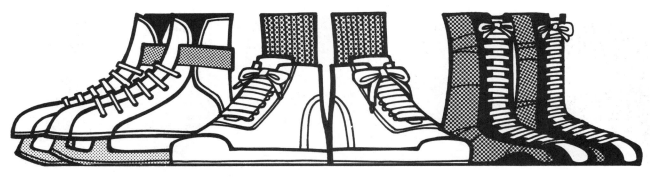

Men in Sports
(continued)

Bob Mathias	Bob Pettit	Roger Staubach
Willie Mays	Richard Petty	Casey Stengel
Bob McAdoo	Laffit Pincay, Jr.	Ingemar Stenmark
John McEnroe	Gary Player	Jackie Stewart
Billy Mills	Pat Riley	Fran Tarkenton
Tommy Moe	Cal Ripken, Jr.	Lawrence Taylor
Joe Montana	Oscar Robertson	Daley Thompson
Edwin Moses	Frank Robinson	Jim Thorpe
Stan Musial	Jackie Robinson	Bill Tilden
John Nabor	Knute Rockne	Y. A. Tittle
Joe Namath	Bill Rodgers	Alberto Tomba
Byron Nelson	Pete Rose	Lee Trevino
John Newcombe	Bill Russell	Gene Tunney
Jack Nicklaus	Babe Ruth	Johnny Unitas
Ray Nitschke	Johnny Rutherford	Al Unser
Matti Nykaenen	Nolan Ryan	Bobby Unser
Al Oerter	Jim Ryun	Fernando Valenzuela
Merlin Olsen	Ulrich Salchow	Peter Vidmar
Bobby Orr	Gale Sayers	Bill Walton
Steve Owen	Tom Seaver	Tom Watson
Jesse Owens	Willie Shoemaker	Johnny Weissmuller
Satchel Paige	Frank Shorter	Jerry West
Arnold Palmer	Don Shula	Ted Williams
Axel Paulsen	Sam Snead	John Wooden
Walter Payton	Warren Spahn	Carl Yastrzemski
Pelé	Mark Spitz	Cy Young
Victor Petrenko	Amos Alonzo Stagg	Pirmin Zurbriggen
	Bart Starr	

Modern Olympic Game Sites

Year	Summer Games	Year	Winter Games
1896	Athens, Greece	1924	Chamonix, France
1900	Paris, France	1928	St. Moritz, Switzerland
1904	St. Louis, Missouri, USA	1932	Lake Placid, New York, USA
1906	Athens, Greece	1936	Garmisch-Partenkirchen, Germany
1908	London, England	1948	St. Moritz, Switzerland
1912	Stockholm, Sweden	1952	Oslo, Norway
1920	Antwerp, Belgium	1956	Cortina d'Ampezzo, Italy
1924	Paris, France	1960	Squaw Valley, California, USA
1928	Amsterdam, Netherlands	1964	Innsbruck, Austria
1932	Los Angeles, California, USA	1968	Grenoble, France
1936	Berlin, Germany	1972	Sapporo, Japan
1948	London, England	1976	Innsbruck, Austria
1952	Helsinki, Finland	1980	Lake Placid, New York, USA
1956	Melbourne, Australia	1984	Sarajevo, Yugoslavia
1960	Rome, Italy	1988	Calgary, Canada
1964	Tokyo, Japan	1992	Albertville, France
1968	Mexico City, Mexico	1994	Lillehammer, Norway
1972	Munich, Federal Republic of Germany	1998	Nagano, Japan
1976	Montreal, Canada		
1980	Moscow, USSR		
1984	Los Angeles, California, USA		
1988	Seoul, Korea		
1992	Barcelona, Spain		
1996	Atlanta, Georgia, USA		
2000	Sydney, Australia		

1. Choose ten of these Olympic sites and locate them on a world map or globe.

2. There were no Olympic Games held in 1916, 1940, or 1944. Do some research to learn the reasons why the Games did not take place in these years.

Olympic Events
Summer Games

archery

badminton

baseball

basketball

boxing

canoeing/kayaking

cycling

diving
platform
springboard

equestrian events
dressage

grand prix jumping
three-day event

fencing
épée
foil
sabre

field hockey

gymnastics, artistic
men
floor exercise
horizontal bar
parallel bars
pommel horse
rings
vault
women
balance beam
floor exercise
uneven parallel bars
vault

gymnastics, rhythmic

handball

judo

pentathlon

rowing

shooting
pistol
rifle
shotgun

soccer

swimming
backstroke
breaststroke
butterfly
freestyle
medley
synchronized

table tennis

track and field
decathlon
discus throw
hammer throw
heptathlon
high jump
javelin throw
long jump
pole vault
running events
100 meters
200 meters
400 meters
800 meters
1,500 meters
3,000 meters
5,000 meters
10,000 meters
hurdles
marathon
relays
steeplechase
shot put
triple jump
walking events

volleyball

water polo

weight lifting

wrestling

yachting

Olympic Events
Winter Games

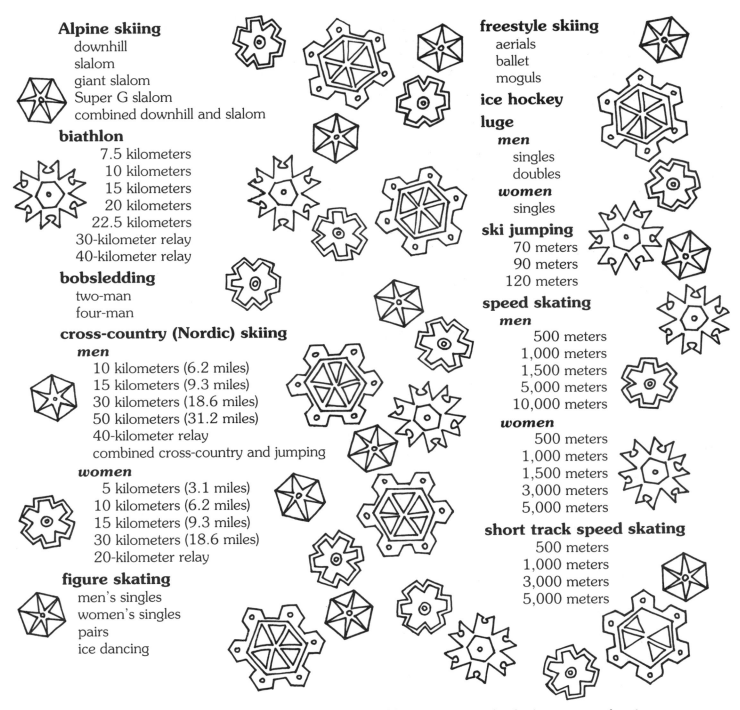

Alpine skiing
  downhill
  slalom
  giant slalom
  Super G slalom
  combined downhill and slalom

biathlon
  7.5 kilometers
  10 kilometers
  15 kilometers
  20 kilometers
  22.5 kilometers
  30-kilometer relay
  40-kilometer relay

bobsledding
  two-man
  four-man

cross-country (Nordic) skiing
  men
    10 kilometers (6.2 miles)
    15 kilometers (9.3 miles)
    30 kilometers (18.6 miles)
    50 kilometers (31.2 miles)
    40-kilometer relay
    combined cross-country and jumping
  women
    5 kilometers (3.1 miles)
    10 kilometers (6.2 miles)
    15 kilometers (9.3 miles)
    30 kilometers (18.6 miles)
    20-kilometer relay

figure skating
  men's singles
  women's singles
  pairs
  ice dancing

freestyle skiing
  aerials
  ballet
  moguls

ice hockey

luge
  men
    singles
    doubles
  women
    singles

ski jumping
  70 meters
  90 meters
  120 meters

speed skating
  men
    500 meters
    1,000 meters
    1,500 meters
    5,000 meters
    10,000 meters
  women
    500 meters
    1,000 meters
    1,500 meters
    3,000 meters
    5,000 meters

short track speed skating
  500 meters
  1,000 meters
  3,000 meters
  5,000 meters

From the lists on pages 240 and 241, select an Olympic event with which you are unfamiliar and do research to learn about it. For example, you might select the **biathlon**, **fencing**, **freestyle skiing**, or the **pentathlon**. Discover when and where this event originated, when it became part of the Olympics, how it is done, and how the winner is determined.

Sports and Athletic Activities

aerobics
alpine skiing
archery
artistic gymnastics
auto racing
badminton
baseball
basketball
bicycling
billiards
boating
bobsledding
bowling
boxing
canoeing
cricket
croquet
cross-country skiing
darts
deck tennis
diving
fencing
field hockey
fishing
football
golf
handball
hiking
horseback riding
horseshoes
hunting
ice hockey
ice skating

jai alai
jogging
judo
jumping rope
karate
kickball
lacrosse
mountain climbing
paddle tennis
polo
racquetball
rhythmic gymnastics
roller blading
roller skating
rugby
running
sailing
shuffleboard
skate boarding
sledding
soccer
softball
squash
surfing
swimming
table tennis
tennis
tetherball
volleyball
walking
water skiing
wrestling
yoga

Sports Teams

Baseball

National League

Atlanta Braves
Chicago Cubs
Cincinnati Reds
Colorado Rockies
Florida Marlins

Houston Astros
Los Angeles Dodgers
Montreal Expos
New York Mets

Philadelphia Phillies
Pittsburgh Pirates
St. Louis Cardinals
San Diego Padres
San Francisco Giants

American League

Baltimore Orioles
Boston Red Sox
California Angels
Chicago White Sox
Cleveland Indians

Detroit Tigers
Kansas City Royals
Milwaukee Brewers
Minnesota Twins

New York Yankees
Oakland Athletics
Seattle Mariners
Texas Rangers
Toronto Blue Jays

National Basketball Association

Atlanta Hawks
Boston Celtics
Charlotte Hornets
Chicago Bulls
Cleveland Cavaliers
Dallas Mavericks
Denver Nuggets
Detroit Pistons
Golden State Warriors
Houston Rockets

Indiana Pacers
Los Angeles Clippers
Los Angeles Lakers
Miami Heat
Milwaukee Bucks
Minnesota Timberwolves
New Jersey Nets
New York Knickerbockers
Orlando Magic
Philadelphia 76ers

Phoenix Suns
Portland Trail Blazers
Sacramento Kings
San Antonio Spurs
Seattle SuperSonics
Toronto Raptors
Utah Jazz
Vancouver Grizzlies
Washington Bullets

National Football League

Arizona Cardinals
Atlanta Falcons
Baltimore Ravens
Buffalo Bills
Chicago Bears
Cincinnati Bengals
Dallas Cowboys
Denver Broncos
Detroit Lions

Green Bay Packers
Houston Oilers
Kansas City Chiefs
Miami Dolphins
Minnesota Vikings
New England Patriots
New Orleans Saints
New York Giants
New York Jets

Oakland Raiders
Philadelphia Eagles
Pittsburgh Steelers
San Diego Chargers
San Francisco 49ers
Seattle Seahawks
St. Louis Rams
Tampa Bay Buccaneers
Washington Redskins

Sports Terms

Baseball

at bat
base hit
bunt
diamond
fly
foul
glove
homer
inning
mitt
pitch
strike
walk

Basketball

air ball
backboard
basket
charging
court
dribble
free throw
guard
hoop
jump shot
key
rebound
slam dunk

Football

block
down
fair catch
gridiron
huddle
kickoff
offside
pass
punt
quarter
safety
tackle
touchdown

Ice Hockey

assist
face-off
goalie
hat trick
high-sticking
icing
offside
pass
power-play goal
puck
shorthanded goal
Stanley Cup
stick

Soccer

chip
dribble
free kick
kickoff
match
offside
pass
pitch
rebound
save
screen
tackle
throw-in

Miscellaneous

alley
Axel
birdie
bogey
chip
gait
love
mogul
parry
putt
rack
schuss
shuttlecock
telemark

1. Often, when the same terms are used in different sports, they have different meanings. Choose two terms (for example, **dribble** and **pitch**) that are used in reference to at least two sports (that is, basketball and soccer, and baseball and soccer). Show that you understand these terms by drawing a picture of each one.

2. Identify the words in the miscellaneous column by matching each one to at least one sport. When you think of sports, don't forget badminton, bowling, fencing, golf, horseback riding, skiing, and tennis.

3. Sometimes, words that are associated with one sport rhyme with words that are associated with another sport (for example, **bunt** and **punt**, **glove** and **love**, **kick** and **stick**). Write a poem in which you make use of some of these rhymes.

Women in Sports

Tenley Albright
Oksana Baiul
Laura Baugh
Joan Benoit
Patty Berg
Bonnie Blair
Valerie Brisco-Hooks
Susan Butcher
Evonne Goolagong Cawley
Nadia Comaneci
Maureen Connolly
Judy Cook
Patty Costello
Margaret Smith Court
Mary Decker
Donna de Varona
Gertrude Ederle
Janet Evans
Chris Evert

Peggy Fleming
Dawn Fraser
Linda Fratianne
Althea Gibson
Steffi Graf
Janet Guthrey
Dorothy Hamill
Carol Heiss
Sonja Henie
Florence Griffith Joyner
Jackie Joyner-Kersee
Karin Kania
Nancy Kerrigan
Billie Jean King
Micki King
Olga Korbut
Elizabeth Manley
Debby Mason
Patricia McCormick
Julianne McNamara

Debbie Meyer
Annemarie Proell Moser
Shirley Muldowney
Martina Navratilova
Mary Lou Retton
Kathy Rigby
Wilma Rudolph
Mary Scharff
Monica Seles
Melanie Smith
Robyn Smith
Debi Thomas
Wyomia Tyus
Grete Waitz
Kathy Whitworth
Helen Wills
Katarina Witt
Sheila Young
Babe Didrikson Zaharias

Bonus Ideas for the Arts and Sports

1. Create a new list related to the arts or to sports. For example, your list might be of
   a. books about dogs
   b. cartoon characters
   c. choreographers
   d. famous cartoonists
   e. famous paintings of people
   f. folk songs

2. Make a poster about a famous architect, artist, author, composer, dancer, sculptor, or athlete whose name appears on one of the lists in this section. Your poster should include a picture of this person and six or more fascinating facts about him or her.

3. Write a letter to one of the people listed in this section. In your letter, tell this person what you most admire about his or her work and achievements. In addition, ask six questions that you would like to have this person answer. If the person is alive and you are able to locate his or her address, mail your letter and see if you receive a reply. If the person is not alive or you are unable to locate his or her address, exhange letters with a friend, and each write a reply to the other's letter.

4. Pick two instruments from the list on pages 215 and 216. Do research to learn what these instruments look like, how they sound, and how they are played.

5. Choose two dances from the list on page 221. Do research to learn the countries in which these dances originated, the celebrations or festivals with which they are associated, and the special clothing or costumes that are worn by dancers who perform them.

6. Select a sport or athletic activity from the list on page 242. Create a list of terms associated with this sport or activity. For example, if you choose baseball, you might list some or all of the following terms:

balk	grounder
bunt	homer
curve	knuckle ball
dugout	out
fly	safe
foul	strike

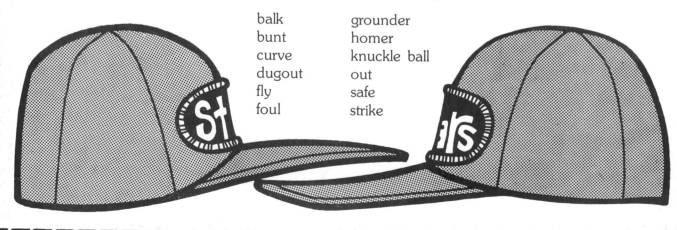

Name _____

Create an Arts or Sports List

Think of a topic in the arts or sports which interests you. On the lines below, create a list that reflects this topic. Illustrate your list and give it a title.

_____

_____

_____

_____

_____

_____

_____

_____

_____

_____

Just for Fun

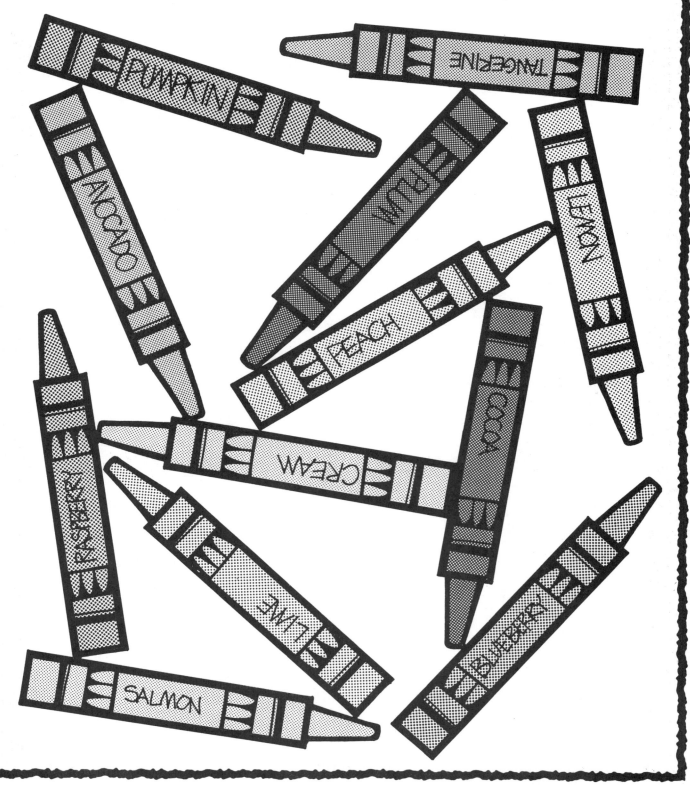

I Love Lists!
© The Learning Works, Inc.

Things That Hold Things

alembic	case	hod	saucepan
amphora	cask	jar	scoup
bag	casket	jigger	scuttle
barrel	chalice	jug	skillet
basin	cistern	keg	stoup
basket	coffer	kettle	tank
bassinet	cradle	krater	tankard
bottle	crate	ladle	test tube
bowl	crock	lecythus	tin
box	cruet	magnum	tray
bucket	cruse	mug	trough
caddy	cup	pail	tub
cage	decanter	pan	tumbler
caisson	demijohn	pitcher	tun
caldron	ewer	plate	tureen
can	flagon	pot	urn
canister	flask	punch bowl	vase
canteen	glass	puncheon	vat
carafe	goblet	rack	vessel
carboy	hamper	retort	vial

1. From this list, select ten words that are unfamiliar to you. Look up the meanings of these words in a dictionary. Then, draw and label a picture of each one.

2. Many of these containers are designed to hold either solids or liquids. Some of them can be used equally well to hold both. Turn these facts into a game. Obtain eighty plain index cards. Print one word from this list in black on one side of each card. On the other side, print in red the word **liquids**, **solids**, or **both**, depending on what that container is designed to hold. Shuffle the cards. Show them one at a time to a friend or classmate, whose task it is to respond by saying whether the named container holds liquids, solids, or both. Set a timer. Allow only a few seconds for each card. Place those cards that are identified correctly in one pile and those that are unidentified or are identified incorrectly in another pile. When all eighty cards have been shown, count the number of cards in the "correct pile" to determine an individual score and/or the overall winner. To increase the challenge, decrease the time allowed for each card.

Things That Measure

accelerometer	electric meter	range finder
altimeter	Fathometer	scale
ammeter	galvanometer	sextant
anemometer	hourglass	speedometer
atomic clock	hydrometer	spirometer
balance	hygrometer	sundial
barometer	light meter	tachometer
caliper	manometer	theodolite
chronometer	micrometer	thermometer
clepsydra	odometer	voltmeter
clock	pedometer	watch
divider	potentiometer	water clock
	quadrant	

1. More than twenty of the terms listed above contain the word **meter**. Why? Where did this word come from? What does it mean?

2. From this list, select five measuring devices with which you are unfamiliar. Do research to learn what they measure and how they work. Then, draw and label pictures or a series of diagrams which will acquaint friends or classmates with these devices.

3. Use at least twenty of these words to create a game in which classmates draw lines or arrange cards to match the name of each device with the name of the thing it is designed to measure.

Things to Collect

antique toys
arrowheads
art
autographs
baseball cards
baskets
bells
books
bottle caps
bottles
bumper stickers
buttons
cartoons
coins
decorated eggs
dolls
fans
feathers
flowers
football cards
fossils
insects
jokes
keys
leaves

marbles
matchbooks
model cars
pennants
photographs
pins
plates
playbills
postcards
posters
postmarks
programs
puppets
riddles
rocks
seeds
shells
stamps
stickers
stuffed animals
tapes
thimbles
ticket stubs
tropical fishes
wind-up toys

Things to Do to Food

When most people think of preparing food, they think of cooking. Below is a list that will broaden your thinking about what to do to food.

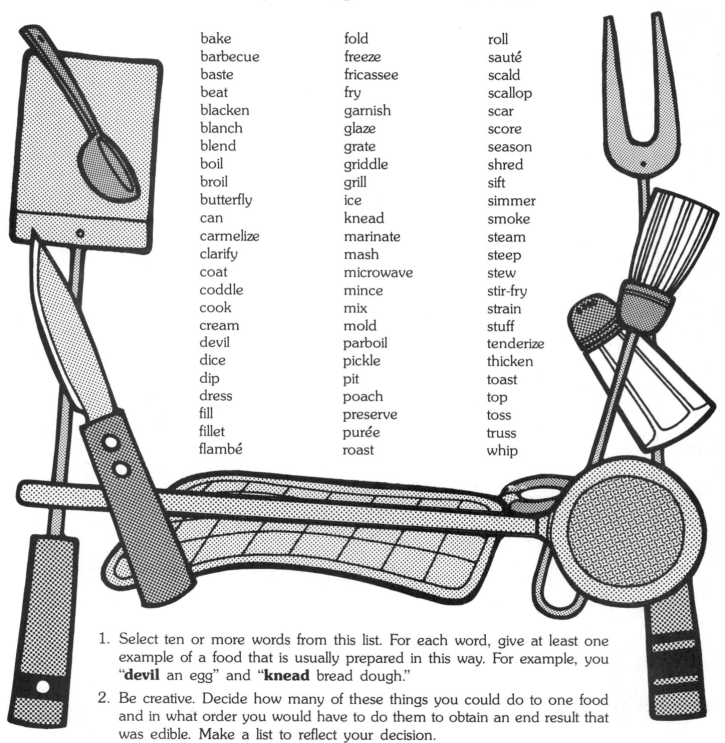

bake	fold	roll
barbecue	freeze	sauté
baste	fricassee	scald
beat	fry	scallop
blacken	garnish	scar
blanch	glaze	score
blend	grate	season
boil	griddle	shred
broil	grill	sift
butterfly	ice	simmer
can	knead	smoke
carmelize	marinate	steam
clarify	mash	steep
coat	microwave	stew
coddle	mince	stir-fry
cook	mix	strain
cream	mold	stuff
devil	parboil	tenderize
dice	pickle	thicken
dip	pit	toast
dress	poach	top
fill	preserve	toss
fillet	purée	truss
flambé	roast	whip

1. Select ten or more words from this list. For each word, give at least one example of a food that is usually prepared in this way. For example, you "**devil** an egg" and "**knead** bread dough."

2. Be creative. Decide how many of these things you could do to one food and in what order you would have to do them to obtain an end result that was edible. Make a list to reflect your decision.

Things to Eat

ambrosia
anise
baklava
béarnaise
béchamel
brittle
casaba
ceviche
chateaubriand
chorizo
codling
compote
costard
couscous
crumpet
daikon
damson

endive
escargot
fennel
filbert
flan
frangipane
gherkin
giblet
goulash
kiss
kohlrabi
kreplach
kumquat
leek
madeleine
marzipan
mousse

napoleon
nougat
piccalilli
pippin
quiche
rosemary
rutabaga
sapodilla
soursop
stroganoff
strudel
succotash
syllabub
thyme
tofu
vichyssoise
whey

Things to Observe and Holidays to Celebrate

January

1 New Year's Day
6 Sherlock Holmes's Birthday
15 Martin Luther King, Jr.'s, Birthday
27 Wolfgang Amadeus Mozart's Birthday
     Chinese New Year**

February

1 National Freedom Day
2 Groundhog Day
4 Boy Scouts of America's Birthday*
     Charles Lindbergh's Birthday
11 National Inventors' Day
     Thomas Alva Edison's Birthday
12 Abraham Lincoln's Birthday
14 Valentine's Day
15 Susan B. Anthony Day
22 George Washington's Birthday
29 Leap Year Day
     Mardi Gras**
     Shrove Tuesday**
     Ash Wednesday**
     Ramadan**

March

3 Alexander Graham Bell's Birthday
11 Johnny Appleseed Day
12 Girl Scout Day
15 The Ides of March
17 Saint Patrick's Day
     Girl Scout Week*
     Vernal Equinox*
     Palm Sunday**

April

1 April Fool's Day
7 World Health Day
13 Thomas Jefferson's Birthday
14 Pan American Day
23 William Shakespeare's Birthday
     Arbor Day*
     Good Friday**
     Easter**
     Passover**
     National Volunteer Week*
     National Library Week*

May

1 May Day
4 Holocaust Day **
5 Cinco de Mayo
22 National Maritime Day
30 Memorial Day
     Armed Forces Day*
     Mother's Day*
     National Music Week*
     National Be Kind to Animals Week*

June

14 Flag Day
27 Helen Keller's Birthday
     Father's Day*
     Summer Solstice*

---

* Date or dates may vary within the indicated month.
** Both month and date may vary.

Things to Observe and Holidays to Celebrate
(continued)

July

1	Canada Day
4	Independence Day
14	Bastille Day in France
24	Amelia Earhart's Birthday

August

12	Ponce de León Day in Puerto Rico
4	Friendship Day*
	Good Nutrition Month

September

17	Citizenship Day
	Labor Day*
	Grandparents' Day*
	Autumnal Equinox*
	American Indian Day*
	Rosh Hashanah**
	Yom Kippur**

---

* Date or dates may vary within the indicated month.
** Both month and date may vary.

October

12	Columbus Day
24	United Nations Day
31	National UNICEF Day
31	Halloween
	National Children's Day*
	Thanksgiving Day in Canada*
	National Fire Prevention Week*

November

5	Guy Fawkes Day in England
11	Veterans' Day
29	Louisa May Alcott's Birthday
	Election Day*
	Thanksgiving Day*
	American Education Week*
	National Children's Book Week*

December

7	Pearl Harbor Day
15	Bill of Rights Day
17	Wright Brothers Day
25	Christmas Day
26	Kwanzaa begins (continues through January 1)
31	New Year's Eve
	Hanukkah*
	Winter Solstice*
	Boxing Day in the British Commonwealth of Nations*

Things to Read

advertisement	formula	poem
agreement	graffiti	portfolio
almanac	greeting card	postcard
anecdote	handbook	poster
anthology	horoscope	program
application	instructions	proposal
atlas	invitation	questionnaire
bill	journal	receipt
billboard	label	recipe
book	letter	register
brochure	limerick	report
bulletin	list	review
bumper sticker	log	riddle
cartoon	magazine	script
catalog	manual	sentence
chart	map	sign
circular	marquee	skywriting
clue	memo	speech
contract	menu	statement
critique	newspaper	story
diary	note	summary
dictionary	notebook	tabloid
digest	obituary	telegram
directory	palindrome	test
encyclopedia	pamphlet	textbook
epigram	paragraph	thesaurus
epigraph	periodical	transcript
epitaph	placard	verdict
essay	play	verse
flier	playbill	will

Things to Wear on Your Body

ascot
balmacaan
bolero
camisole
cardigan
chesterfield
cloak
cravat
cummerbund
dickey
djellaba
farthingale
furbelow
garibaldi
greatcoat
guernsey
jabot
jersey
jodhpurs
joseph
kimono
knickers
Macfarlane
mackinaw
mackintosh
mantle
mantua
palatine
peignoir
polonaise
puttee
rabato
raglan
roquelaure
sari
sarong
smallclothes
tabard
toga
tunic
ulster
waistcoat

Select fifteen things to wear from this list and do research to learn more about the people and places for which these things were named.

Things to Wear on Your Feet

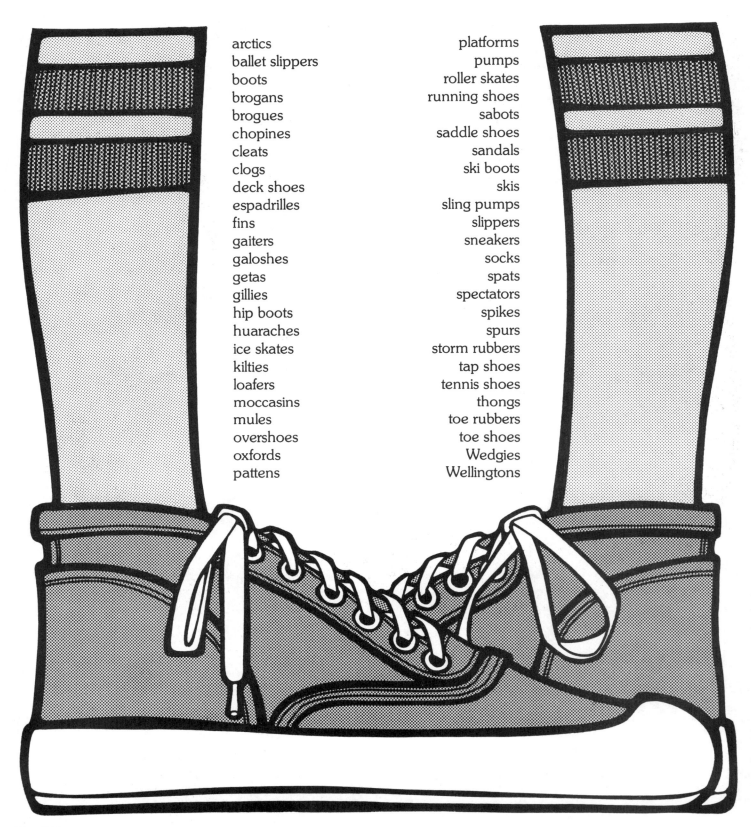

arctics
ballet slippers
boots
brogans
brogues
chopines
cleats
clogs
deck shoes
espadrilles
fins
gaiters
galoshes
getas
gillies
hip boots
huaraches
ice skates
kilties
loafers
moccasins
mules
overshoes
oxfords
pattens

platforms
pumps
roller skates
running shoes
sabots
saddle shoes
sandals
ski boots
skis
sling pumps
slippers
sneakers
socks
spats
spectators
spikes
spurs
storm rubbers
tap shoes
tennis shoes
thongs
toe rubbers
toe shoes
Wedgies
Wellingtons

Things to Wear on Your Head

balaclava
Balmoral
bangkok
bathing cap
beanie
beret
biretta
bonnet
bowler
busby
calot
cap
chapeau
cloche
cowboy hat
crown
derby
fedora
fez
gibus
Glengarry
hard hat
havelock
helmet
homburg
Jinnah cap
kepi

mantilla
miter
mortarboard
opera hat
Panama hat
peruke
pith helmet
pixie
porkpie
sallet
scarf
shako
shower cap
skullcap
snood
sombrero
Stetson
stocking cap
tam-o'-shanter
tiara
top hat
toque
turban
visor
wig
yarmulke
zucchetto

1. Design a hat to be worn by all people who share a particular occupation or profession, such as computer programmers or doctors. Make a detailed drawing of your design and label the various special features and parts. Give your design a name.

2. Make a montage using pictures of hats found in magazine ads. See how many different kinds of hats you can find and include.

3. Pretend that you are a hat sitting on someone's head. For example, you might choose to be a fire fighter's helmet or a king's crown. Write a diary entry or narrative about all of the things that happen to you and your wearer during one twenty-four-hour period.

Things to Write About
Animal Stories

1. Watson, the Worm
2. Horse Fever
3. The Blue Ribbon Pet
4. Puppy Power
5. A Turtle in Trouble
6. The Baboon That Loved Bubble Gum
7. The Empty Cage
8. Pet Problems
9. The Burglar and the Bear
10. The Pet Store Window
11. The Goofy Gopher
12. A Skunk in the Trunk
13. Rhino on the Run
14. A Visit to the Zoo
15. Pick of the Litter
16. The Laughing Lion
17. One Puppy Too Many
18. Horace, the Roller-Skating Hippo
19. Tale of the Giant Gorilla
20. Cat in the Candy Store
21. Fido to the Rescue
22. Noah, the Boa
23. How the Dalmatian Got Its Spots
24. Monkey Business
25. Mrs. Rich and the Rhino

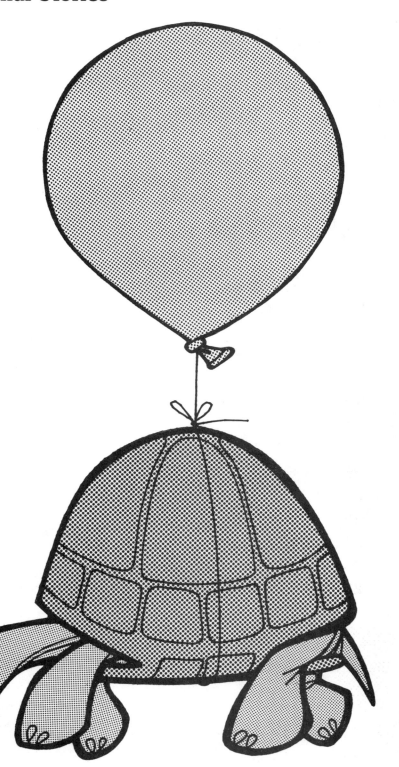

Things to Write About
Just for Fun

1. Giggling Gus of Gatorville
2. The Magical Mirror
3. An Ingenious Invention
4. Mummy on the Loose
5. Wish upon a Unicorn
6. The Whistling Wopperbopper
7. When Numbers Disappeared
8. A Glimpse of the Future
9. The Tri-Eyed Slitherwart
10. The Secret Formula of Dr. Ficklepickle
11. A Ride on the Rainbow
12. The Practical Joke
13. Backwards Day
14. The Blue Balloon Escape
15. The Purple House on Murple Street
16. Miss Mandy and the Candy Machine
17. A Cow on the Roof
18. The Surprise Package
19. The Chocolate Chip Gang
20. The Kid with the Green Face
21. The Popcorn That Wouldn't Stop Popping
22. The Bubble Gum Disaster
23. The Magical Lollipop Tree
24. How the Toad Got Its Tongue
25. The Time Machine

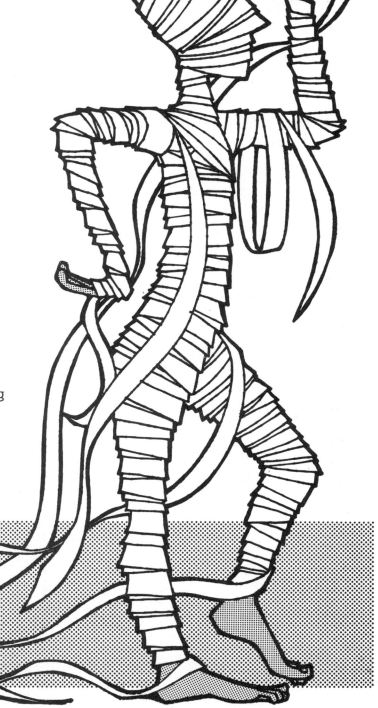

Things to Write About
Miscellaneous

1. Decisions, Decisions
2. Lost at Sea
3. A Special Secret
4. Conquer the Waves
5. To the Rescue
6. Wally, the Wizard
7. When the Sun Disappeared
8. A Kid in Trouble
9. The Spider That Grew and Grew
10. A Narrow Escape
11. Climb to the Peak
12. Without a Warning
13. On the Island of Goochie-Geechie
14. The Happiest Day
15. Trapped
16. The Hot-Air Balloon Ride
17. A Skunk in My Tub
18. Was I Ever Mad!
19. The Magical Ladder to Nowhere
20. Visitor from Another Planet
21. Mable in Muddville
22. All in a Day's Work
23. A Friend in Need
24. Stranded in the Desert
25. A Day I'll Never Forget

Things to Write About
Mysteries

1. The Fortune Cookie Caper
2. Super Spy for the FBI
3. Revenge of the Raven
4. A Scream in the Night
5. The Creature of Willow Creek
6. Up from the Deep
7. The Secret of Timber Tunnel
8. The Groaning Ghost
9. The Phone Booth Mystery
10. The Empty Room
11. Swamp Creature
12. The Monster That Took over the Earth
13. Happenings in the Haunted House
14. The Creepy Claw
15. The Nightmare
16. Not a Second Too Soon!
17. The Cave of the Dragon
18. The Case of the Stolen Key
19. Schoolroom Mystery
20. The Vanishing Footprints
21. The Howl of the Hound
22. The Mysterious Mirror
23. Detective Donna Solves the Mystery
24. Night of the Fog
25. The Ghost in the Attic

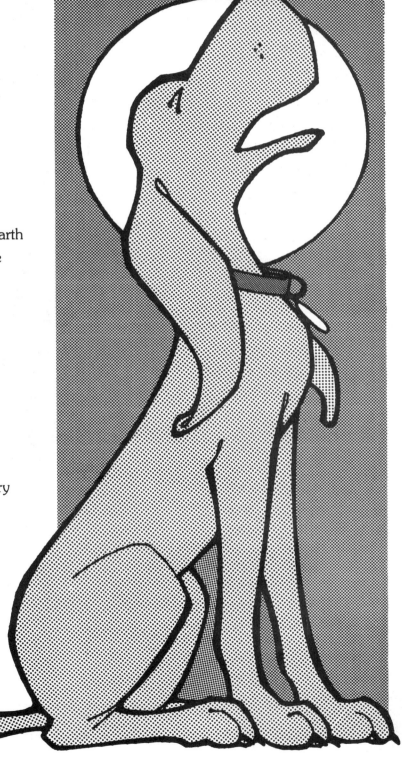

Things to Write About
Sports Stories

1. The Tryouts
2. My Turn to Bat
3. When the Crowds Went Wild
4. Scoring Secrets
5. Tops on the Team
6. How I Saved the Game
7. Slugger Strikes Out
8. The Day of the Championships
9. The Winning Goal
10. Super Stars
11. Bessie of Baseball Fame
12. Touchdown Troubles
13. On the Run
14. The Champ
15. The Soccer Star
16. The Stringers Meet the Wingers
17. The Play that Changed the Game
18. Race Against the Clock
19. How I Survived My Rookie Year
20. Newcomer to the Team
21. A Crack at the Bat
22. Wrestlemania
23. The Volleyball Victory
24. My Basketball Blunder
25. The Hockey Hoax

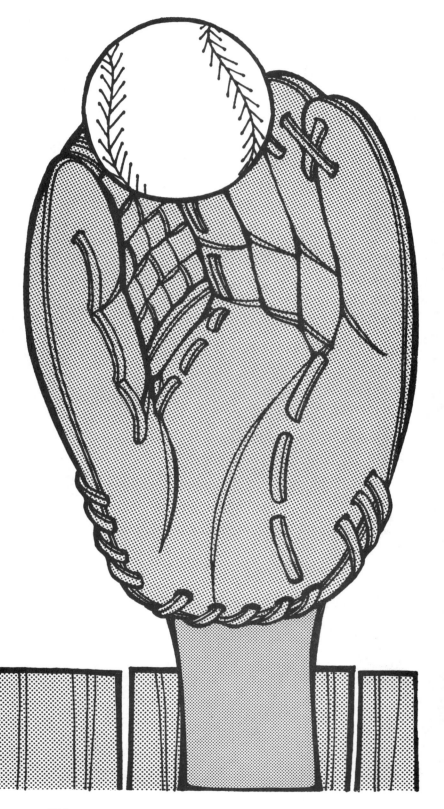

Things with Holes

bagels
balloons
basketball hoops
beads
beanshooters
belts
bowling balls
button-down collars
buttons
chicken wire
chimneys
collanders
computer paper
doughnuts
drains
electrical outlets
eyedroppers
faucets
floppy disks
funnels
golf courses
graters
handcuffs
hollow logs
honeycombs
hoops
inner tubes
laces
lace-up-shoes
life preservers
Life Saver candies
locks

macaroni
needles
nets
noses
nozzles
nuts
pegboards
pencil sharpeners
pierced ears
pipes
records
rings
rubber bands
salt and pepper shakers
scissors
screen doors
sieves
sifters
socks
spigots
sponges
spools
spouts
squirt guns
strainers
straws
swiss cheese
teeth (sometimes)
tennis rackets
washers
wind instruments
window screens

Braille Alphabet

Louis Braille was a French organist and teacher of the blind. He developed a system of raised-dot writing for literature and music. This remarkable system, called the Braille alphabet, makes it possible for people who cannot see to read with their fingertips.

The Braille alphabet is based on a rectangle made up of six dot positions. By changing the number of dots used and varying their positions within the rectangle, Louis Braille was able to come up with enough variations to represent twenty-six letters, ten numerals, and all needed punctuation marks.

Within the rectangle, each dot position has a number. Different combinations of these positions represent different letters, numerals, and punctuation marks, and even indicate when a letter should be capitalized. For example, a dot in position 1 represents the letter **a**. A combination of dots in positions 2, 5, and 6 stands for a period. A dot in position 6 *before* a letter indicates that the letter should be capitalized.

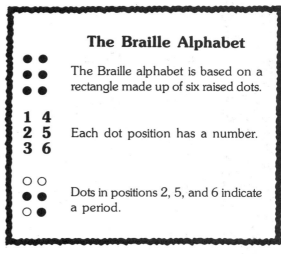

The Braille Alphabet

The Braille alphabet is based on a rectangle made up of six raised dots.

Each dot position has a number.

Dots in positions 2, 5, and 6 indicate a period.

Braille Alphabet Chart

a	b	c	d	e	f	g	h	i	j	k	l	m

n	o	p	q	r	s	t	u	v	w	x	y	z

Greek Alphabet

A α	alpha		N ν	nu
B β	beta		Ξ ξ	xi
Γ γ	gamma		O o	omicron
Δ δ	delta		Π π	pi
E ε	epsilon		P ϱ	rhō
Z ζ	zēta		Σ σ ς	sigma
H η	ēta		T τ	tau
Θ θ	thēta		Y υ	upsilon
I ι	iota		Φ φ	phi
K κ	kappa		X χ	chi
Λ λ	lambda		Ψ ψ	psi
M μ	mu		Ω ω	ōmega

International Morse Code

Letters

Letter	Code		Letter	Code		Letter	Code		Letter	Code
A	• —		G	— — •		N	— •		U	• • —
B	— • • •		H	• • • •		O	— — —		V	• • • —
C	— • — •		I	• •		P	• — — •		W	• — —
D	— • •		J	• — — —		Q	— — • —		X	— • • —
E	•		K	— • —		R	• — •		Y	— • — —
F	• • — •		L	• — • •		S	• • •		Z	— — • •
			M	— —		T	—			

Numbers

Number	Code		Number	Code
0	— — — — —		5	• • • • •
1	• — — — —		6	— • • • •
2	• • — — —		7	— — • • •
3	• • • — —		8	— — — • •
4	• • • • —		9	— — — — •

Punctuation Marks

Mark	Code		Mark	Code
period (.)	• — • — • —		semicolon (;)	— • — • — •
comma (,)	— — • • — —		colon (:)	— — — • • •
question mark (?)	• • — — • •		apostrophe (')	• — — — — •
hyphen (-)	— • • • • —			

Because it can be difficult to tell where one Morse code letter ends and another begins, people writing in this code often place a single slash (/) between letters and a double slash (//) between words.

Manual Alphabet

Some people who cannot hear learn to spell and speak with their fingers. The alphabet for finger spelling is called the manual alphabet. It is pictured below. Use this alphabet to spell your name, a greeting, and a word that names a feeling.

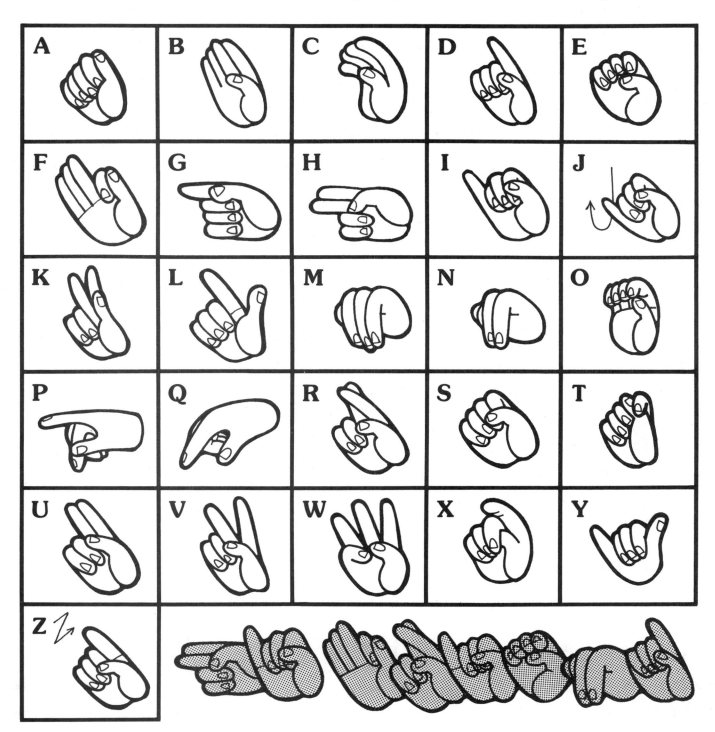

Map Symbols

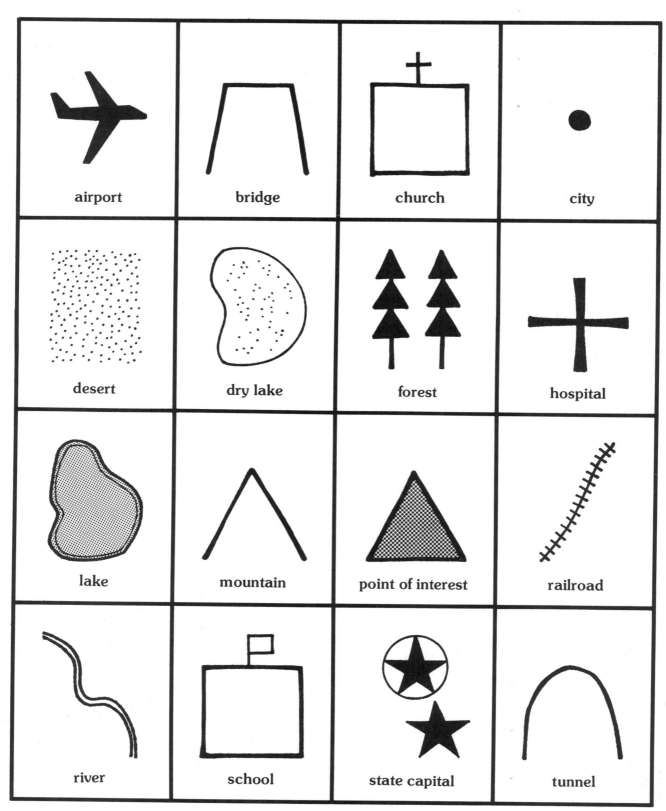

airport	bridge	church	city
desert	dry lake	forest	hospital
lake	mountain	point of interest	railroad
river	school	state capital	tunnel

Proofreaders' Symbols

Symbol	Meaning
⁋	begin a new paragraph
cap or ≡	capitalize a lowercase letter
lc or /	lowercase a capital letter
ℌ	delete
∧	insert
#	insert space
⌣	close up; delete space
⊐	move right
⊏	move left
⊓	move up
⊔	move down
⊐⊏	center
‖	align vertically
⋏	insert a comma
⋎	insert an apostrophe
⋎⋎	insert quotation marks
⊙	change the existing punctuation mark to a period; insert a period
sp	spell out (of a number or abbreviation); verify and/or correct spelling
stet	let it stand without making the indicated change or correction
tr or ⊓⊔	transpose

⁋ Proof͡ reading is a tedius sp
task⊙ a proofreader must
≡
carefully compare type͡ set
material with the original
⊙ sp
(MS) to see if the compositer
o
has "followed copy. He or
∧
she must also determine if
#
the correct͜type face, size⋏
∧
and weight have been used
and if the column width
sp
matches the (specs⊙) These
things can⌐only⌐be determined⌐
by lo͜king carefully at the
o
designer's and editors⋎ marks
on the edited manuscript.

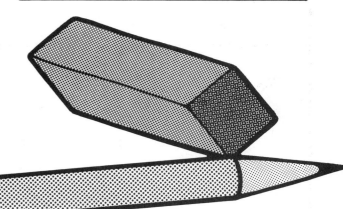

Sports Symbols
Basketball

Holding

Pushing

Traveling

Personal Foul

Player Control Foul

Technical Foul

Illegal Dribble

Illegal Use of Hands

Time Out

Cancel Score

Sports Symbols
Football

Dead Ball **Time Out** **Start the Clock** **First Down** **Safety** **Touchdown or Field Goal**

Offside **Illegal Procedure** **Illegal Motion** **Illegally Passing or Handing Ball Forward** **Illegal Use of Hands and Arms**

Ineligible Receiver Down Field on Pass **Forward Pass or Kick-Catching Interference** **Intentional Grounding** **Ball Illegally Touched, Kicked, or Batted** **Incomplete Forward Pass, Penalty Declined, No Play, or No Score**

Clipping **Unsportsmanlike Conduct** **Personal Foul** **Roughing the Kicker**

Weather Symbols

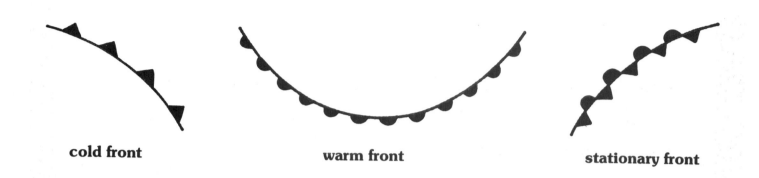

cold front   **warm front**   **stationary front**

cloudy   **partly cloudy**   **clear**   **fog**   **snow**   **rain**

low   **high**   **wind direction**   **hurricane**

hail   **frost**   **haze**   **sleet**   **thunder**

wind (1-4 mph)   **wind (15-20 mph)**   **partly cloudy**
wind (21-31 mph)

I Love Lists!
© The Learning Works, Inc.

Book Report Brainstorms

After you have read a book, choose one of these ways to share your book with other members of the class.

- Draw a cartoon strip of the most important events in the story.

- Make a soap, wood, or clay model to illustrate a character from the book.

- Write a different ending for the story.

- Make a list of questions you think everyone should be able to answer after reading the book.

- Make a diorama depicting the most exciting part of the book or the part you liked best.

- Compare a character in the story with a person you actually know. Write a paragraph or two in which you describe the ways in which they are alike and the ways in which they are different.

- Make a word search puzzle using vocabulary words from the book.

- Make a time line of events in the story.

- Make a crossword puzzle using words from the book.

- Make a stitchery sampler to illustrate a scene from the book.

- Write a letter to a friend telling why you recommend the book.

- Pretend that you are the main character and write several diary pages describing an important event in the book.

- Make a shoe box filmstrip of an exciting event in the story.

- Use a wire coat hanger and string to make a mobile based on the book.

- Design a bookmark that tells something about the story.

- Make a poster to advertise the book.

- Write a one-act play based on the book.

- Make a puppet to represent a character in the book.

- Tape-record an interview in which you or a friend acts as the author of the book.

- Write a review of the book for a magazine or newspaper.

Children's Periodicals

American Girl
Pleasant Company Publications, Inc.
8400 Fairway Place
Middleton, WI 53562
(Blend of historical fiction and nonfiction for
    girls age 7 and older)

Bananas
Scholastic, Inc.
730 Broadway
New York, NY 10003

Boys' Life
Boy Scouts of America
1325 Walnut Hill Lance
Irving, TX 75038-3096

*Bugs Bunny Presents Looney Tunes
    Magazine*
Welsh Publishing Group
300 Madison Avenue
New York, New York 10017-6216
(Bugs, Daffy, and the gang star in this
    magazine packed with zany games, comics,
    stories, and puzzles)

Jack and Jill
Children's Better Health Institute
1100 Waterway Blvd.
Indianapolis, IN 46202

The Children's Album
(Stories, plays, poetry, crafts)
EGW Publishing Company
Box 6086
Concord, CA 94524

Cobblestone
(American history for young people age 8-14)
Cobblestone Publishing, Inc.
20 Grove St.
Peterborough, NH 03458

Creative Kids (Chart Your Course)
GCT Inc.
Box 6448
Mobile, AL 36660-0448
(Original works of gifted, creative, and talented
    young people age 5-18)

Cricket
Open Court Publishing Company
315 Fifth Street
Peru, IL 61354

Disney Adventures
Walt Disney Publications
500 South Buena Vista
Burbank, CA 91521
(For young people age 7-14; includes music,
    movies, trends, science, travel, gadgets,
    games, heroes, explorers, and more)

The Dolphin Log
The Cousteau Society
8440 Santa Monica Blvd.
Los Angeles, CA 90069

Dr. Jim's PETZINE for Kids
Good Dog!
P.O. Box 31292
Charleston, SC 29417
(A fun and educational monthly newsletter
    that helps kids learn about pets and respon-
    sible pet care)

Children's Periodicals
(continued)

Ebony, Jr.
820 South Michigan Ave.
Chicago, IL 60605

Faces: The Magazine About People
Cobblestone Publishing, Inc.
7 School Street
Peterborough, NH 03458-1470
(Cultural anthropology for young people age
　8-15; published in cooperation with the
　American Museum of Natural History)

Fast Forward
Opportune Press
79 Walnut
Mill Valley, CA 94941
(By kids, for kids, and about kids growing up
　in the 90's)

Garfield Magazine
Welsh Publishing Group
300 Madison Avenue
New York, NY 10017-6216
(Quarterly magazine for children age 6-12;
　includes stories, puzzles, jokes, and comics)

Highlights for Children
803 Church St.
Honesdale, PA 18431

Hopscotch, The Magazine for Girls
Bluffton News Publishing and Printing
　Company
Box 164
Bluffton, OH 45817-0164

Hot Dog
Scholastic Inc.
730 Broadway
New York, NY 10003-9511

Kid City (Electric Company)
Children's Television Workshop
1 Lincoln Plaza
New York, NY 10023-7129

Kids Discover
Kids Discover
170 Fifth Avenue
New York, NY 10010
(For children age 5-12; each issue covers a
　single topic in nature, science, geography,
　or manmade wonders)

Ladybug: The Magazine for Young Children
Carus Publishing Corporation
315 5th Street
Peru, IL 61354-2859
(For children age 2-6)

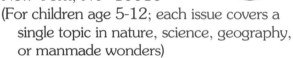

MAD
E. C. Publications
485 MADison Avenue
New York, NY 10022

McMag
McDonald's Corporation
Publications Department
1 Kroc Drive
Oak Brook, IL 60521
(Puzzles, games, and articles for children)

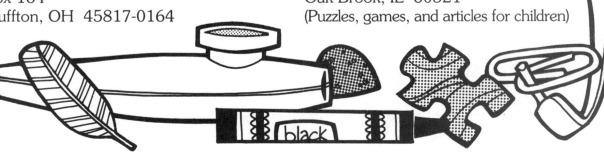

Children's Periodicals
(continued)

Mickey Mouse
Welsh Publishing Group
300 Madison Avenue
New York, NY 10017-6216

Monkey Shines on America
N.C. Learning Institute for Fitness and
    Education
Box 10245
Greensboro, NC 27404-0245
(A children's magazine focusing on American
    history, geography, folklore, people, etc.;
    each issue covers a different state)

Muppet Magazine
475 Park Avenue South
New York, NY 10016

National Geographic World
National Geographic Society
17th and M Streets, N.W.
Washington, D.C. 20036

News for Kids
D.M. Publishing, Inc.
400 Heliotrope Avenue
Corona Del Mar, CA 92625-2921
(A news magazine for children age 7-12;
    encourages reader contributions)

Noah's Ark
(A monthly newspaper about Jewish history,
    holidays, and laws)
7726 Portal
Houston, TX 77071

Odyssey
Kalmbach Publishing Company
1027 N. Seventh St.
Milwaukee, WI 53233
(For children age 8-12; emphasizes astronomy
    and outer space)

Owl Magazine
(discovery magazine for children)
The Young Naturalist Foundation
56 The Esplanade, Suite 306
Toronto, Ontario M5E 1A7
Canada

Peanut Butter
Scholastic Inc.
555 Broadway
New York, NY 10012
(For children age 4-6)

ProAction
Marvel Entertainment Group
387 Park Avenue, South
New York, NY 10016-8810
(Combines characters from Marvel comics
    with NFL football stars; features sports and
    fashion news)

Ranger Rick
National Wildlife Federation
1412 16th St., N.W.
Washington, D.C. 20036

Spider, the Magazine for Children
Carus Publishing Group
315 5th St.
Peru, Il 61354-2859
(For children age 6-9)

Children's Periodicals
(continued)

Sports Illustrated for Kids
500 Office Park Drive
Birmingham, AL 35223

Stone Soup, the Magazine by Children
Children's Art Foundation
Box 83
Santa Cruz, CA 95063-0083
(A collection of poems, stories, book reviews,
   and art by children age 13 and younger)

Storyworks
Scholastic Inc.
555 Broadway
New York, NY 10012
(A literature-based magazine for children
   age 8-11)

3-2-1 Contact
Children's Television Workshop
One Lincoln Plaza
New York, NY 10023

Wow
Scholastic, Inc.
730 Broadway
New York, NY 10003

Young American
(Newspaper for kids)
Young American Publishing Company
Box 12409
Portland, OR 97212

Young Author's Magazine
(Features work of gifted kids)
Theraplan, Incorporated
3015 Woodsdale Blvd.
Lincoln, NE 68502

Zillions (Penny Power)
Consumer Reports Books
9180 LeSaint Drive
Fairfield, OH 45014
(Consumer advice for young people age
   8-14 from *Consumer Reports*)

Zoobooks
930 W. Washington, Suite 6
San Diego, CA 92103

Clubs and Organizations for Kids

Entries for this list are based on information contained in the *Encyclopedia of Associations* (29th ed.; Detroit, MI: Gale Research Co., 1995). This multi-volume guide includes the names, addresses, and brief descriptions of more than 23,000 national and international organizations. If you have a special interest that is not included in the list on pages 280-281 and you want to know if there is a club or organization for people who share this interest, consult the *Encyclopedia of Associations* in the research section of your public library.

Academy of Model Aeronautics (AMA)
5151 E. Memorial Drive
Muncie, IN 47302
(317) 287-1256

Amateur Athletic Union of the
    United States (AAU)
3400 West 86th Street
Indianapolis, IN 46268
(317) 872-2900

American Youth Hostels (AYH)
P.O. Box 37613
Washington, DC 20013-7613
(202) 783-6161

American Youth Soccer Organization (AYSO)
5403 West 138th Street
Hawthorne, CA 90250
(310) 643-6455

Big Brothers/Big Sisters of America
230 North 13th Street
Philadelphia, PA 19107
(215) 567-7000

Boys and Girls Clubs of America
12330 W. Peachtree Street, N.W.
Atlanta, GA 30309
(404) 815-5700

Boy Scouts of America (BSA)
1325 W. Walnut Hill Lane
P.O. Box 152079
Irving, TX 75015
(214) 580-2000

Camp Fire Boys and Girls
4601 Madison Avenue
Kansas City, MO 64112-1278
(816) 756-1950

Children's Alliance for the Protection
    of the Environment
P.O. Box 307
Austin, TX 78767
(512) 476-2273

4-H Program
Extension Service
U.S. Department of Agriculture
Washington, DC 20250
(202) 447-5853

Future Farmers of America (FFA)
National FFA Center
5632 Mount Vernon Memorial Highway
Alexandria, VA 22309-0160
(703) 360-3600

Gifted Children's Pen Pals International
c/o Dr. Debby Sue Vandevender
166 East 61st Street
New York, NY 10021-8509
(212) 355-2469

Girl Scouts of the U.S.A. (GSUSA)
420 Fifth Avenue
New York, NY 10018-2702
(212) 852-8000

Clubs and Organizations for Kids
(continued)

International Soap Box Derby, Inc.
P.O. Box 7233
Akron, OH 44306
(216) 733-8723

Junior Philatelists of America
P.O. Box 850
Boalsburg, PA 16827
(814) 466-3171

"Just Say No" International
2101 Webster Street, Suite 1300
Oakland, CA 94612
(510) 451-6666

Kids for Saving Earth
P.O. Box 47247
Plymouth, MA 55447-0247
(612) 525-0002

Little League Baseball (LLB)
P.O. Box 3485
Williamsport, PA 17701
(717) 326-1921

National Association of Rocketry
P.O. Box 177
Altoona, WI 54720
(715) 832-1946

National Association of Youth Clubs (NAYC)
5808 16th Street, N.W.
Washington, DC 20011
(202) 726-2044

National Audubon Society (NAS)
950 Third Avenue
New York, NY 10022
(212) 832-3200

National Campers and Hikers Association
(NCHA)
4804 Transit Road, Building 2
Depew, NY 14043
(716) 668-6242

Pop Warner Football (PWF)
920 Town Center Drive
Suite I-25
Langhorne, PA 19047
(215) 752-2691

Puppeteers of America (PA)
Five Cricklewood Path
Pasadena, CA 91107
818-797-5748

Ranger Rick's Nature Club
8925 Leesburg Pike
Vienna, VA 22184-0001
(703) 790-4274

Special Olympics, Inc.
1350 New York Avenue, N.W., Suite 500
Washington, DC 20005
(202) 628-3630

Student Letter Exchange
630 Third Avenue
New York, NY 10017
(212) 557-3312

World Pen Pals
1694 Como Avenue
St. Paul, MN 55108
(612) 647-0191

YMCA
101 N. Wacker Drive
Chicago, IL 60606
(312) 977-0031

Dewey Decimal Classification
The One Hundred Divisions

000 Generalities
010 Bibliography
020 Library and information sciences
030 General encyclopedic works
040 [unassigned]
050 General serial publications
060 General organizations and museology
070 Journalism, publishing, newspapers
080 General collections
090 Manuscripts and book rarities

100 Philosophy
110 Metaphysics
120 Epistemology, causation, humankind
130 Paranormal phenomena and arts
140 Specific philosophical viewpoints
150 Psychology
160 Logic
170 Ethics (Moral philosophy)
180 Ancient, medieval, Oriental
190 Modern Western philosophy

200 Religion
210 Natural religion
220 Bible
230 Christian theology
240 Christian moral and devotional theology
250 Local church and religious orders
260 Social and ecclesiastical theology
270 History and geography of church
280 Christian denominations and sects
290 Other and comparative religions

300 Social Sciences
310 Statistics
320 Political science
330 Economics
340 Law
350 Public administration
360 Social problems and services
370 Education
380 Commerce (Trade)
390 Customs, etiquette, folklore

400 Language
410 Linguistics
420 English and Anglo-Saxon languages
430 Germanic languages—German
440 Romance languages—French
450 Italian and Romanian languages
460 Spanish and Portuguese languages
470 Italic languages—Latin
480 Hellenic languages—Greek
490 Other languages

500 Pure Sciences
510 Mathematics
520 Astronomy and allied sciences
530 Physics
540 Chemistry and allied sciences
550 Sciences of the earth and other worlds
560 Paleontology
570 Life sciences
580 Botanical sciences
590 Zoological sciences

600 Technology (Applied Sciences)
610 Medical sciences—Medicine
620 Engineering and allied operations
630 Agriculture and related technologies
640 Home economics and family living
650 Management and auxiliary services
660 Chemical and related technologies
670 Manufactures
680 Manufacture for specific uses
690 Buildings

700 The Arts
710 Civic and landscape art
720 Architecture
730 Plastic arts—Sculpture
740 Drawing, decorative and minor arts
750 Painting and paintings
760 Graphic arts—Prints
770 Photography and photographs
780 Music
790 Recreational and performing arts

800 Literature (Belles-Lettres)
810 American literature in English
820 English and Anglo-Saxon literatures
830 Literatures of Germanic languages
840 Literatures of Romance languages
850 Italian and Romanian literatures
860 Spanish and Portuguese literatures
870 Italic literatures—Latin
880 Hellenic literatures—Greek
890 Literatures of other languages

900 General Geography and History
910 General geography—Travel
920 General biography and genealogy
930 General history of ancient world
940 General history of Europe
950 General history of Asia
960 General history of Africa
970 General history of North America
980 General history of South America
990 General history of other areas

The Parts of a Book

half-title page	The first printed page in a book and the page on which only the main part of the book title is listed. Both the subtitle and the author's name are omitted from this page.
title page	The second printed page in a book and the page on which the full title of the book, the name of the author, the name of the illustrator, and the name of the publisher are listed.

author   the person who wrote the book
illustrator the person who drew the pictures
publisher   the company that printed the book

copyright page	Usually the back of the title page, this page includes the copyright notice, the name of the person or publishing company holding the copyright, and the year in which the book was copyrighted.
dedication page	Page that carries a brief statement in which the author inscribes or addresses his book to someone as a way of recognizing or complimenting that person.
table of contents	A list of the significant parts of a book by title and page number in the order in which they appear. It is usually near the front of the book and includes the introduction, all chapter titles, the bibliography, and the index (if there is one).
preface	A statement by the author telling how or why he or she wrote the book and acknowledging any help he or she had in doing so.
introduction	An essay that sets the scene for the book, explains the subject or format of the book, or tells how to use the book.
body or text	The main part of the book.
notes	Additional explanatory information about facts in the text or about the sources from which they have been gathered.
glossary	An alphabetical listing of the difficult, special, or technical words used in a book with their definitions and, sometimes, their pronunciations.
bibliography	A list of articles and other works referred to in the book or used by the author in writing it, or a list of writings relating to the same subject as the text. The works in a bibliography are usually arranged in alphabetical order based on the authors' last names.
index	An alphabetical list of the names or topics covered in a book, together with the numbers of the pages on which they are defined, explained, or discussed. The index usually appears at the end of the book.

A Hundred Holiday Words

Valentine's Day

arrow
bow
candy
cards
caring
cookies
cupid
February
flowers
hearts
lace
love
red
sweetheart
valentines

Halloween

apples
bats
black
broom
candy
cats
costumes
ghosts
goblins
jack-o'-lanterns
makeup
masks
monsters
night
October
orange
pumpkins
skeletons
spooky
treats
tricks
witch

Thanksgiving

corn
cornucopia
cranberries
fall
feast
football
gathering
gravy
harvest
Indians
Mayflower
November
Pilgrims
Plymouth Rock
pumpkin
pumpkin pie
stuffing
turkey

Hanukkah

candles
dreidel
eight
festival
gelt
Hanukkah
latkes
lights
Maccabees
menorah
miracle
oil
presents
songs
temple

Christmas

angel
bells
candles
candy canes
carols
chestnuts
crèche
December
elf
gifts
green
holly
lights
mistletoe
ornaments

parades
popcorn
red
reindeer
Rudolph
Santa Claus
shopping
sleigh
snow
stockings
toys
tree
wassail
winter
wreath

Use some of the words on this list and the grid on page 304 to create a crossword puzzle or a word search for a family member for one of these holidays.

Colors

alabaster	canary	crow	lake
amber	carmine	cyan	lapis lazuli
amethyst	celadon	damask	lavender
apricot	cerise	delft	lemon
aquamarine	cerulean	drab	lilac
aubergine	champagne	dun	lime
auburn	charcoal	ebony	madder
avocado	chartreuse	ecru	magenta
azure	cherry	emerald	mahogany
bay	chestnut	fawn	malachite
beet	chocolate	fuchsia	maroon
beige	cinnabar	gold	mauve
bice blue	cinnamon	gray	navy
bice green	coal	green	ocher
black	cobalt	hazel	olive
blood	cocoa	heliotrope	orange
blue	coffee	henna	orchid
brick	copen	indigo	peach
bronze	copper	ink	peacock
brown	coral	ivory	pearl
buff	cream	jet	periwinkle
cadmium	crimson	khaki	pink

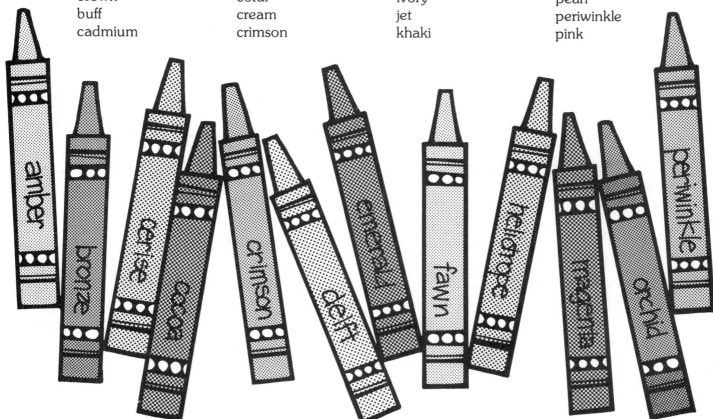

Colors
(continued)

pitch	russet	soot	ultramarine
plum	sable	sorrel	umber
puce	saffron	spice	vermilion
purple	salmon	tan	vert
red	sapphire	tangerine	violet
rhodamine	scarlet	taupe	walnut
rose	sepia	tawny	white
royal blue	sienna	teal	xanthic
royal purple	silver	titian	yellow
ruby	slate	turquoise	

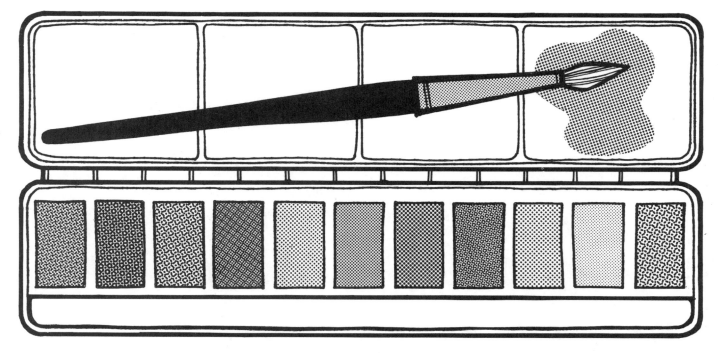

1. Make a chart on which you classify these colors as either **reds, oranges, yellows, greens, blues, purples, browns, blacks,** or **whites**.

2. Use crayons, marking pens, or paints to show subtle differences in shade within a single color classification, such as reds or blues.

3. Write a descriptive poem or paragraph in which you use some of the color words from this list.

4. Pick ten of the color words on this list which are new to you. Use a dictionary to discover where these words came from and to write descriptions of the colors to which they refer.

5. Many compound words contain the names of colors. Examples are *blackmail, blueprint, greenhorn, silverware,* and *Yellowstone.* See how many color compounds you can add to this list.

Famous Detectives in Fiction

Detective or Agent	Author
Lew Archer	Ross Macdonald
Mack Bolan	Don Pendleton
Inspector Napoleon Bonaparte	Arthur W. Upfield
James Bond	Ian Fleming
Encyclopedia Brown	Donald Sobol
Nick Carter	John Coryell
Charlie Chan	Earl Derr Biggers
Nancy Drew	Carolyn Keene
Peter Gunn	Henry Kane
Mike Hammer	Mickey Spillane
Joe Hardy	Frank Dixon
Sherlock Holmes	Sir Arthur Conan Doyle
Travis McGee	John D. MacDonald
Phillip Marlowe	Raymond Chandler
Jane Marple	Agatha Christie
Hercule Poirot	Agatha Christie
Horace Rumpole	John Mortimer
Sam Spade	Dashiell Hammett
Spenser	Robert B. Parker
Dick Tracy	Chester Gould
Lord Peter Whimsey	Dorothy Sayers
Nero Wolfe	Rex Stout

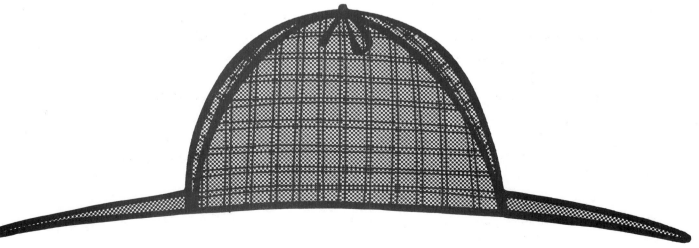

Famous Pairs

Abbott and Costello

Adam and Eve

Alfredo and Violetta

Amos and Andy

Antony and Cleopatra

Elizabeth Barrett and Robert Browning

Batman and Robin

Beauty and the Beast

Bonnie and Clyde

Archie and Edith Bunker

George Burns and Gracie Allen

Rhett Butler and Scarlett O'Hara

Calvin and Hobbes

Cheech and Chong

Cyrano and Roxane

Dagwood and Blondie

Dick and Jane

Donald and Daisy Duck

Don Quixote and Dulcinea del Toboso

Nelson Eddy and Jeannette MacDonald

Fred and Wilma Flintstone

Gilbert and Sullivan

Hansel and Gretel

Famous Pairs
(continued)

Henry Higgins and Eliza Doolittle

Jack and Jill

Kermit and Miss Piggy

Lady and the Tramp

Laurel and Hardy

Lerner and Lowe

Lucy and Desi

Mickey and Minnie Mouse

Napoleon and Josephine

Othello and Desdemona

Ozzie and Harriet

Radames and Aïda

Robin Hood and Maid Marian

Rodgers and Hammerstein

Rodgers and Hart

Romeo and Juliet

Franklin and Eleanor Roosevelt

Sonny and Cher

Superman and Lois Lane

Tarzan and Jane

Tristan and Isolde

Hobbies and Occupations

Field	Person	Subject of Study or Interest
agronomy	agronomist	soil
anthropology	anthropologist	man
archaeology	archaeologist	ancient civilizations
astronomy	astronomer	celestial bodies
audiology	audiologist	hearing
biology	biologist	living organisms, both plant and animal
botany	botanist	plants
cardiology	cardiologist	heart
conchology	conchologist	shells
criminology	criminologist	crime
dermatology	dermatologist	skin
endocrinology	endocrinologist	glands
entomology	entomologist	insects
etymology	etymologist	word origins and histories
genealogy	genealogist	families and ancestors
geology	geologist	rocks
geophysics	geophysicist	earth
graphology	graphologist	handwriting
helminthology	helminthologist	parasitic worms
hematology	hematologist	blood and blood-forming organs
herpetology	herpetologist	amphibians and reptiles

Hobbies and Occupations
(continued)

Field	Person	Subject of Study or Interest
horticulture	horticulturist	growth and cultivation of fruits, vegetables, flowers, or ornamental plants
hydrology	hydrologist	water
ichthyology	icthyologist	fish
malacology	malacologist	mollusks
mammalogy	mammalogist	mammals
numerology	numerologist	numbers
numismatics	numismatist	coins, tokens, medals, and paper money
ophthalmology	ophthalmologist	eye
ornithology	ornithologist	birds
osteology	osteologist	bones
otology	otologist	ears
paleontology	paleontologist	fossils
pathology	pathologist	diseased tissues
philately	philatelist	stamps
philology	philologist	literature or linguistics
phrenology	phrenologist	skulls
podiatry	podiatrist	feet
psychology	psychologist	mind; mental processes and activities
zoology	zoologist	animals

Interview Questions

Early Years

1. Where were you born?
2. Do you have any brothers or sisters?
3. Did you have a pet as a child? If so, what kind?
4. What special memories do you have of your childhood?
5. What was your favorite toy?
6. Did you collect anything as a child? If so, what?
7. Who were your close friends while you were growing up?
8. What things did you and your family enjoy doing together?

Education and Career

1. Where did you go to school?
2. What was your favorite subject in school?
3. What person influenced your life the most?
4. How old were you when you started your career?
5. What made you choose your present vocation?
6. What special training and/or education is needed for your job?
7. Describe a typical day on your job.
8. What do you like most about your work?
9. What do you like least about your work?
10. What is the most exciting or gratifying thing that's happened to you on your job?

Special Interests

1. What hobbies and special interests do you enjoy in your spare time?
2. What is the best book you've ever read?
3. What is your favorite food?
4. What three words best describe you?
5. What is one thing you would like to change about yourself?
6. What is one thing you would do differently if you could start over?

Monsters and Creatures

Abominable Snowman

Argus

basilisk

Big Foot

centaur

Cerberus

Chimera

Cyclops

Dracula

dragon

Frankenstein

gargoyle

giant

Gorgons

griffin

Harpies

Hydra

kraken

manticore

Medusa

Minotaur

Nessie (or Loch Ness monster)

Nessus

phoenix

roc

Sasquatch

Sphinx

Titans

vampire

werewolf

wyvern

yeti

1. Design a poster advertising one of these monsters or creatures for sale.

2. Make a monster mobile using six or more of the creatures listed.

3. Read some of the Greek epics or myths in which many of these monsters appear.

4. Use some of the creatures on this list and the grid on page 304 to create a crossword puzzle or a word search.

Movie Stars from A to Z

F. Murray Abraham
Dan Akroyd
Alan Alda
Woody Allen
Julie Andrews
Ann-Margaret
Fred Astaire
Lauren Bacall
Kevin Bacon
Alec Baldwin
Anne Bancroft
Brigitte Bardot
Lionel Barrymore
Kim Bassinger
Warren Beatty
Candice Bergen
Ingrid Bergman
Humphrey Bogart
Shirley Booth
Ernest Borgnine
Marlon Brando
Jeff Bridges
Charles Bronson
Pierce Brosnan
Yul Brynner
George Burns
Ellen Burstyn
Richard Burton
Gabriel Byrne
James Cagney
Michael Caine
Leslie Caron
Jim Carrey
Charles Chaplin
Cyd Charisse
Maurice Chevalier
Julie Christie
Claudette Colbert
Ronald Colman

Sean Connery
Gary Cooper
Joseph Cotten
Jeanne Crain
Joan Crawford
Hume Cronyn
Bing Crosby
Tom Cruise
Tony Curtis
Geena Davis
Doris Day
Olivia de Havilland
Catherine Deneuve
Robert De Niro
Danny DeVito
Marlene Dietrich
Kirk Douglas
Michael Douglas
Richard Dreyfuss
Faye Dunaway
Clint Eastwood
Douglas Fairbanks
Douglas Fairbanks, Jr.
Peter Falk
Mia Farrow
Sally Field
W. C. Fields
Peter Finch
Carrie Fisher
Henry Fonda
Glenn Ford
Harrison Ford
Jodie Foster
Michael J. Fox
Morgan Freeman
Clark Gable
Greta Garbo
Ava Gardner
Judy Garland

Teri Garr
Greer Garson
Janet Gaynor
Mitzi Gaynor
Lillian Gish
Whoopi Goldberg
Louis Gossett, Jr.
Elliott Gould
Betty Grable
Stewart Granger
Cary Grant
Hugh Grant
Lee Grant
Kathryn Grayson
Melanie Griffith
Alec Guinness
Gene Hackman
Tom Hanks
Rex Harrison
Goldie Hawn
Rita Hayworth
Audrey Hepburn
Katharine Hepburn
Charlton Heston
Dustin Hoffman
William Holden
Bob Hope
Anthony Hopkins
Rock Hudson
John Hurt
William Hurt
Angelica Huston
Betty Hutton
Timothy Hutton
Glenda Jackson
James Earl Jones
Jennifer Jones
Danny Kaye
Diane Keaton

Movie Stars from A to Z
(continued)

Michael Keaton	Jack Nicholson	Omar Sharif
Gene Kelly	David Niven	Simone Signoret
Grace Kelly	Donald O'Connor	Jean Simmons
Deborah Kerr	Laurence Olivier	Frank Sinatra
Nicole Kidman	Ryan O'Neal	Maggie Smith
Val Kilmer	Jennifer O'Neill	Ann Sothern
Alan Ladd	Peter O'Toole	Sylvester Stallone
Dorothy Lamour	Al Pacino	Barbara Stanwyck
Burt Lancaster	Geraldine Page	Rod Steiger
Jessica Lange	Gregory Peck	Jimmy Stewart
Angela Lansbury	Anthony Perkins	Meryl Streep
Charles Laughton	Michelle Pfeifer	Donald Sutherland
Bruce Lee	River Phoenix	Keifer Sutherland
Janet Leigh	Mary Pickford	Jessica Tandy
Vivien Leigh	Brad Pitt	Elizabeth Taylor
Jack Lemmon	Sidney Poitier	Shirley Temple
Jerry Lewis	Jane Powell	Emma Thompson
Sophia Loren	Anthony Quinn	Gene Tierney
Shirley MacLaine	Tony Randall	Marisa Tomei
Dean Martin	Robert Redford	Lily Tomlin
Lee Marvin	Christopher Reeve	Spencer Tracy
James Mason	Keanu Reeves	John Travolta
Marlee Matlin	Burt Reynolds	Kathleen Turner
Walter Matthau	Debbie Reynolds	Liv Ullmann
Victor Mature	Tim Robbins	Peter Ustinov
Marcello Mastroianni	Cliff Robertson	Dick Van Dyke
Bette Midler	Ginger Rogers	Jon Voight
Ray Milland	Mickey Rooney	Denzel Washington
Ann Miller	Katherine Ross	John Wayne
Liza Minnelli	Jane Russell	Sigorney Weaver
Demi Moore	Meg Ryan	Raquel Welch
Dudley Moore	Winona Ryder	Richard Widmark
Mary Tyler Moore	Eva Marie Saint	Cornell Wilde
Roger Moore	Susan Sarandon	Gene Wilder
Eddie Murphy	Roy Scheider	Robin Williams
Bill Murray	Arnold Schwarzenegger	Shelley Winters
Patricia Neal	Paul Scofield	Joanne Woodward
Liam Neeson	George C. Scott	Keenan Wynn
Paul Newman	Randolph Scott	Loretta Young

Mythological Gods and Goddesses

Greek Deity	Description or Area of Responsibility	Roman Deity
Gaea	Earth (or Mother Earth)	Tellus
Uranus	Heaven (or Father Heaven); husband of Gaea	
Cronos	son of Uranus and Gaea; youngest of the Titans	Saturn
Rhea	daughter of Uranus and Gaea; wife of Cronos; mother of Demeter, Hades, Hera, Hestia, Poseidon, and Zeus; goddess of the earth	Ops
Zeus	son of Cronos and Rhea; ruler of heaven; god of rain; king of the gods	Jupiter
Hera	daughter of Cronos and Rhea; sister and wife of Zeus; mother of Ares, Hebe, and Hephaestus; goddess of marriage and womanhood; queen of the gods	Juno
Aphrodite	created from the remains of Uranus, which had been thrown into the sea; goddess of love and beauty; patroness of seafarers and of war; most beautiful of all the goddesses; had the power to grant irresistible beauty to mortals	Venus
Athena	sprang forth fully grown and in complete 'armor from the forehead of Zeus; goddess of truth and wisdom, justice and war; defender of Athens; patroness of the arts and trades	Minerva
Poseidon	son of Cronos and Rhea; husband of Gaea (Mother Earth); originally lord of earthquakes and freshwater streams; later god of the sea and of horses and horse racing	Neptune
Hades	son of Cronos and Rhea; husband of Persephone; king of the lower world; giver of all blessings that come from within the earth, including both crops and precious metals; god of wealth; also called Aides, Aidoneus, Orcus, Tartarus, and Pluto	Dis *or* Dis Pater
Demeter	daughter of Cronos and Rhea; sister of Zeus; mother of Persephone; goddess of the earth's fruits, especially corn	Ceres
Apollo	son of Zeus and Leda; twin brother of Artemis; patron of archery, music, and medicine; protector of law and defender of the social order; closely associated with the sun	Apollo
Artemis	daughter of Zeus and Leda; twin sister of Apollo; originally associated with birth and care of the young; later viewed as protector of maidens and goddess of the hunt; often represented by a bear or bow; closely associated with the moon	Diana
Ares	son of Zeus and Hera; handsome but savage god of the warlike spirit	Mars
Hermes	son of Zeus and Maia; herald of Zeus; messenger of the gods; god of eloquence, prudence, and cleverness; inventor of the alphabet, astronomy, gymnastics, weights, measures, and the lyre; god of the roads; protector of travelers	Mercury
Hephaestus	son of Zeus and Hera; god of fire; skilled worker in metals who made armor, weapons, and ornaments for the gods	Vulcan
Hestia	daughter of Cronos and Rhea; sister of Zeus; maiden goddess of the fire burning on the hearth and of domestic life in general	Vesta
Hebe	daughter of Zeus and Hera; goddess of youth; waited upon the gods, filling their cups with nectar; had the power to make old people young again	Juventas

Palindromes

The English word **palindrome** comes from the Greek word ***palindromos***, meaning "running back again." A palindrome is a word or group of words that reads the same both forward and backward. Examples of palindromes are listed below.

bib	gag	pop	rotor
bob	level	pup	sees
civic	mom	race car	solos
dad	noon	radar	toot
did	not a ton	refer	we sew
eve	peep	repaper	wet stew

Able I was ere I saw Elba.

A dog—a panic in a pagoda!

A man, a plan, a canal—Panama!

Madam, I'm Adam.

Too hot to hoot.

Was it a cat I saw?

WET STEW

1. Add to this list of palindromes.

2. According to the *Guinness Book of World Records*, Edward Benbow of Bewdley, England, invented the longest English palindrome. Containing 65,000 words, it begins with the words "Rae hits Eb, sire . . . " and ends with the words "Beer is best, I hear." See how long a palindrome you can invent.

3. Words are not the only palindromes. Numbers can be palindromes, also. For example, in every year there is one day whose date is a palindrome. In 1987, this day was July 8—7/8/87. Discover and write the palindrome dates for the current year, the year in which you were born, and the year in which your school building was constructed.

Proverbs

A **proverb** is a brief saying that states a universal truth or expresses a choice morsel of folk wisdom.

A bird in the hand is worth two in the bush.

A fool and his money are soon parted.

All that glitters is not gold.

An apple a day keeps the doctor away.

A rolling stone gathers no moss.

As the twig is bent, so grows the tree.

A stitch in time saves nine.

A thing of beauty is a joy forever.

A watched pot never boils.

Be it ever so humble, there's no place like home.

Better late than never.

Better safe than sorry.

Don't count your chickens before they're hatched.

Don't cross the bridge until you come to it.

Don't cry over spilt milk.

Don't judge a book by its cover.

Don't look a gift horse in the mouth.

Don't put all of your eggs in one basket.

Early to bed, early to rise, makes a man healthy, wealthy, and wise.

Half a loaf is better than none.

Haste makes waste.

Look before you leap.

Love is blind.

Make hay while the sun shines.

Necessity is the mother of invention.

Never leave 'till tomorrow what you can do today.

Nothing is certain but death and taxes.

Nothing succeeds like success.

One bad apple doesn't spoil the bunch.

One picture is worth more than ten thousand words.

On the day of victory, no one is tired.

Pride goeth before a fall.

The pen is mightier than the sword.

Variety is the spice of life.

Whatever is worth doing at all is worth doing well.

When poverty comes in at the door, love flies out the window.

TV Network Addresses

ABC-American Broadcasting Company
77 West 66th Street
New York, NY 10023

A&E-Arts and Entertainment Network
235 East 45th Street
New York, NY 10017

AMC, BRV-American Movie Classics, Bravo
Rainbow Programming Holdings, Inc.
150 Crossways Park, W.
Woodbury, NY 11797

BET-Black Entertainment Television
1232 31st Street, N.W.
Washington, DC 20007

CBS-Columbia Broadcasting System, Inc.
51 West 52nd Street
New York, NY 10019

**CNBC-Consumer News and
   Business Channel**
2200 Fletcher Avenue
Fort Lee, NJ 07024

CNN-Cable News Network
One CNN Center, Box 105366
Atlanta, GA 30348-5366

**C-SPAN-Cable Satellite
   Public Affairs Network**
400 North Capitol Street, N.W., Suite 650
Washington, DC 20001

DIS-The Disney Channel
3800 West Alameda Avenue
Burbank, CA 91505

ESPN-ESPN, Inc.
ESPN Plaza
Bristol, CT 06010-9454

Fox Television
205 East 67th Street
New York, NY 10021

MTV-Music Television
MTV Networks, Inc.
1515 Broadway
New York, NY 10036

NBC-National Broadcasting Company
30 Rockfeller Plaza
New York, NY 10112

NICK-Nickelodeon/Nick at Nite
1515 Broadway
New York, NY 10036

PBS-Public Broadcasting Service
1790 Broadway
New York, NY 10019

SC-Sports Channel
3 Crossways Park., W.
Woodbury, NY 11797

TBS-Turner Broadcasting System
1050 Techwood Drive, N.W.
Atlanta, GA 30318

TDC-The Discovery Channel
Discovery Networks
7700 Wisconsin Avenue
Bethesda, MD 20814-3522

USA-USA Networks
USA Networks
1230 Avenue of the Americas
New York, NY 10020

**Westinghouse Broadcasting
   and Cable, Inc.**
888 7th Avenue
New York, NY 10106

Water Words

water	waterfowl	water-repellent
water balance	waterfront	water-resistant
water ballet	water gap	watershed
waterbed	water gas	waterside
water beetle	water gate	water ski
water biscuit	water glass	waterspout
water blister	water hole	water strider
waterborne	water lily	water system
water boy	waterline	water table
waterbuck	waterlogged	watertight
water buffalo	waterloo	water tower
water chestnut	water main	water turkey
water closet	watermark	water vapor
watercolor	watermelon	water wagon
water cooler	water moccasin	waterway
watercourse	water ouzel	waterwheel
watercraft	water pipe	water wings
watercress	water polo	water witch
waterfall	waterpower	waterworks
	waterproof	

Use some of these words and their definitions to create a matching game. In **Column A**, list at least twelve words from this list. In **Column B**, write simple definitions for these words in random order. Follow the form and format of the example below. When you have finished creating your puzzle, ask a friend to match the words with their definitions by writing the correct letter on each line.

Column A

____ 1. water biscuit

____ 2. water closet

____ 3. waterfowl

____ 4. watermark

____ 5. water strider

Column B

A. an aquatic bird

B. a design pressed in paper

C. a bathroom

D. a cracker

E. a long-legged bug that moves about on the surface of the water

What's Up?

The versatile word **up** can be a noun, a verb, an adjective, an adverb, or a preposition, depending on how it is used. Here is a list of words that begin with **up**.

up-and-coming	upon	upshot
up-and-down	upper	upside
up-and-up	uppercase	upside down
upbeat	upper class	upstage
upbraid	upper crust	upstairs
upbringing	uppercut	upstart
update	upper hand	upstate
upend	uppermost	upstream
upgrade	uppity	upstroke
upheaval	upraise	upswing
uphill	upright	uptake
uphold	uprising	uptight
upholster	uproar	up-to-date
upkeep	uproot	up-to-the-minute
upland	ups and downs	uptown
uplift	upscale	upturn
upmost	upset	upwind
	upshift	

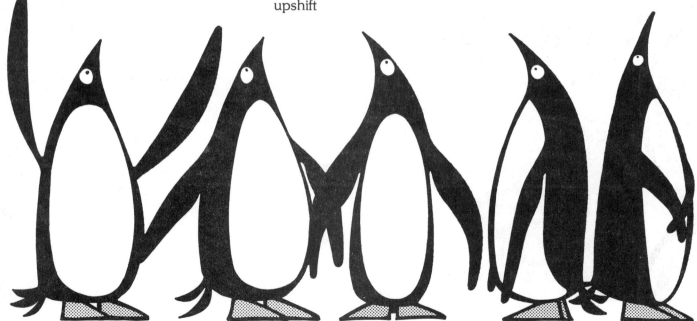

1. Write a humorous story using as many of these **up** words as possible.

2. Pick one of the following words and use it to create your own list like the one above: **day**, **double**, **down**, or **ice**.

Bonus Ideas Just for Fun

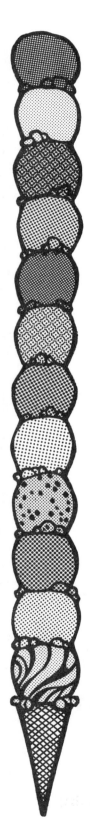

1. Select six unusual objects from the Things That Hold Things list on page 249. Do research to discover what these objects look like. Draw and label a picture of each one.

2. From the list on pages 254 and 255, choose a holiday you would like to learn more about. Do research to discover the origin of this holiday and the specific foods and customs associated with its celebration.

3. Select a creative writing title from one of the lists on pages 260 through 264. Working with a partner, write and illustrate a short story inspired by the title you have selected.

4. Exchange creative writing papers with a classmate and each proofread the other's work. Where appropriate, use the symbols listed on page 271.

5. Select one thing from the list of Things with Holes on page 265. On a sheet of white art paper, draw a picture of this thing. Cut out the hole. Color your picture. Write a paragraph describing this thing. Pretend that you are describing it to a person who has never seen one. Tell what it is made of, how big it is, and what it is used for.

6. A proverb is a brief saying that states a universal truth or expresses a choice morsel of folk wisdom in words that are simple and easy to understand. Select a proverb from the list on page 298. Using a thesaurus, rewrite this proverb to make it sound much more complex. For example, you might rewrite *Don't cry over spilt milk* to be *Refrain from engaging in lacrimation in response to the inadvertent wasting of a dairy product.*

7. Using a sheet of lined paper or the form on page 303, create a list of your own. For example, you might list
    a. board games,
    b. candy bars,
    c. famous animals on television or in the movies,
    d. ice cream flavors,
    e. kinds of shelters,
    f. nursery rhymes,
    g. things that are a particular color, such as red,
    h. things that are round,
    i. things that are sold in tubes, or
    j. words with the word *down* in them.

Name _____

Create a Just-for-Fun List

Think of a just-for-fun topic that interests you. On the lines below, create a list that reflects this topic. Illustrate your list and give it a title.

_____

_____

_____

_____

_____

_____

_____

_____

_____

Create a Puzzle

Use this grid to create a crossword puzzle or a word search based on one of the lists in this book. Print the title of your puzzle on the line below. On the back of this page, write instructions, clues and definitions, and/or a list of words for which students are to search. On a separate sheet of paper, provide an answer key.

_____

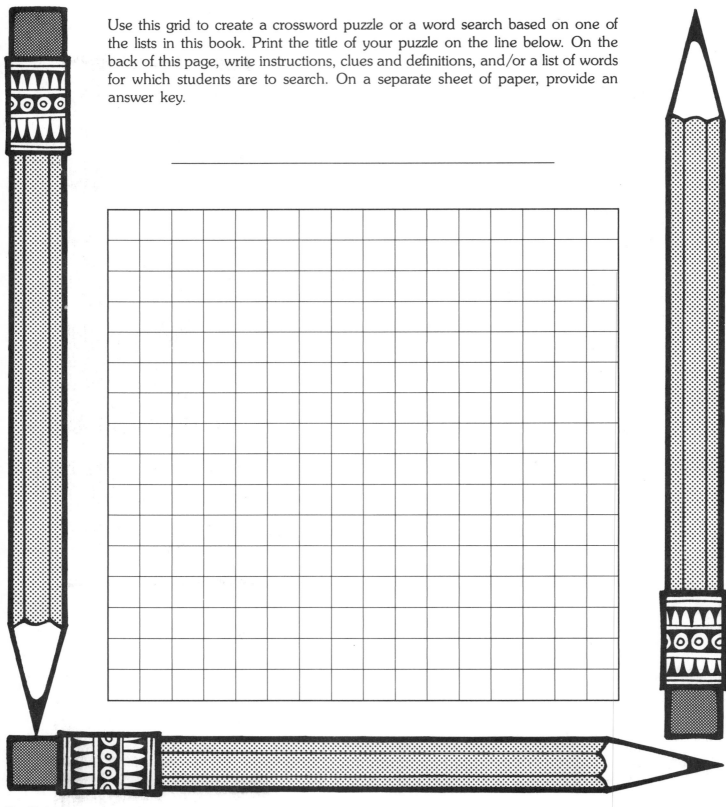